Ethical Issues in the Communication Process

LEA'S COMMUNICATION SERIES
Jennings Bryant/Dolf Zillmann, General Editors

Selected titles include:

Berger • Planning Strategic Interaction: Attaining Goals Through Communicative Action

Christ • Media Education Assessment Handbook

DeWerth-Pallmeyer • The Audience in the News

Gershon • The Transnational Media Corporation: Global Messages and Free Market Competition

Greene • Message Production: Advances in Communication Theory

Webster/Phalen • The Mass Audience: Rediscovering the Dominant Model

For a complete list of other titles in LEA's Communication Series, please contact Lawrence Erlbaum Associates, Publishers.

Ethical Issues
in the Communication Process

J. Vernon Jensen

University of Minnesota

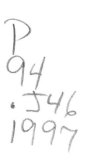

LEA LAWRENCE ERLBAUM ASSOCIATES, PUBLISHERS

1997 Mahwah, New Jersey

Lawrence Erlbaum Associates, Inc., Publishers
10 Industrial Avenue
Mahwah, New Jersey 07430

Cover design by Kathryn Houghtaling

Library of Congress Cataloging-in-Publication Data

Jensen, J. Vernon (John Vernon), 1922–
    Ethical issues in the communication process / J. Vernon Jensen.
        p. cm.
    Includes bibliographical references and index.
    ISBN 0-8058-2035-3 (cloth : alk. paper). — ISBN 0-8058-2036-1
    (pbk. : alk. paper)
    1. Communication—Moral and ethical aspects. I. Title.
    P94.J46   1997
    175—dc21   96-46360
                                                                 CIP

Books published by Lawrence Erlbaum Associates are printed on acid-
free paper, and their bindings are chosen for strength and durability.

Printed in the United States of America
10 9 8 7 6 5 4 3 2 1

To Khin Khin

Contents

7

8

Appendix A

Appendix B

Preface

An upsurge of interest in applied ethics is apparent today throughout academia and society. The enlarging role of communication in all its forms (oral, written, nonverbal, pictorial), formats (interpersonal, public speaking, small group, organizational, intercultural, mass communication), and purposes (persuasive, informative, entertaining) demands a deeper than usual sensitivity to ethical considerations. Students and the general public look for thoughtful analyses and guidance in these areas. Because only a very few books in the communication field have been entirely devoted to ethics, I hope that this book fills the real need.

Ethical Issues in the Communication Process attempts to digest and synthesize the research, writing, and thinking on the subject without bogging down readers in many long footnotes. The References and Suggested Additional Readings at the end of the book give readers an idea of this book's many sources, and provide ample avenues for further exploration. Drawing from works in the humanities and social sciences, I have put the scholarly literature into nontechnical and familiar language. To avoid being time bound, I have used examples from contemporary life to illustrate discussion of other times, places, and people. I have tried to be as objective and fair as possible and encourage readers to think through the various issues for themselves. The book offers food for thought to help us conscientiously evaluate our everyday decisions in communicative transactions.

Ethical Issues is intended for advanced undergraduate students, graduate students, and general readers interested in this subject. This book offers a helpful overview of college and university students' communications studies and brings coherence and depth understanding of ethical issues. Although intended as the sole text for a course in speech communication ethics, *Ethical Issues* can supplement readings in other speech communication courses and in journalism and mass communication courses. Preprofessional students planning to become engineers, doctors, counselors, businesspeople, public servants, lawyers, as well as practicing professionals can also find the book relevant.

The introductory chapter focuses on overall considerations, and the second chapter contains a survey of the roots for ethical guidance on which human beings consciously or unconsciously draw, when making decisions in communication. Following chapters are devoted to ethical issues revolving around the communicator, the message, the medium, the receiver, and the situation, with a final chapter of summary. Exercises at the end of each chapter are designed for class discussions or writing assignments.

Throughout a lifetime of teaching including fifteen years of teaching courses in communication ethics, my many students have contributed to my ideas: Much material here is an outgrowth of our stimulating interchanges. I am grateful for the long association with colleagues in the speech communication profession here and abroad, especially those in the Commission on Communication Ethics in the Speech Communication Association. I also want to express my gratitude to the citizens of Minnesota, who have been supportive and generous contributors to my life and learning. Hollis Heimbouch and Kathleen O'Malley, senior editors, and Larry Hayden IV, book production editor, of Lawrence Erlbaum Associates, and others of the editorial staff have been helpful and supportive. I wish to commend and thank the copyeditor of this volume, Ann Farkas, for excellent detailed scrutiny of the manuscript and helpful sugestions for its improvement.

I am deeply grateful for the constant love and support of my wife, Irene Khin Khin, who has shared not only our personal family life but also our dual careers in higher education with grace and with excellence. This and the love of our son, Donald, and our daughter, Maythee, and their respective families, make this endeavor and all others worthwhile.

1

Introduction

ETHICS LANDSCAPE

In virtually all areas of society ethical issues are mushrooming. Professionals in the health field grapple with ethical questions about transplants, abortion, birth control, life-support systems, informed consent, human genetics, patient privacy, malpractice suits, and high costs of insurance and care in general. Ethical concerns about oil spills, nuclear power accidents, defense weaponry, disposal of industrial waste, acid rain, lead and asbestos poisoning, and ecological balance confront those in science, technology, and industry. People in the political arena deal with ethical questions about homelessness, unemployment, welfare reform, Social Security, foreign policy decisions, law enforcement practices, electioneering costs, racial and gender discrimination, Central Intelligence Agency (CIA) activities, drugs, crime, immigration control, and lobbying activities. The legal profession is accused of unethical practices like charging exhorbitant fees, stimulating an unhealthy litigious spirit, engaging in questionable plea-bargaining practices, and advertising improperly. The business and corporate world is challenged on lack of truth in advertising, selling unsafe products, committing white collar crimes, practicing insider trading, being involved in savings and loan scandals, and giving unbridled allegiance to the profit motive. In mass communications an overwhelming concern with profit produces demeaning entertainment, sensationalism, dramatic investigative reporting, manipulation of photography, invasion of privacy, little interest in truth telling, suspect allocation of resources, and questionable editorial decisions. "Never in the history of our profession have editors and reporters been more aware of the need for ethical behavior and the ethical treatment of stories," wrote McMasters (1996, p. 17). Academia is plagued by accusations of questionable research procedures, an interest in furthering personal research rather than honoring good teaching, engaging in excessive outside consulting, pandering to contemporary trends, and bowing to business demands. Irresponsible individualism

1

and unbridled greed seem to be on the increase, not only in the United States but also in former Communist countries like Russia. These widespread conditions have stimulated an intense interest in ethics, and an indignant citizenry is demanding a more ethical standard of behavior.

Legislative ethics committees in state and national government have been making serious efforts to increase ethical standards. In February 1996 Congress passed and President Clinton signed the historic, sweeping Communications Decency Act, which includes requiring the V-chip in television sets, and thus permits parents to block out objectionable programs. But in June 1996, a panel of three federal judges in Philadelphia castigated the Act and "declared the internet a medium of historic importance, a profoundly democratic channel for communication that should be nurtured, not stifled" (Quittner, 1996, p. 56). Strident and reckless rhetoric, many feel, have helped to create an atmosphere conducive to violent acts, like the assassination of the Israeli prime minister Yitzhak Rabin in November 1995. In January 1996, a group of moderates in the U.S. House of Representatives formulated a bipartisan resolution calling for a more civil discourse in their proceedings, and the British House of Commons has recently done the same. Some corporations and even cities have set up ethical practices boards to monitor the ethical atmosphere and to investigate specific complaints. Communities have set up a special "values week", hospitals have created ethics committees, and car dealers have held special workshops on increasing ethical behavior in selling practices. Programs on ethics have appeared on television, and magazines and newspapers have allocated space to discussing ethics. Books and articles have been devoted to discussions of ethics in various professions, and a few journals about ethics in specific professions have appeared in the last decade.

College mission statements now include an emphasis on ethics and values, and commencement addresses not infrequently dwell on the importance of ethical commitment. New courses in applied ethics, are appearing throughout academica, for instance, in schools of law, medicine, dentistry, engineering, business, and social work. By the mid-1990s, 90% of the business schools offered courses in business ethics, with a total of about 500 such courses (Hausman, 1995). Departments of philosophy, where ethics have traditionally been studied, are being asked to create courses in applied ethics for engineers, lawyers, and doctors. Departments of political science, mass communication, and others have constructed courses in ethics relevant to their areas of study. Newly endowed chairs in ethics have been created, some on an interdisciplinary arrangement. Applicants for graduate school have been including an ethical dimension in their program projections. Job openings in colleges and universities have begun listing an interest in ethics as a desired qualification.

Ethics centers, independent or attached to a college or university, have been created and are increasingly active. A number of such centers are listed in Appendix A, and another list appears in the Spring 1995 issue of *Ethically Speaking*, the semiannual publication of the Association for Practical and Professional Ethics. The programs of many ethics centers include awarding research grants for studies in ethics. These centers and other sponsoring agencies have increasingly set up conferences, seminars, and workshops about ethics in the fields of medicine, engineering, technology, business, law, education, and other professions.

The field of speech communication shares this strong interest in ethics. Speech communication departments are creating undergraduate and graduate courses in ethics, and are including sections on ethics in other courses. More Master's theses and Doctoral dissertations on communication ethics are appearing. International, national, regional, and state speech communication associations are increasing their activities on ethical issues. For example, in 1985 the Speech Communication Association created a Commission on Communication Ethics that, among other projects, holds a biennial conference on communication ethics, sponsored in part by Western Michigan University in Kalamazoo. Publications in speech communication now deal with ethics. New textbooks or new editions of popular textbooks, especially in public speaking but also in discussion, interpersonal, organizational and intercultural communication, are including new chapters or sections on ethics. Ethics in speech communication, in academia, and in the larger society will be in the forefront of concerns as we enter the 21st century.

Through the centuries, ethics has been a central emphasis of the field of rhetoric. For example, Aristotle insisted that a rhetorician's personal character, or ethos, was crucial to effectiveness, and Quintillian asserted that a good orator is a "good man speaking well". Hugh Blair, the 19th century British rhetorical theorist, wrote: "In order to be a truly eloquent or persuasive speaker, nothing is more necessary than to be a virtuous man" (Golden & Corbett, 1968, p. 458). In the mid-20th century, Thonssen and Baird (1948) concluded in their classic work, *Speech Criticism:* "The cultivation of a sense of responsibility for the uttered statement is a crying imperative for public speakers today—just as it was yesterday and will be tomorrow" (p. 470). Today people in high and low places are using their natural and carefully honed communication skills in demeaning ways for dehumanizing and often cruel ends. Those of us in speech communication must live up to D. K. Smith's (1979) observation: "I think it is good that we have never ceased to engage our students in confronting the eternal ambiguities linking effective speech practice to ethical speech practice" (p. 103). We have excessively focused on achieving *effectiveness*—on convincing audiences, converting skeptics, winning the debates—without balancing these aims with the ethical commitment. We must blend proficiency and ethics, skills and compassion. As the Association of Communication Administrators stated in their 1995 definition of their profession: "The field of communication focuses on how people use messages to generate meanings within and across various contexts, cultures, channels, and media. The field promotes the effective *and ethical* (italics added) practice of human communication."

KEY TERMS

I define *ethics* as the *moral responsibility to choose, intentionally and voluntarily, oughtness in values like rightness, goodness, truthfulness, justice, and virtue, which may, in a communicative transaction, significantly affect ourselves and others.* Ethics refers to theory, to abstract universal principles and their sources, whereas *morals* implies practicing those principles of applied ethics, our culture-bound modes of conduct.

The ethical dimension affects decision making when two or more options are viable and can be freely chosen. Pike (1966) put it well: "There is no point in analyzing what men [*sic*] ought to do if they are powerless to choose what they will do" (p. 1). Choice must be *intentional* and *voluntary*: The communicator can then be evaluated by relevant values. Unintentional misrepresentation of facts marks an intellectual, not a moral, failing. When choice is by chance unintentional, a communicator's ethical judgment is meaningless. A communicator's intention is a prime consideration in ethical judgment. When a communicator is coerced to engage in an involuntary communicative transaction, normal ethical standards hardly apply. Furthermore, we should "view intentionality as existing in varying degrees and, as we interact, we may engage in multiple intentions" (Sharkey, 1992, p. 271).

Oughtness is at the heart of ethics, and thus ethics are inevitably involved with prescriptiveness. Prescriptive ethics, guided by the highest ideals, measure acts accordingly: descriptive ethics emphasize that as ideals are usually unattainable, we must focus on what "is" rather than what *ought to be*, on what ethical guidelines people actually use. Although the descriptive approach has helped to stimulate ethical analysis, we must ultimately grapple with oughtness. In fact, descriptive ethics are insufficient. Their blind allegiance to the status quo rests on several factors: chance (what mores have been established and why); power (who exerted the influence to establish the norms—bullies, people of wealth, an occupying military force); chronology (who first established the norms); majoritarianism (quantity does not necessarily imply quality); and tradition ("it has always been done that way"). What *is* continues to operate; the status quo does not change for the better unless human agents intervene; and such intervention arises from prescriptive oughtness.

Oughtness does battle over *values*. We struggle to understand right and wrong, good and bad, true and false, just and unjust, virtuous and corrupt. In dealing with these ends, we assume that we seek the right, the good, the true, the just, and the virtuous rather than their opposites. Himmelfarb (1995) wrote about the shift in vocabulary and mind-set from *virtues* to *values*. Virtues which flowered in the Victorian era, were fixed and clear, she contended, whereas values are vague. Although I do not share her interpretation and her anxiety, her point deserves consideration. Values, abstract conceptions that people consider desirable, do not usually act in isolation from one another; for several intertwined values often affect decision making, with one or more taking precedence at any moment. Often two or more "good" values clash. For example, *peace* is sometimes willfully violated by social activists seeking *justice* in the political and social arenas. Freedom of expression may conflict with social responsibility; liberty, with safety. The legitimate journalistic goal of getting a good story may collide with values of privacy, honesty, and compassion. This clash of values creates *issues*. Values in conflict are like natural laws in conflict. For example, icycles are temperature's triumph over gravity, but gravity still exists even though it does not take precedence at that moment.

The Josephson Institute of Ethics, in Marina del Ray, California, has generated what the Institute calls core values, six "pillars of character": respect, responsibility, trustworthiness, caring, justice and fairness, and civic virtue and citizenship. Searching for core values on the international scene, Rushworth Kidder and his Institute for Global Ethics, in Camden, Maine, has arrived at eight: love, truthfulness, fairness, freedom, unity, tolerance, responsibility, and respect for life. Defining each value and distinguishing between almost synonymous terms and concepts is difficult. *Fairness* or example, is sometimes used interchangeably with *equality*, but the former is a qualitative conception and the latter a quantitative one. Parents may justify giving different sized weekly allowances to their 12-year-old and their 6-year-old, because of the children's varying needs, household chores, and ability to handle money responsibly. Traffic lights are adjusted to give more time to a major thoroughfare than to minor cross streets with few cars—unequal but fair and reasonable for traffic control. Giving equal television time to every political party on television means giving each one not only the same number of minutes but also the same quality of broadcast time.

This book deals with verbal, nonverbal, written, and pictorial *communicative transactions*, direct or mediated via an electronic means, with the circular dynamic of both senders and receivers as potentially active participants. It covers the entire landscape of interpersonal communication, public speaking, small group communication, mass communication, and intercultural communication. This provides us the opportunity to bring together the divergent courses in our field, to be a cohering force, to create an umbrella under which we see the interrelatedness of the many areas of our profession. The organizing framework of this book is the fundamental paradigm of the communicative process: the ethical concerns revolving around the *communicator*, the *message*, the *mediums* (the plural *mediums* is used here rather than the often used Latin form *media*, for the latter is so embedded in our lexicon to mean electronic mass media), the *receivers* and the *situations*. I focus on the ethical tensions within the familiar question: "Who said what through what medium to whom in what context with what effect?"

Of central concern is the *effect* of the communicative act. What is the effect on immediate and long-range audiences? Centuries ago, Augustine (1949) warned rhetoricians racing after superficial superiority to look deeply into the potential harm of their remarks:

> In quest of the fame of eloquence, a man standing before a human judge, surrounded by a human throng, declaiming against his enemy with fiercest hatred, will take heed most watchfully, lest, by an error of the tongue, he murder the word "human being"; but takes no heed, lest, through the fury of his spirit, he murder the real human being. (p. 22)

Are people with whom we are intimately identified—family, relatives, friends, fellow employees, club members, religious affiliations—honored or ashamed by our communicative efforts? How are we ourselves affected by our communicative acts?

ETHICAL QUALITY (EQ) SCALE[1]

Throughout this book I emphasize the need to think in terms of the *degree* of ethical quality, not in terms of simplistically labeling words or deeds as either ethical or unethical, automatically eliciting a yes or no response. Setting up only two options, one totally good and one totally bad, we must instead ask, "How ethical is it?" This question elicits a statement of degree, a degree of *ethical quality (EQ)*. On a seven-point Ethical Quality Scale, a communicative act can be highly ethical (7), moderately ethical (6), slightly ethical (5), neutral (4), slightly unethical (3), moderately unethical (2), or highly unethical (1).

Ethical Quality Scale

Unethical			Neutral			Ethical
Highly	Moderately	Slightly	Neutral	Slightly	Moderately	Highly
1	2	3	4	5	6	7

By refining our judgments, we can continually probe the possible variables, nuances, and consequences that may alter our evaluation. For example, lying to a thief may warrant an EQ *7*, because of the dangers involved: lying in other circumstances may call for an EQ *1* or *2* rating. We thus can appreciate the complex milieu of most communicative transactions. By avoiding hasty categorical judgments and pronouncing the case closed, we can continue to analyze and then communicate our specific evaluation. The EQ Scale stimulates us to note positive as well as negative instances. The latter usually capture our full attention; we are drawn to ethics only when a grievous negative instance occurs. The EQ Scale also helps us to see that we are generating opportunities for communicative acts that enrich the lives of many. In the familiar Latin terms, a *5* is cum laude (with praise), a *6* is magna cum laude (with great praise), and a *7* is summa cum laude (with highest praise). Likewise, a *3* is with condemnation, a *2* with great condemnation, and a *1* with greatest condemnation.

As Hausman (1995—1996) has written, we must dwell on those gray areas in the middle as well as on the two extremes. Most of the action in

---

[1]This section draws on my 1985 article, Teaching Ethics in Speech Communication. *Communication Education, 34*, 324–331. Used by permission of the publisher.

a football game takes place between the two 10-yard lines, yet we tend to highlight the action inside the 10-yard lines. We need to pay more attention to mid-field play, where our ordinary communicative experiences fall. Case studies all too often conjure up major dramatic *goal line* episodes far removed from the small but significant decision-making tasks of everyday life. Dorff and Newman (1995) put it this way: "We misrepresent the moral life when we focus only on dramatic choices and overlook the many attitudes and values that express themselves in everyday life and which shape our sense of ourselves" (p. 247).

The EQ Scale gives us the opportunity and encouragement to voice our displeasure (at a 2 or 3 rating), without calling something unethical when that is the only terminology available. Using a scale gives a sense of freedom as well as precision within evaluative processes.

CAUSES OF LOW ETHICAL QUALITY BEHAVIOR

Most people acknowledge that we all have moral shortcomings, but simply viewing evil as caused by evil people is obviously incomplete and inadequate. A host of mixed motives, many of which are good, usually operate. Acting on narrow loyalties may be one motive. Secretaries may lie out of loyalty to a boss, and be disloyal at the same time to the broader society. Members of a sorority or fraternity may feel pressured to conform to their group's mores rather than to the values of the larger society. Engineers may put loyalty to their company above their commitment to safety values protecting consumers and the general public. Mixed with the honorific value of loyalty in these and similar instances are such motives as fear of losing a job or of ostracism by a group. People may justify their behavior by telling themselves they benefit others, feed their families, increase their companies' profits, and make their stockholders happy. A desire for material gain, prestige, and power may well be operating. People also seem to be capable of selective compassion of mourning the death of someone in the United States but not in another country, or of lamenting the falling profits of a company they work for, but not those of a competitor. Sometimes people are driven by the expediency of getting a job done, of reaching an objective with as little time and effort as possible.

Poor time management can cause low ethical behavior. Because a speech deadline was at hand, a speaker inserted some unverified figures and facts. A doctor did not have time to communicate important information in an empathic manner to a patient. A student late for an important meeting parked in a *No Parking* area broke the law—not because of a dark criminal urge, but simply because of not allowing enough time to find legitimate parking. Thus, in some instances, people must not only emphasize moral commitments but also must manage time carefully.

"RIGHTSABILITIES" AND OPPORTUNITIES

The First Amendment in the U.S. Constitution articulated boldly our fundamental rights: "Congress shall make no law respecting an establishment of religion, or prohibiting the free exercise thereof; or abridging the freedom of speech, or of the press; or the right of the people peaceably to assemble, and to petition the government for a redress of grievances." The French Declaration of the Rights of Man and of the Citizen asserted that "free communication of thought and opinion is one of man's most precious rights." In an historic court battle in England in 1792 over Thomas Paine's publications, Lord Erskine defended the premise of the freedom of the press: "I am not insisting upon the infallibility of Mr. Paine's doctrines; if they are erroneous, let them be answered, and truth will spring from the collision" (*British orations*, 1960, p. 137). Indeed, John Milton's mid-17th-century advocacy of the crucial importance of the free marketplace of ideas has been a strong thread in Western democracies. In the mid-20th-century, the United Nations General Assembly's Universal Declaration of Human Rights provided a ringing re-affirmation and summary of the many fundamental rights of human beings. Articles 18 and 19 are particularly relevant here:

> "Everyone has the right to freedom of thought, conscience and religion; this right includes freedom to change his *[sic]* religion or belief, either alone or in community with others and in public or private, to manifest his *[sic]* religion or belief in teaching, practice, worship and observance. Everyone has the right to freedom of opinion and expression; this right includes freedom to hold opinions without interference and to seek, receive and impart information and ideas through any media and regardless of frontiers."

Henkin (1990) defined human rights and insisted on their universal application: Human rights are those benefits deemed essential for individual well being, dignity, and fulfillment, and that reflect a common sense of justice, fairness, and decency. . . . Human rights are universal; they belong to every human being in every human society. They do not differ with geography or history, culture or ideology, political or economic system, or stage of social development. (p. 2)

That all societies do not agree on the universality of human rights was made very clear at the United Nations Conference on Women in Beijing in 1995.

It is quite clear that we do not focus nearly as much on responsibilities as on rights. Glendon (1991) asserted in her chapter, "The Missing Language of Responsibilities": "Each day's newspapers, radio broadcasts, and television programs attest to our tending to speak of whatever is most important to us in terms of rights, and to our predilection for overstating the absoluteness of the rights we claim. Our habitual silences concerning responsibilities are more apt to remain unnoticed" (p. 76).

People constantly struggle with the tension between rights and responsibilities, and conscientious people seek to balance the tensions in meaningful and fair ways. Individuals demand the right of free expression, but society demands that individual freedom not harm the larger community. The courts have ruled that the right to free speech does not include falsely yelling "Fire" in a crowded theater. Citizens demand the right of privacy, but law enforcement agencies claim they must breach that right under certain circumstances to apprehend dangerous people who threaten the life of the community.

Rights and responsibilities are not separate entities; the metaphor of two sides of the same coin is inadequate to depict their intimate enmeshing. A single concept, a single term, is needed. I suggest *"rightsabilities."* Although the term may not become widely adopted, it does communicate the total integration of rights and resonsibilities, like the intertwining strands of a rope or the encircling figures on a totem pole or a Hindu temple. The two words characterize the yin and yang in Eastern cultures, the supposed opposites that are really complementary, each contributing to the other's fulfillment, much like inhalation and exhalation, night and day, male and female. I constantly stress this reciprocal relationship throughout this book.

Furthermore, I urge in that we go beyond rightsabilities to emphasize opportunities. We need to see more clearly the opportunities for enhancing life all around us through our communication, and we need to act more readily on those observations.

OBJECTIVES

The objectives of this book, and an academic course based on it include 11 aims. First, people must seek to broaden and deepen their command of many sources for ethical standards to enlarge the resources for guidance in decision making and communicating.

Second, people must sharpen their ethical sensitivities so that we may "see" and understand the issues and problems calling for ethical judgment. (Lind and Rarick [1994, 1995] have led in exploring this important dimension.) People must stretch themselves beyond a comfortable moral plateau and open their eyes to communication that can bring potential harm. Nehru (1942) poignantly expressed this ideal in his autobiography when he wrote that in human affairs violence of the sword is obviously to be condemned, "but what of the violence that comes quietly and often in peaceful garb and.... without any outward physical injury, outrages the mind and crushes the spirit and breaks the heart" (p. 312). May ethical sensitivity glorify the mind, bolster the spirit, and heal the heart of those with whom people communicate.

Third, people must develop a set of ethical guidelines to use for confronting ethical dilemmas. Guidelines must be flexible, but they represent tools created from past experience, thoughtful insight, and high aspiration, and enable people to avoid being immobilized by the tension and urgency of situations calling for immediate ethical judgments. People need to develop a mind-set enabling them to routinize loving and humane behavior.

Fourth, the partnership between ethics and reasoning, must be furthered as reflected in terms like *principled reasoning, moral reasoning, moral argumentation, and rational ethics*. Sharper analytical skills help people to see what claims are being made, what evidence is brought to bear in developing those claims, and what conclusions are reached. People must be accustomed to ferret out underlying, usually unstated, assumptions and likely motives of communicators. Although finding "right" answers is difficult, people can at least employ careful reasoning to choose the best option available.

Fifth, going beyond reasoning and communicating skills, people must deepen the *will* to communicate with increasingly high ethical quality. In the conclusion of her intercultural communication study, Steglitz (1993) warned that a person with high intercultural adaptability skills need not necessarily use them for "ethical, non-exploitative, and generally benevolent intercultural practice" (p. 194). For example, a person might use such intercultural sophistication to take unfair advantage of someone in a cross-cultural business negotiation. Thus, sound reasoning and skilful communication do not necessarily imbue communicative transactions with high ethical quality.

Sixth, people need to note the metaphorical language they use in this abstract enterprise of ethics. Vertical images include "building" character, laying good moral "foundations," "elevating" the soul, "uplifting" human personality, developing "higher" standards, and experiencing consciousness "raising." Closely related is the "growth" metaphor, such as to grow in wisdom and compassion, to mature, to increase moral "development," to "mold" character. The "health" metaphor is also frequent: People talk of making life healthier for individuals and for society, of "strengthening" moral fiber and reasoning ability, and of "empowering" personality. Metaphors with the *en-* prefix are often employed: the wish to "enrich" the communication experience, to "enlighten" discourse, "enhance" self-esteem, "ennoble" the communication transaction, and "enlarge" the human capacity for compassion. The qualities may remain fuzzy, but the metaphors help to obtain an approximate view of the objectives in pursuing communication ethics. Underlying the values and objectives is the obvious assumption that people favor life, seek to further and sustain it, to better fulfill it, to show reverence toward it, to dignify it. Common metaphors also refer to ethical lapses in communication: the credibility "gap" between the populace and their elected officials, the "torn," "frayed," or "loosened" "fabric" of society, "shattered" or "eroded" trust. The bridges of society are "undermined," the well or circulation "poisoned." Confidence is "lowered"; there is a "breakdown" of communication. People "short-circuit" reasoning with emotionalism, "retard" values, or "circumvent" the issue at hand. Studying the metaphors commonly used to describe the role of ethics in communication, elucidates underlying assumptions about ethical behavior.

Seventh, people need better insight into themselves, to perceive their values clearly, to be willing and able to engage in self-examination, and to strenthen ethical commitment. People need to focus on the first person, *I,* rather than the second person, *you,* and the third person, *they.* It is easier to discuss ethical shortcomings in others, less painful to look at cases where "they"—government officials, celebrities, relatives, business tycoons, mass media moguls—have behaved questionably. Others should be honest, open-minded, and fair. But are we? As has been frequently observed, many people want to change the world, but only a few want to change themselves. Introspection is painful, but leads to high ethical quality in communicative contexts, and increases the courage to engage in risk taking to fulfill ethical guidelines. Introspection can also produce the pleasurable experience of building inner integrity, self-esteem, inner peace. People need to be strong enough to do highly ethical acts even when no one notices, when "no one is counting." A cartoon portrayed a gentleman glumly looking out the living room window, while his wife responded to a visiting friend's query, "What's he so despondent about?" with the answer, "Today he stood up to be counted, and no one was counting!"

Eighth, people must come to appreciate, tolerate, and understand others with different views. It has been said that it is good to live and let live, but better to live and help live. To demonstrate a sincere desire to work in concert with, and enhance the well-being of, those with whom we may drastically disagree is obviously easier said than done, but it is a challenging objective. Dag Hammarskjold (1964), the Swedish diplomat who served as secretary-general of the United Nations, wisely admonished "You can only hope to find a lasting solution to a conflict if you have learned to see the other objectively, but, at the same time, to experience his *[sic]* difficulties subjectively" (p. 114).

Ninth, people must be able and willing to be proactive, to engage in behavior that lessens the likelihood of low ethical quality communication's occurring. Instead of focusing only on unfortunate episodes, people must seek to forestall them.

Tenth, people must be exposed to examples of high ethical communication acts as well as of low ones. The mass media focus on ethical shortcomings of people in high places, not on their commendable actions, on social problems, not solutions, and thus increase the awareness of negative ethics.

Finally, by viewing the ethical dimension in all areas of human communication—interpersonal, small group, organizational, public speaking, intercultural, and mass communication—people may sense the unity of the field of speech communication and the many opportunities to enrich life as rhetors, audiences, and critics.

TEACHING ETHICS

Scholars, teachers, parents, and the general citizenry are increasingly pondering whether ethics can or should be taught in schools. Some parents want very much to make teaching ethics mandatory in secondary schools, but some teachers oppose this. Nazario (1990) pointed out that teachers may fear lack of funding, lack of follow-through, extra responsibilities and burdens, loss of an existing course in the curriculum, parental complaints, and possible lawsuits. Also, and ironically, teachers worry about success: if students' moral standards rise considerably above those of their parents, family discord could well result.

This book, however, focuses on the college and university level. Rest, a scholar who has long and carefully researched the teaching of ethics in higher education, has concluded that college and university students are still in a formative stage, that a formal education setting enhances moral reasoning, and that after people leave school, they reach a moral plateau. He has refuted the claim that by the time young people arrive at college their character development is established and little ethical growth is possible. Rest (1988) found that "formal education (years in college / professional school) is a powerful and consistent correlate"(p. 23) to positive changes in moral problem solving. This improvement, he stated, can be linked to actual behavior in subsequent life experiences. Rest maintained that whatever the deficiencies of the teaching process, they "do not foreclose the prospect of more penetrating analyses of professional ethics, more dynamic teaching, and more helpful curriculum materials being developed" (p. 26). Rest and Narvaez (1994) presented a collection of research studies showing that ethics can be learned and that subsequent moral development can be discerned in the professions of teaching, nursing, counseling, accounting, auditing, dentistry, medicine, veterinary medicine, sports, and journalism. Included in Rest and Navarez's volume is McNeel's (1994) finding that at a specific college at which students were taught ethics, a strong growth in their moral judgment from the first to the fourth year was documented. In studying ethics training and dentistry, Bebeau (1994) concluded: "Our ongoing studies .... demonstrate that a curriculum of rather modest duration can influence ethical development in measurable ways, provided that curriculum incorporates the elements of effective instruction" (p. 138). Self and Baldwin (1994) asserted that medical education "must teach students to clarify and understand the ethical standards of the profession and of society; to seek and develop insight into one's personal values; to acquire a method of apprehending and appreciating the values and expectations of patients, families, and society" (p. 146). Thoma (1994) concluded that there is a definite link between moral judgment and action.

As for the practical proceedings of teaching ethics, there are several possibilites. A special course could be created, or ethics units could be inserted into existing courses. Class work could include discussion of readings on ethics drawn from scholarly books and periodicals in speech communication or related fields. Students could also read fiction in which communication ethics are an important dimension. For example, J. Black (1995) suggested analyzing "ethical dilemmas raised in numerous novels in which journalists are central characters and find themselves making 'tough calls'...[on] questions of accuracy and fairness, objectivity and truth-telling, conflicts of interest, deception, diversity, invasion of privacy, relationships with sources, and just about every other interesting dilemma facing journalists" (p. 9). Guest lecturers could be drawn from academia and from practitioners in various fields. Classes could include small group discussions, student debates on issues and cases, role playing, and discussions of real or hypothetical cases created by teacher or students. Cases could be open-ended and deal with ambiguities or closed, that is, students could choose between two or more proposed solutions and defend their choices. Such classes as communication ethics could be a "safe," mutually supportive atmosphere in which students could grapple with ethical dilemmas rather than doing so for the first time alone on the job.

Whether a course in speech communication ethics should be mandatory is open to debate. If mandatory, all graduates in the department will be familiar with this increasingly important subject. But mandatory courses frequently generate resentment, and nonmotivated, hostile students scarcely contribute to a healthy atmosphere in class. Classes may be too large for the students to be fully involved or discuss issues in depth. I prefer that such a course be an elective, for it is too important to be thrust on thoughtful students unless they freely choose it.

Students should take an ethics course shortly before graduation, after they have a grounding in the theory, concepts, and terminology of the portion of the field on which they have focused. The ethics course, touching on all areas of the field, then serves as a synthesis and gives students an opportunity to reflect on, and probe more deeply into, their educational experience.

Many people have objected to the teaching of ethics. Dogmatic teachers, whose private value systems could dominate the class proceedings, could create a rigid atmosphere and sharply curtail openness and a range of viewpoints. At the other extreme, exceedingly open-minded teachers could convey to students a wishy-washy approach in which a particular ethical choice would not make much difference because of the many but equally acceptable divergent views. Instructors might be unqualified, with little knowledge of ethics or little training in teaching the subject. Students might be left more confused than committed and might learn only clever ways to justify low ethical quality behavior. The course might become a politicized version of a national value system, feed a provincial attitude of self-righteousness, and portray other countries as possessing inferior, even dangerous values. After the defeat of Japan in World War II, the U.S. occupation government forbade the teaching of ethics in Japanese schools because of the strong nationalistic and militaristic tone of their prewar ethics, which contributed greatly to the aggressive policies of the Japanese government. Because of political and business corruption changes, contemporary Japan is witnessing a resurgence of interest in ethics; but efforts to reinstate ethics courses in their schools created sharp controversy. Some observers feared a return of nationalistic militarism; others welcomed an effort to build a responsible social conscience. The United States, too, might nationalize its ethical thrust into a superficial flag-waving exercise. Some people consider ethics and moral development as entrenching the social mores of the status quo and stifling individualism and pluralism.

Before leaving this section on teaching ethics in colleges and universities, I must emphasize that after the years of formal education, there is a strong need to continually upgrade ethical commitments. Backsliding can easily develop. Periodic workshops and seminars for doctors and other professionals help to update and energize their skill and will to communicate as ethically as possible, after attitudes learned in their professional training begin to wither away. Alumni groups could be well served by continuing education on the subject, and professors and teaching assistants in speech communication departments would be wise to arrange for on-going workshops to keep themselves ethically alert.

As a society, we need to continually educate ourselves to exert ethical leadership. Paul Mann (1995) pointed out that "when noble minds shrink from the task of leadership ignoble minds will rush to fill the vacuum" (p. 28). Derek Bok (1988), former President of Harvard, clearly enunciated the role of higher education: "A university that refuses to take ethical dilemmas seriously violates its basic obligations to society" (p. 15).

EXERCISES

1. Explore the interest in ethics on your campus. For example, survey the course offerings in departments, look for ethics centers (biomedical

ethics center, mass media ethics center), check on special seminars, programs, and lectures, on applied ethics, and find out whether informal or formal faculty networks share an interest in ethics. Write a summary report, give a speech in your class, or both.

2. Explore indexes to journals in the various areas of communication (see the References and Suggested Additional Readings at the end of this text for some relevant journals) for articles about ethics. Summarize your findings in a written report.

3. In a printed program of a recent or upcoming convention in an area of communication, note how many panels and individual papers are devoted to ethics. List the authors and titles of papers. Write to at least one author to secure a copy of the paper if it is available. Eventually share your findings with your classmates in a written report, an oral communication format, or both. For instance, four or five students might explore different professional associations related to communication (e.g., Speech Communication Association and its four regional associations, International Communication Association, associations in journalism and mass communication, public relations, business) and share their findings in a panel discussion.

4. Linger on some of the assertions made in this chapter, such as "A good orator is a good man speaking well," or "In order to be a truly.... persuasive speaker, nothing is more necessary than to be a virtuous man." Develop a case enlarging on one such assertion, develop a case against one assertion, or in a jocular vein play around with such a claim in a humorous presentation. Present your effort in a class speech or a written paper.

5. Write a paper in which you dwell on the different aspects of the definition of ethics given in this chapter, and agree or disagree as you see fit. As a conclusion, construct your own definition of ethics.

6. Write a paper, give a speech, or both, in which you illustrate at length the contention that ethical dilemmas are often a conflict between two good values, not necessarily between good and bad values.

7. Write a paper, in which you discuss Josephson's six "pillars of character". Would you want to phrase the six differently? Would you want to add to the list? Why?

8. Write a paper in which you discuss the pros and cons of utilizing the EQ Scale.

9. Write a paper in which you develop the notion of rightsabilities, that is, the intertwining of rights and responsibilities. Evaluate the way the notion is developed in this chapter, and suggest a better way of handling the idea.

10. Write a paper on your main objective in taking this course or in reading this book. Why is that objective important to you? Construct a list of what you would consider to be your five most important objectives.

2

Sources For Ethical Guidelines

Where can we find guidance when grappling with decision making about ethics in communication? In a paraphrase of the Golden Rule, Communicate unto others as

1. your religion would have you do,
2. a person would have you do,
3. a group to which you give loyalty would have you do,
4. your society's values would have you do,
5. your society's laws would have you do,
6. consequential principles would have you do,
7. nonconsequential principles would have you do,
8. the enhancement of human nature would have you do,
9. the dialogical spirit would have you do,
10. The Golden Rule would have you do.

In this chapter, these many sources of guidance are explored to lay the groundwork for discussions of ethical issues embedded in the communicative process in later chapters.

RELIGIOUS ROOTS

Millions of people on this planet are guided by religious admonitions of ancient heritages whose organizational frameworks have perpetuated their teachings, values, and rules for centuries—for better or for worse, depending on a person's viewpoint.[1] Although their origins are far removed from us in time and place, these ancient religions speak to people today in a prescriptive and compelling fashion about communi-

---

[1]This section draws on one of my articles (1992, June): Ancient eastern and western religions as guides for contemporary communication ethics. In J. A. Jaska (Ed.), *Conference proceedings of the second national communication ethics conference* (pp. 58–67). Annandale, VA: Speech Communication Association. Used by permission of publisher.

19

cating at a high ethical quality level. Jews, Christians, and Muslims with the same monotheistic heritage trace their roots to Abraham and Jehovah—God—Allah, and honor their respective scriptures as being uniquely inspired by the Creator. In Asia, Hinduism, Buddhism, Taoism, and Confucianism have dominated the religious and cultural landscape. Admittedly, Confucianism is less a religion than a humanistic, psychological, sociological body of thought; indeed, the People's Republic of China excludes it from the listing of religions in China (Information Office of the State Council, 1991, p. 30). But Confucianism's orientation and commitment to all of life make it a religion in the eyes of many despite debates about its religious nature. (Ames, 1984; Overmyer, 1995; Taylor & Arbuckle, 1995).

People often ignore Eastern religions' rich resources, perhaps from a justifiable concern about mixing church and state, perhaps from a less justifiable ignorance of, or lack of interest in, those religions outside the Western heritage and from a general disdain for what may be perceived to be outdated, irrelevant, "primitive" admonitions and claims. Without being believers, people can still appreciate to some degree the power of the values expressed in these various traditions and can learn from them. It is worth sifting the chaff—admittedly abundant—from the wheat to gain an appreciation for human beings' centuries-old struggle toward ethical communication as part of their coping with life in all its dimensions.

A few cautions are in order. First, singular labels, like *Christianity* or *Islam*, do not acknowledge the diverse schisms and factions within each heritage that have developed because of religious and ideological emphases as well as political, economic, sociological, and cultural factors. Second, although I am here trying to synthesize similarities in the teachings of major religions, there are large differences—vast gulfs—separating them. Religions create tight, unified in -groups of adherents, bodies of believers, and thus strong out -groups of nonbelievers, with resulting pity, disdain, and even hatred between the religious communities. Third, cutting across religious frameworks are different motivations behind the ethical admonishments, from a mature sense of cosmic linkage, to sincere devotion, to blind submission, to primitive fear. Such disparate motives suggest considerable variance in different strands within each religion in addition to those between the religions. Finally, the works cited in my discussion are of course only hints of the resources available and are not exhaustive.

These religious heritages share several communicative characteristics. First, argument from authority dominated their mode of reasoning:

Ethical admonitions issued ultimately from deities or revered sages, who revealed their will and wisdom through holy or venerated documents. Second, admonishments were frequently cast in terse, two -valued, negative commandments. Moses did not submit the "ten suggestions"! Third, teachings were often embedded in a narrative form, like parables, legends, fables, colloquies, anecdotes, aphorisms, proverbs, or analogies, designed to make concepts and values readily understandable and easily remembered. Fourth, a sense of intimate linkage between the divine or sage communicator and the human communicatee emerged. A covenant or contract involving reciprocal promises and mutual commitments allowed the adherents to concentrate on following the wishes of the creator or sage rather than on practicing the mores of contemporaries. Fifth, ancient religions, especially the monotheistic Judaism, Christianity, and Islam, projected a strong sense of an omnipresent audience, emphasizing that the anthropomorphic Jehovah–God–Allah was an ubiquitous eavesdropper, cognizant of, and judging, people's every word, act, and thought. Sixth, a central motivator in these religious perspectives was an explicit promise of rewards and punishments, both in this life and in a life after death. Finally, religious traditions stressed individual responsibilities, not rights.

Against this backdrop, certain central admonitions for ethical communication were embedded in these heritages. First, an important issue was telling the truth, avoiding deception. In biblical literature some admonitions were positive (i.e., truth or a truthful person was praised); but more often sharp negative warnings are uttered against lying (Lev. 19:11 (Revised Standard Version); I Kings 22:16; 2 Chron. 18:15; Pss. 5:6, 15:1–3, 24:4, 52:2–3, 59:12, 63:11, 120:2–4, 140:11; Prov. 6:17, 19, 14–25, 30:8; Eccles. 12:10; Isa. 59:14–15; Jer. 7:28, 9:3–5; Dan. 8:12; Zech. 8:16–17, 19; Mark 7:22; John 8:44; 2 Cor. 6:7; Eph. 4:15, 25; Col. 3:9). The book of Proverbs warned against "the getting of treasures by a lying tongue" and urged hearers and readers to "buy the truth, and sell it not" (21:6, 23:23). Falk (1995, pp.5 -6) cited a number instances where Jewish scripture deprecated lying. Islam likewise honored truthfulness and expressed faith in its triumph over falsehood: "We hurl the truth against falsehood and it crashes into it, and lo! it vanishes" (Palmer, 1947, 21:18; see also 34:47). As Kirkwood (1989) discussed, truth has been at the center of values in Hinduism, and one of the five Precepts of Buddhism was "to abstain from false speech" (Conze, 1984, p. 70; see also pp. 76–78, 83). Mencius (372–289 B.C.E.), who was to Confucius as Paul was to Jesus, reminded followers of the proper motivation: "One must always speak the truth, but it is not with a view to become famous for upright conduct" (Mencius, 1960, p.162). Kühn and Kuschel (1993) emphasized how the various religions were concerned with truthtelling. A second heavily emphasized admonition about communication ethics was that of not slandering another person. The Ninth Commandment stated: "Thou shalt not bear false witness against thy neighbor" (Exod. 20:16; Deut. 5:20), and biblical writers generally decried slander (Pss. 15:1–3, 101:5; Prov. 10:18, 30:10; Jer. 6:28, 9:4; Matt. 15:19; Rom. 1:29–30, 3:8; Titus 2:3, 3:2). The Koran warned: "And those who malign believing men and believing women undeservedly, they bear the guilt of slander and manifest sin" (Pickthall, 1953, 33:58). Buddhism likewise deprecated slander. The Buddha said in a sermon: "The slanderer is like one who flings dust at another when the wind is contrary; the dust does but return on him who threw it" (Lin, 1942, p. 363). Buddhism, Taoism, and Confucianism all stressed living in harmony and speaking ill of no one. In short, these ancient religions emphasized that the gift of human communication was not to be used to injure other human beings. Defamation in writing—libel—was hardly yet a concern, but oral defamation—slander—certainly was.

A third major admonition was the warning not to blaspheme God or other sacred aspects or figures of the religion. Blasphemy is speaking irreverently about something sacred, profaning, dishonoring, reviling, or being contemptuous toward it. According to the Third Commandment, "Thou shalt not take the name of Jehovah thy God in Vain" (Exod. 20:7; Deut. 5:11). Jesus warned his hearers not to blaspheme (Matt. 12:31–32). The Koran admonished likewise: "Lo! those who malign Allah and His messenger, Allah hath cursed them in the world and the Hereafter, and hath prepared for them the doom of the disdained" (Pickthall, 1953, 33:57). Some contemporary Muslim countries still mete out mandatory death penalties for blasphemy. Buddhism clearly warned against speaking disrespectfully of the Buddha, his teachings, and the Buddhist order. Secular religions like contemporary Communism likewise brook no blasphemy, and those who speak against the Party are sent to prisons or to the countryside to be re-educated. Ancient Roman emperors were masters at punishing those who spoke disparagingly about the state or the divine emperor.

Fourth, believers were urged to avoid numerous other inappropriate uses of speech which were judged to be demeaning to others and to life in general. They were to avoid speech that was evil, shameful, foolish, clever, cunning, glib, vain, or too wordy (Pss. 34:3, 140:11; Eccles. 5:2,

10:12; Matt. 6:7; Eph. 4:14, 5:4; Col. 3:8; 1 Pet. 2:1; see also Confucius, 1938, 15:26; Lin, 1942, p. 678; Palmer, 1947, 23:3). Flattery was denigrated (Pss. 5:9, 7:21), and Confucius provided an interesting reason why: " I detest flatterers out of fear that they become confused with propriety" (Mencius, 1960, p. 164). Buddhist writings warned against being taken in by insincere praise (Oliver, 1971, p. 82). Biblical writers expressed disapproval of gossipmongering (Lev. 18:16; Prov. 16:28; Matt. 12:36; Rom.1:28; 2 Corin. 3:8, 12:20), and seductive speech (Pss. 55:27; Prov. 7:21; Rom. 16:18; Eph. 5:6).

Fifth, these religious traditions stressed the need to earn the trust of others to communicate effectively and ethically. Adherents were to demonstrate ethical qualities by example, by their very lives, not just by their words. Jesus made this point by asserting that evil people bring forth evil things including evil speech and good people bring forth good things including good speech (Matt.12:33–35). In Taoist literature, Chuang Tzu said: "The Sages of old first strengthened their own character before they tried to strengthen that of others" (Lin, 1942, p. 645). Confucius emphasized the importance of trust in human interactions: "A gentleman obtains the confidence of those under him, before putting burdens upon them. If he does so before he has obtained their confidence, they feel that they are being exploited. It is also true that he obtains the confidence [of those above him] before criticizing them. If he does so before he has obtained their confidence, they feel that they are being slandered" (Confucius, 1938, 19:10).

Finally, these ancient religions admonished communicators to enhance the lives of those around them. In this they went beyond the three fundamental purposes of rhetoric set forth by Aristotle—to inform, to persuade, and to please—and added a fourth, to edify. In his letters, Paul admonished: "Let no corrupt speech proceed out of your mouth, but such as is good for edifying as the need may be, that it may give grace to them that hear" (Eph. 4:29; see also Eph., 4:15; Col. 4:6). As expressed by Christians, Rotzoll, and Fackler (1995, p. 17) the Judeo -Christian ideal was "giving and forgiving with uncalculating spontaneity and spending oneself to fulfill a neighbor's well -being." The Koran presented a vivid image: "A good word is like a good tree whose root is firm, and whose branches are in the sky; it gives its fruit at every season" (Palmer, 1947, 14:29–30). The ultimate objective of ethical communication in these Eastern and Western religions was for people to examine and improve their ethical behavior as much as possible to glorify the Creator.

PERSONAL ROLE MODELS

People can draw on broad, abstract religious guidelines, and also look to concrete, specific human beings as models for guidance in decisions and actions. What would our parents, siblings, relatives, or close friends do in a situation? What would they think of us when we behave in a certain manner? We would not want to disappoint a person in the community whom we respect, and whom we feel respects us, be it the grocer, hardware store owner, banker, mechanic, or a worker. A federal judge, Miles Lord, ilustrated the power of the small community in which he grew up: Often in making judicial decisions he said, "I take myself back to this little town. 'Wonder what would the people in Crosby/Ironton [Minnesota] say about this?' I'm able to get a good deal of help in deciding what I think is right, fair, appropriate and just" (Corgan, 1995, pp. 24–25). For those with dysfunctional families or uninspiring community experiences, role models can be impressive public figures, government officials, business executives, labor leaders, or athletes, who are respected as highly ethical. Teachers or clergy are often role models. In addition to contemporaries, historical figures may serve as standards for decisions and actions. What would Jesus, Confucius, Francis of Assisi, Erasmus, Mahatma Gandhi, Eleanor Roosevelt, Martin Luther King, Jr. have done in this situation? Even a fictional hero or heroine may be a role model.

The potential dangers of hero worship ought not to be overlooked; in many contexts hero worship signals abandoning individual responsibility. Religious or political groups may try to inculcate hero worship, sometimes to a ludicrous degree, to further their own interests. For example, Communist regimes systematically created *hero workers* portrayed as superhumanly perfect, for the citizenry to emulate (Chen, 1993). Despite potential dangers, people depend on, and can profit from, individual embodiments as guides when striving for high ethical quality communication. People should also turn their gazes inward and remind themselves that they are potential role models for others and that the examples they set may have far reaching chain effects. Are we today the person we had wanted to be in our childhood idealism?

GROUP LOYALTIES

People often use as ethical standards the guidelines and expectations of groups with which they are closely linked and whose culture they respect or feel obligated to uphold. In addition to families and religious affiliations, tightly knit groups like sororities, fraternities, or coworkers often play a powerful role. Students may cheat on exams, lie to instructors, or engage in other questionable behavior that is accepted by "brothers" or "sisters." The implicit or explicit standards of behavior in the workplace may be used to justify decisions and actions because "that is the way it is done around here." Some companies have found it wise to construct a statement of values. Ethical tone is enhanced when top leadership in an organization demonstrates by example that high ethical quality is expected. Professions—medical, legal, academic, public relations, mass media journalism—may have written codes of ethics to which those practicing in these areas are expected to live up. Gorlin (1994) brought together many codes in areas of law, health, education, government service, and business.

Codes of ethics have many positive effects. The very task of creating a code can be a profitable experience for an organization: Objectives are crystallized and verbalized, grounds for standards are studied, and obligations to customers or clients, employees, management, stakeholders, and the general public are made explicit. Well-constructed codes can be particularly helpful to new members of a profession or business: Ethical expectations are stated at the outset, the historical roots of an organization become appreciated, and specific issues can be addressed. Codes help organizations see a broad landscape by turning from detailed, day-to-day focus on profits to a long-range view of the reason for their existence. Well-written codes suggest that a profession or business can police the behavior of its members, and can forestall damaging attacks from outsiders like government or concerned citizens. Consumers may be significantly protected. Codes may encourage members of a group not only to do or to avoid doing certain things, but also to be living examples of highly ethical people, contributing positively to the organization and to the general public.

Written codes of ethics can also have drawbacks that bring into question their actual worth. Their language may be so abstract and ambiguous that their meaning and application can be easily manipulated to mean almost anything. Enforcement is often difficult, and codes must be periodically updated. Critics assert that codes have not noticeably elevated the ethical behavior of the groups using them. Outsiders may view codes as smoke screens. Furthermore, in a profession like journalism, practitioners may claim that their constitutional freedom of expression is curtailed by a code. Finally, codes are easily forgotten, and certainly need to be prominently publicized and revisited periodically to keep ethical sensitivity sharp. Seminars, retreats, workshops, or brief meetings, held at least annually, could serve as ethical audits much like annual financial audits.

Johannesen (1996, pp. 197–220) summarized guidelines for constructing a meaningful and effective ethical code. These guidelines include using clear language, speaking to the specific concerns of a particular profession or business, stating realistic goals, honoring specific values, revealing true concern for the well -being of the general public, and being enforceable.

Members of groups need to recognize that their loyalties go beyond their groups to encompass all humankind. Cult and gang members, fraternity or sorority members, students at military academies, business employees, professional people, and all other examples of group identities must avoid the dangers of inward-looking parochialism and group-think. Loyalty can lead one to dangerous acts as well as to lofty behavior.

SOCIETY'S VALUES

Beyond a person's group is the broad political, social, and cultural landscape of society. Social values are another powerful source of guidelines for ethical decision making. These deeply embedded cultural values and traditions are not always positive. Although values are sometimes nebulous, they can be articulated with a considerable degree of accuracy and meaning.

Values in the U.S. cultural milieu are numerous and complex. Joseph (1995) stated: "What makes one an American is not genetics, ideology or theology. What Americans share in common is a set of values" (p. 12). U.S. society emphasizes individualism, the dignity and intrinsic worth of each person, and honors freedom and mutual respect. There is a commitment to blending freedom and responsibility, to understanding that self -government takes work and effort by the governed as well as by the governors. Without waiting for, or depending on, government to provide all the answers to society's needs, this society honors citizen -initiated programs and volunteerism. It asserts that people are capable of governing themselves, that they can think through issues and arrive at solutions to society's problems; it honors rationality and openness in public discourse. The citizenry should be free from coercion, should have unrestricted access to information to make wise decisions, and should not be impeded in analyzing issues from divergent standpoints.

A free and vigorous press is fundamental. Democracy honors the secret ballot, free and open debate, freedom of dissent, assembly, and worship. The outcomes of these freedoms and procedures are unknown, but people assume that the results are worthwhile, more so than if those freedoms and procedures were not in place. People are willing to live with this ambiguity and enter into the social contract that recognizes a need to give up some freedoms to the state for the general good. Majority rule is honored although people realize that the majority is not necessarily right and that in the future today's minority may become the majority. Hence it is important to protect the minority. People's ancestors, and contemporary immigrants, came here looking for equality of opportunity for all regardless of their initial station in life, for an honoring of fairness, egalitarianism, and diversity. Fairness injects a qualitative dimension beyond the quantitative sense of equality. Hubert Humphrey (1976) closed his memoirs with this summary statement: "Our democracy is the most exceptional attempt at popular governance in the history of the world" (p. 438). These values form a crucible in which people absorb their impact. Public and interpersonal discourse, draws on these societal values, norms, and expectations, often unconsciously and automatically. Of course, just because values are extolled does not mean they are practiced, or that everyone is committed to them. Strong minority pockets within any society are greatly at variance with its major value premises. Some states or regions have—or claim to have—a special sense of civic virtue, a sense of right and wrong. Indeed, the Supreme Court has sidestepped defining obscenity, and has left it up to the operative community standards. A recent resurgence of states rights, a return of power to the states, emphasizes that states rather than the federal government know what is best. Whether this move reflects a growing provincial fragmentation of values remains to be seen.

Behaviors, specifically communicative acts, that strengthen society's values are ranked high on the Ethical Quality (EQ) Scale. Common metaphors expressing this belief show that whatever furthers the *health* and *growth* of society, whatever preserves its *fabric*, is good, is high on the EQ Scale. This assumes that a given status quo is worthy of continuation. But some political regimes have been established through force and other unprincipled means, often by a self -serving clique. Why should people hope that their fabric remains strong? In the last few decades people have witnessed dehumanizing cruel political value systems, which fortunately ended. Hitler's Germany, Mussolini's Italy, Imperial Japan, military dictatorships, apartheid society in South Africa, and the Soviet Union. Vaclav Havel (1992), president of the Czech Republic, wrote a devastating critique of Communist society:

> Life in the system is so thoroughly permeated with hypocrisy and lies: government by bureaucracy is called popular government; the working class is enslaved in the name of the working class; the complete degradation of the individual is presented as his [sic] ultimate liberation; depriving people of information is called making it available; the use of power to manipulate is called the public control of power, and the arbitrary abuse of power is called observing the legal code; the repression of culture is called its development; the expansion of imperial influence is presented as support for the oppressed; the lack of free expression becomes the highest form of freedom; farcical elections become the highest form of democracy; banning independent thought becomes the most scientific of world views; military occupation becomes fraternal assistance. (pp. 135–136)

The deterioration of such value systems' health and growth, and the destruction of their fabric are cause for gratitude. In evaluating a society's values we need to be alert to the likelihood of an egocentric mindset. Tuan (1977), a contemporary geographer, wrote: "Human groups nearly everywhere tend to regard their own homeland as the center of the world. A people who believe they are at the center claim, implicitly, the ineluctable worth of their location" (p. 149). This tendency was expresed by the 5th century B.C.E. Greek historian, Herodotus (trans. 1947):

> (Nations) honour most their nearest neighbors whom they esteem next to themselves; those who live beyond these they honour in the second degree; and so with the remainder, the further they are removed, the less the esteem in which they old them. The reason is, that they look upon themselves as very greatly superior in all respects to the rest of mankind, regarding others as approaching to excellence in proporation as they dwell nearer to them; whence it comes to pass that those who are farthest off must be the most degraded of mankind. (p. 75)

Thus, the values of a society need to be constantly evaluated as worthy or unworthy guides, as do religious, personal, and organizational or professional ideals.

LEGAL STATUTES

People in developed and cohesive societies construct rules, regulations and laws, to function successfully in reasonable harmony and happiness. Laws are reactive responses to correct the ills and meet the needs of societal life. They are the price of living communally. Laws set forth the impermissible and carry with them the power to enforce punishments: thus they are another source of ethical guides in human communication under the premise that to obey legal statutes is ethical. For example, there are laws stating that in the presence of a third party a person cannot make statements that are false and injurious to another person's reputation. Such statements are defamatory, whether in written (libel) or spoken form (slander). A person accused and convicted in a court of law could be subject to heavy fines or a prison sentence. Federal and state laws and court rulings seek to deal with obscenity, pornography, and deceptive advertising. On the other hand, "we cannot necessarily settle moral questions by settling the legal questions. The law may permit immoral behavior, the law may require immoral behavior, or the law may be morally justified but circumstances may be such that transgressing the law is permissible or even morally required"(J. Callahan, 1988, p. 11). Using civil disobediance to overturn racial segregation laws in parts of the United States or to counteract apartheid laws in South Africa illustrates such situations.

In many religions, judgments of right and wrong are based on moral criteria in their holy writings; legal criteria are based on collections of laws, for instance, a book of statutes. In the United States a legislative body, composed of representatives of the people put by majority vote a law in the book of statutes. Legislative bodies often claim that the voice of the people is the voice of God, an echo and rephrasing of the old claim that the voice of the king or the voice of the emperor is the voice of God of the voice of Heaven. Such claims are not merely exuberant expressions of democratic arrogance but statements that the voice of the majority of the people's representatives freely elected and assembled is as close to the universal voice of God as humans can be. For example, a law in which the maximum speed on a given stretch of highway is set at 65 miles per hour is a response to a specific, identifiable, recurring problem in society (people driving dangerously) and states in specific, measureable, and enforceable language the admonition to drive safely. Legal codes thus become an explicit and enduring source of ethical practices.

Legal criteria are the lowest common denominators of society, below which any behavior is unacceptable. But to do only what is legal is to stop at the elementary school level of moral behavior. Just as learning to read and write are lifelong processes of improvement and refinement, so too do people progress to higher and higher levels of ethical development and commitment beyond the level of guidance in legal codes.

CONSEQUENTIALISM

The possible consequences of our communicative acts often affect our ethical decision making. Under this ends -based criterion, for example, if we lie or withhold information, we wonder who will be affected. We think about the consequences not only on our immediate audience, but also on unseen audiences distant in place and time. We realize that our behaior may affect ourselves, by lowering or raising self -esteem, strengthening or weakening integrity. Oliver (1971) wrote that in Buddhism "whatever may be said has direct consequences not alone (not even especially) for the hearer, but most explicitly and inevitably for the speaker himself [sic]. This is vastly different from the Western ethics" (p. 77). Actions may affect family, friends, work associates, and other groups by bringing shame or prestige to them. The general public may be significantly affected. Often people try to predict the quantitative dimension, that is, does an act benefit many more than those who are adversely affected? The greatest good to the greatest number is the familiar source of justification in this context. What is meant by *good* introduces a qualitative aspect; the consequentialist guideline adds a concern for the minority involved, that is, the greatest good for the greatest number, but with the least possible harm to those not benefitting. When elevated to a philosophical level, this judgment becomes consequentialism or utilitarianism. Whatever has social utility and usefulness, whatever brings the most happiness and well -being to the most people, gains a high ethical quality rating. Increased sensitivity to the consequences of communication attitudes and acts is a desirable goal. For example, when three U.S. servicemen stationed on Okinawa raped a 12 -year -old girl, a fierce anti -American feeling erupted throughout Japan. We all too often lamely lament, "If I had only known what the consequences would have been.... ." Assessing the results of actions is a flexible guideline; certain communicative acts might bring highly positive consequences in one situation but not in another. This fact is both a strength and a weakness of consequentialism and emphasizes the need for the guideline of nonconsequentialism.

NONCONSEQUENTIALISM

Whereas the consequential criterion is result oriented, nonconsequentialism is rule oriented. Consequentialism focuses on what comes out of the tunnel, the finish line; nonconsequentialism focuses on what goes into the tunnel, the starting line. The latter focuses on a principle, and insists that it is our duty to live up to that ideal, independent of the outcome. For instance, in nonconsequentialism, the commandment "Thou shalt not lie" should universally govern and should not be rationalized away depending on the variables in a particular situation. With this deontological focus, something ought to be done simply because it is right, not because of other considerations. People have an obligation to follow a rule, wherever it leads, without thinking of the costs and the results, without asking what others may say or do, who may be disadvantaged, who will approve, or how variable factors will balance. The only question in inconsequentialism is, "Is it right?"

HUMAN NATURE ENHANCEMENT

We are, or should be, led by the desire not only to preserve human life but to enhance it. We thus focus on the essence of human nature, on ontology. *Onto* is the Greek term for "being" or "existence." Whatever furthers these characteristics of human nature is deemed to be highly ethical; whatever weakens human "beings", is a dehumanizing act low on the ethical scale. Of course, those who do not subscribe to the premise that we ought to care about the worth, dignity, and preservation of humanity, never could be convinced to worry about its enhancement.

What are the attributes unique to human beings? We possess the intellectual ability to reason, and whatever shakes this capacity, whatever weakens this cognitive power, whatever tempts us to bypass the use of rationality, is of low ethical quality. We have the capacity and compulsion to communicate via symbols and thus to contribute to our personality development and our creative powers unless debilitating ailments like a stroke, aphasia, or Alzheimer's disease destroy our speaking and cognitive abilities. Scientists studying chimpanzees and other animals increasingly teach us to be humbler and more accurate in our claims to superiority. Other animals have rudimentary communicating abilities, but they do not approximate the complexity of human communication or reflect the human compulsion to interact. Human beings possess a concern for values and judge things to be good or bad. We experience a wide range of feelings, like pride, guilt, joy, sorrow, pity, love, friendship, despondency, and humor. We can imagine, hope, and appreciate beauty. We have a concern for rights and responsibilities. We embrace freedom as well as community. We have the capacity for self -control, and as Willard Gaylin (1990), a psychiatrist and president of the Hastings Center, wrote, "One of the primary aspects of our humanness is the capacity to modify ourselves" (p. 21). Ramsey (1978), writing as "a Christian ethicist" (p. xiii) insisted that "the notion that an individual human life is absolutely unique, inviolable, irreplaceable, noninter-changeable, not substitutable, and not meldable with other lives is a notion that exists in our civilization because it is Christian" (p. xiv). Whether or not we attach a religious connotation to the human nature standard, communicative acts that weaken human attributes are to be deprecated, and those that strengthen them are high on the Ethical Quality (EQ) Scale.

DIALOGICAL SPIRIT

Coalescing many of the previously discussed ideas about communicative characteristics brings into focus a single identity emphasizing true dia-logue between participants. Dialogue here refers to a spirit, an attitude, a mind -set that is reflected by the techniques and behaviors, the verbal and nonverbal cues, of those who are interacting. The degree of ethicality in a communicative exchange rests on how close to the dialogical char-acteristics the participants come. The characteristics are usually clarified by contrasting them with the monological attitude, and many commu-nication texts, especially in interpersonal communication, include a discussion of these contrasting spirits.

From a dialogical viewpoint, communicators should look upon their communicatees as humans, not things or objects, and should treat them accordingly. Dialogue reflects a mutual sense of equality, respect, and communion and a genuine supportive and loving responsibility each for the other. Dialogue implies showing a concern for possible consquences and employing honesty, directness, frankness, and spontaneity. Dialogue reflects authenticity, inclusion, and confirmation but avoids manipula-tion, pretense, self -centeredness, and defensiveness. Dialogue does not impose one speaker's views, but encourages a free choice among poten-tial options, and is willing to delay final judgment. Dialogue is advisory rather than directive. Self-scrutiny of claims, motives, reasoning, and evidence is unhesitatingly entered into, and there is a willingness to admit error if it is demonstrated. The dialogical spirit gives full concentration to the present interaction, contributes fully, avoids distractions, and genuinely tries to exhibit empathy for others' views. A person engaged in true dialogue tries to "see" the other person's "place" of view, much like an adult lying on the floor sees the surroundings from the viewpoint of a small child. (Johannesen [1996, pp. 66–68] and Arnett [1992, pp.

10–11] summarized and categorized the dialogical characteristics succinctly.) Seldom would *pure* dialogical or monological attitudes be totally present, but communicators can reflect as fully as possible the dialogical spirit, and use it as their guide.

These attitudes and ideals are always easier to list than to embody, and one or more of these qualities can be employed superficially or irresponsibly. The dialogical emphasis has been criticized as too utopian, assuming that people are by nature good and that progress is inevitable. Furthermore, entering into another person's views and desires is not as simple as it may seem. We probably can never completely feel what another feels, but we can aim at a *reasonable zone of empathy* that enables all participants to interact lovingly, to be nurtured, and to attain more and more understanding and self -fulfillment.

THE GOLDEN RULE

Philosophical positions, religious admonitions, moral codes, cultural values are often difficult to practice; they can be nebulous, overwhelming, even oppressive. For centuries people have frequently relied on the simple rule: Do unto others what you would want them to do unto you. Jesus preached this guideline to his disciples as the summary of the Law and the Prophets (Matt. 7:12; Luke 6:31). Confucius gave the same admonition in the negative: "Do not do to others what you would not like yourself" (Confucius, 1938, 12:2; See also 5:11, 15: 23). Küng (1993, pp. 54, 71–72) listed the presence of the golden rule in Confucianism, Judaism, Christianity, Islam, Jainism, Buddhism, and Hinduism. The adjective *golden* became attached to this rule. Gold has long signified the highest possible quality in many cultures, as in sporting competitions, where the gold medal, first place, is the competitors' goal. Part of the golden rule's value and appeal is its simplicity and its evidence of people's capacity to reverse roles, to place themselves imaginatively and empathically into the place of others, an attitude fundamental to developing high ethical quality communication.

This golden rule, however, is basically a secular and selfish guide, centered on one's self, on one's self -respect, on personal standards and values at the moment, values that have been partly formulated through exposure to a specific culture. How sound is the Golden Rule? People may have very different standards (e.g., a macho person compared to one who is easily intimidated). Scholars in intercultural communication have suggested this limitation to the Golden Rule, and Bennett (1979), for one advocated the Platinum Rule instead: A communicator should be guided by doing unto others as *they* would want him or her to do. That is, communicators should apply their audiences' cultural mores, not their own. Although "When in Rome, do as the Romans do" sounds empathic and adaptive, what if the "Roman" values include head hunting, apartheid, ethnic cleansing, punishment by severing of hands, or flogging? Both the Platinum and the Golden Rules are helpful, but the ultimate agonizing over ethical decision making remains with us.

Readers might feel that I have omitted another common source of ethical guidance—our conscience. "Let your conscience be your guide," we say. But the conscience is a summary, an internalization of most, if not all, of the approaches earlier discussed, a composite of moral development built slowly through varying experiences and ethical decision making.

EXERCISES

1. Search for relevant quotations from one ancient religious document, such as the Bible, the Koran, the analects of Confucius, Buddhist or Hindu scriptures, and record the admonitions related to communication ethics. List your quotations and comment on their strengths and weaknesses as guides for contemporary communicators.

2. Write a paper or give a speech describing a person, contemporary or historical, who serves as an important ethical role model for you.

3. Write an essay in which you summarize the connection of specific U.S. values to communication ethics.

4. Study a current or fairly recent libel case, and analyze the claims and counterclaims and the evidence produced for both sides. If you were the judge, how would you decide the case? Defend your decision.

5. Write an essay in which you trace the consequences of a communicative act. Consider both immediate and potential long -range consequences.

6. Defend a basic principle, such as "One should never tell a lie"; explicitly fend off any moderating considerations depending on possible consequences.

7. Reflect on instance(s) in which you experienced a tension between adhering to the mores of a group and adhering to the mores of a larger context, for example, the dilemma of keeping secret the questionable behaviors in your fraternity or sorority when you know the larger

campus community would condemn such behaviors. Write an essay exploring the ethical dimensions involved.

8. Applying the human nature enhancement guideline to a contemporary, ethically suspect communicative experience you have observed or read about. Write a paper in which you analyze the ethical quality of the act.

9. Employing the dialogical measuring stick, evaluate a communicative act you have experienced or read about recently. Include a section in your paper in which you comment on the *reasonable zone of empathy* factor as it applies to this episode.

10. Write an essay in which you evaluate general features of the Golden Rule and the Platinum Rule. Apply the rules to a communicative experience.

3

Ethical Issues Revolving Around The Communicator: General Aspects

In chapters 3 and 4 I explore the ethical dimension of the communicator's roles. In this chapter I discuss overarching concerns and data gathering and processing. In chapter 4 I discuss ethical considerations involved in specific communicator roles such as ghostwriters, hemispheric communicators, and whistleblowers.

In the section on overarching concerns, I will look at freedom of expression, prioritizing of purposes, conflict of interests, gatetenders, manipulators of ethos, communicator shrinkage, the act of noncommunicating, and the effects of low ethical quality communication on the communicator. In the section on ethical concerns involved in data gathering and processing, I discuss this subject as related to students (plagiarism), reporters, legislative bodies, academic researchers, government agencies, law enforcement agencies, business and professional groups, parents, and general initiators of communicative transactions.

OVERARCHING CONCERNS

Freedom of Expression

The centerpiece of a democratic society has been for centuries the flowering of human beings' freedom of expression, considered desirable and necessary for personal self-fulfillment and for a safe, healthier society. Humans need freedom to speak, freedom to write, and freedom to assemble, that is, to express themselves orally, nonverbally, in writing, and in concert with others. In the United States, the First Amendment to the Constitution has enshrined this basic value: "Congress shall make no law respecting an establishment of religion, or prohibiting the free exercise thereof; or abridging the freedom of speech, or of the press; or the right of the people peaceably to asemble, and to petition the Government for redress of grievances." This negative command inhibits the freedom of Congress and enshrines the essence of individuals' right to express themselves without societal (i.e., any governmental body) prohibitions. William O. Douglas (1974), a former Supreme Court justice, closed his autobiography in this manner: "In the oscillating movement of the planets man [sic] is a tiny speck— a microscosm. We seek truth, and in that search, a medley of voices is essential. That is why the First Amendment is our most precious inheritance. It gives equal time to my opponents, as it gives to me" (p. 470). "The Supreme Court handles more First Amendment cases than any other type of case" (Westbrook, 1994, p. 189).

But are there no limitiations to freedom of expression? The familiar court ruling that a person does not have the freedom to falsely yell "Fire" in a crowded theatre and to potentially endanger the patrons indicates that in certain situations some freely expressed statements would be of low ethical quality, even illegal and punishable by the courts. In other sections of this book, I look at situations in which unrestricted expression may well have low ethical quality, but I finally strongly reaffirm the centrality and preciousness of freedom of expression. The right to be heard, however, does not guarantee that a person is taken seriously; serious consideration as a communicator must be *earned*.

The mass media have used the familiar metaphor that any infringement on freedom of expression would have a chilling effect not only on their enterprises but on the democracy's health. The metaphor of temperature is apt: Flowering plants may freeze and die, or the flowing waters of the democracy's stream may freeze to a halt. Another familiar metaphor—the free market place of ideas—likewise suggests that a democratic society must permit people to show their wares, to express their ideas. Supposedly the best product sells, the best, most truthful ideas sell. This last is an article of faith: In many instances, the best ideas did not, at least immediately, win out. Furthermore, as Sunstein (1993) reminded us, the flood of expression does not necessarily mean the presence of thoughtful deliberation, which was, in the Madisonian concept of free political speech, considered central to democratic self-government. Today some observers warn of the danger that "the marketplace of ideas, become[s] so cacophonous that neither the vendors nor the shoppers hear or understand one another" (J. Black, 1994, p. 134). Some critics contend that freedom of the press means merely the freedom to write and broadcast what sells. Thus democracies are re-stricted, although not in the same fashion as in totalitarian regimes that have freedom to criticize foreign power but not the repressive regime, or as in religious cultures where freedom does not extend to saying negative things about the established religion. Nevertheless, what better article of faith than to build on the First Amendment?

Freedom of expression is crucial in academia. Natural scientists must be free to search for new discoveries and to publicize the results of their experiments. Scholars in the humanities and social sciences need free-dom in their realms to seek and publish new insights, even as they work more with probabilities than with certainties. Future scholarship will sustain or overturn present findings to the benefit of all. The freedom to publicize scholarly findings, despite any irritation or threat to pow-erful forces in the status quo, must be kept sacred.

An axiom in free journalism growing out of this freedom of speech premise is that those outside the media industry should not be permitted to dictate what is to be printed or broadcast— not governments or advertisers or other powerful segments of society— or criminal ele-ments. The agonizing decision made by the *Washington Post* and the *New York Times* to accede to the demands of a bomb terrorist who promised not to kill again if the newspapers published his manifesto is a case in point. Will this unusual instance set a precedent for criminal elements to blackmail the media and society? (In this instance, it actually strength-ened the case against the arrested suspect, for the published document bore great similarity to his other writings confiscated by law enforce-ment officials.)

The familiar idea that people have freedom to swing their arms until they come into contact with another person illustrates where freedom ends and responsibility begins. As discussed in chapter 1, this eternal balancing of rights and responsibilities teeter-totters its way through communicative interactions each day and year of life.

Prioritizing Purposes

Communicators, be they individuals or mass communication organiza-tions, have an ethical responsibility to know and honor the multiple purposes present in their messages; they must prioritize and appropri-ately balance their stress on each purpose. For instance, a college pro-fessor giving a lecture presumably should chiefly inform the students; entertaining or persuading should be decidedly subordinate to the major purpose. In a television news program, a newspaper, or a news magazine, the producers likewise should inform, even though an entertaining quality helps to secure and hold communicatees. The media should fulfill their multiple roles with ethical sensitivity, whether in mirroring society (reflecting what people do or believe); in being a conduit of information (news, editorials, advertisements); in acting as an advocate (for parks, social reforms, etc.); in acting as a watchdog (over people in power); or in entertaining (giving events a humorous twist).

Communicators need to realize that multiple objectives and motives constantly operate within every communicative act. They ought not be deluded into thinking they are moved by only one motive, although at any given moment a dominant motive may be operating. For instance, a newspaper eagerly supporting the city's endeavor to clean up its urban environment may do so not only from altruistic motives but also to create good will toward itself and increase sales. But such multiple motives are not necessarily bad, for people are rarely, if ever, driven by a single motive. People go to college for many reasons, to enrich their lives, to qualify for a better job, to make more money, to satisfy nagging relatives, to have fun, to find a compatible spouse, to engage in athletics. But not all motives are created equal. People must decide which motives take priority and not be too quick to claim that their motives are righteous and someone else's are dastardly. Dag Hammarskjold (1964), a secretary general of the United Nations, wrote: "In any crucial decision, every side of our character plays an important part, the base as well as the noble. Which side cheats the other when they stand united behind us in an action?" (p. 65).

Conflict of Interests

Most of us at various moments and in various situations have had to juggle and somehow resolve a conflict of interests within us before we constructed our eventual message. Communicators who live with this internal tension perhaps more than most are newspaper reporters and editors. Reporters by definition must discover and report what is happening around them. Investigative reporters have even more intensive and complex tasks. All those who report for and edit newspapers try to discover and fit the pieces of the "news" into a coherent, understandable, meaningful, fair, and "sellable" narrative. All those involved in this story-telling process have to watch themselves carefully to avoid letting internal conflicts of interest distort their product.

Some critics think that people like newspaper personnel should not be involved in community groups, whether profit or nonprofit, to avoid biasing their selecting, reporting, and editing. Others contend that participating in community events would isolate these people from common concerns, and activities. But reporters or editors might find it difficult to be fair in news coverage when they take sides in a local effort. For instance, taking a stand against a local school board's request for a bond issue to raise more money for the city's schools may result in slanted news, when the readership expects and is entitled to fair, objective reporting. When a newspaper's editorial staff takes a stand against introducing gambling casinos in the city, the reporters may find it difficult to report positively on casinos for fear of stirring the ill will of their employers.

A reporter is supposed to be outside the event, a nonparticipant observer who writes about the news but is not a part of the news. A reporter is a storyteller, not a character in the story. Bernard Shaw, returned from his CNN assignment in Baghdad during the Persian Gulf War early in 1991, described the terrible conflict when he and his CNN colleagues experienced the Allied bombing of Baghdad while they were reporting it to the world. Torn or not, however, the thrill of such a scoop under such dangerous conditions no doubt gave these reporters an inner sense of professional pleasure and accomplishment. Nevertheless, those in the news-selling industry must be constantly alert not to let their opinions or community activities and allegiances color their messages: their consumers have the right to receive unbiased accounts.

Gatetenders

Gatetenders need to be sensitive to the ethical considerations of their role in whatever communication context it appears. Secretaries may say that their employer is not in when the latter is in but does not want to be disturbed. Truthfulness should be better honored, and if the deception is discovered, a decline in trust is inevitable. People may set themselves up as "mindguards" in group decision-making situations, stop ideas and information from entering a discussion, and shield a group from data and views that would run counter to the prevailing mood or policy. In a small group discussion, one person might inappropriately cut off the remarks of another, inappropriately change the subject, distract by nonverbal means, or verbally shift the flow of conversation. A person who intentionally and inappropriately channels the flow of communication, may well have low ethical quality. On the other hand, distracting someone in a conflict situation may not only be an efficient ploy but a highly ethical act. Suppose, for instance, that parents, instead of arguing with their children about cleaning their room, picking up their toys, or eating, simply shift a child' s attention by talking of something else or doing something else. When they eventually return to the original subject, the child may be easier to deal with. Tension may have been significantly reduced and relationships strengthened. When a conflict occurs between siblings, parents may "tend the gate" by suggesting an alternative such as a pleasant task or a favorite game. An alert gatetender may enrich relationships by anticipating trouble, and initiating preventive distractions—a highly ethical act.

Communicators often have the power and responsibility to determine when and under what circumstances they should express themselves or open the gate. Efficiently and sensitively minimizing interferences in a communicative transaction earns a high ethical rating. One should avoid talking to a person who is intensely involved in an activity—watching a television program, reading a newspaper, or fixing a broken object. When a receiver is physically too far away, or a distracting noise makes it difficult for the intended audience to hear and understand a message, communicators ought to be sensitive to the obstacles. Waiting until such physical or psychological distractions are eliminated or conditions are altered may well reduce the likelihood of irritation developing between the parties and increase the likelihood of a mutually satisfying communicative transaction.

People expect communicators to be clear. Textbooks on speech and composition admonish students to avoid ambiguity and vagueness at all costs. When communicators tend the gate in such a way as to muddy intentionally the clarity of the message, they must justify their behavior to the receivers who expect a clear message. A low ethical rating is warranted for communicators who are intentionally vague.

Manipulators of Ethos

Along with logos and pathos, the ancient Greeks greatly stressed the role of ethos in effective rhetoric. Ancient Asian philosophy and religion also emphasized the claim that people should be trustworthy and live exemplary lives if they wished to persuade others. *Ethos* refers to credibility, reputation, and prestige of the communicator; when the audience perceives that ethos is impressive, a communicator is likely to be successful. In modern scholarship the ethos has been further analyzed and refined, and today we can view ethos as having the five dimensions of the intellectual (expertness, competence, intelligence, experience, training, knowledge); the moral (trustworthiness, honesty, integrity, sincerity, good will, courage, fairness, patience, open-mindedness); the managerial (dynamism, problem-solving capability, alertness, managing ideas and people); the social (likeability, friendliness, courtesy, humor, frankness, modesty); and the psychological.

I include the dimension of suffering in the last category. Suffering has not been considered in the literature as part of ethos, but it seems relevant to me. A person who has suffered for a cause may be strengthened by suffering. People running for high political office have stressed, in direct or subtle ways, justifiably or questionably, their having suffered: Benazir Bhutto, prime minister of Pakistan whose father had been killed by the people in power, Corazon Aquino former president of the Philippines whose husband had been assassinated, presumably by the government; and other world leaders. In the United States, George Bush made much of his having been shot down in the Pacific theater during World War II; Bob Dole frequently mentioned his WWII wounds and long hospitalization (reinforced nonverbally by his damaged right arm); President Clinton emphasized his early childhood suffering (death of his father, maltreatment by his step-father, low family income); and Vice-President Gore told of the near-fatal automobile accident of his young son and the death of his sister from lung cancer caused by smoking. Some political leaders or social advocates have highlighted their own battle to overcome the same evil they are trying to eliminate, such as drugs, alcohol, poverty, ill health, and broken homes. Anita Hill and others who told of being sexually harassed have gained a boost in ethos. Nelson Mandela' s almost three decades of imprisonment in South Africa, Martin Luther King, Jr.'s imprisonment, and Franklin Delano Roosevelt's battle with polio and its after effects all added to their stature. Their suffering added to their ethos. For maximum appeal, all three factors—suffering, devotion to a cause, and growing stronger—should be present. Those who have truly grieved, rather than harboring a grievance, whether they were 19th-century African-American leader Frederick Douglas or the 20th-century Mother Teresa, bring a unique quality to their rhetorical or poetic utterances and acquire an added power in their ethos. Such rhetors can eloquently empathize with audiences in their plight, without forgetting Wiesel's

(1990) cautionary comment on his Holocaust nightmare: "I have also learned that suffering confers no privileges; it depends upon what one does with it" p. 175).

Critics sometimes charge that communicators manipulate their claims about themselves to create a higher credibility than is deserved. Communicators have sometimes padded their curriculum vitae, for instance by suggesting they have graduated from college when they actually only *attended* for a year or so, and by exaggerating the amount and significance of their experience. People, including some posing as professionals like doctors, lawyers or counselors, have gone so far as to present phony college transcripts. A public speaker may assume a carefully rehearsed facade of confidence, courtesy, and friendliness. Communicators may inflate their suffering; for example, they may indeed have served in the armed services but always worked in an office stateside far from any danger zone.

Another misuse of ethos is communicators' excessive pandering to an audience' s emotional attachment to them. When a communicator is held in awe, the temptation to draw on that reservoir of prestige and good will rather than on reason and substantial material is great. A renowned scholar, a revered religious leader, a famous athlete, a successful corporation executive, or a charismatic military figure may fall prey to their own strengths and produce messages weak in substance. A powerful government official may overwhelm a legislative committee by bringing great prestige but little substance to committee testimony. Irrational argumentation has all too frequently been used by respected orators who relied mainly on their fame. Ironically, a great strength may become a great weakness.

People often mistakenly assume that when they are sincere their messages are highly ethical. But a "sincere" message that is inaccurate, incomplete, or excessively emotional can hardly be commended. Sincere stupidity merits little praise.

Highly experienced speakers may also fall into the trap of not preparing very carefully and choosing to improvise, to coast on their past accomplishments. Their audiences may be cheated of a substantive presentation. When lax preparation is consistent, a communicator' s ethos begins to slip. Public speakers who might repeat past presentations, such as a clergyperson, who repeats the same sermons to different congregations or a professor who reuses old lectures, cheat their audiences. Such presentations may lack updated information and insights. Such communicators let their high ethos make them lazy. A repetition of past lectures or sermons could be partly justified by their careful and succinct preparations and by the presence of new audiences. But we must question the ethical quality of such repetitious messages by those perceived to possess high ethos.

A communicator who transfers one's high ethos from one area to another may reduce the ethical quality of the message. For example, a medical doctor who seeks to speak authoritatively on nonmedical social issues might inappropriately transfer ethos, as might a movie star who speaks out on a political subject. People obviously might be highly qualified to speak on subjects in more than one field of endeavor, but communicators must be fair with their audiences and acknowledge that expertise in one area does not necessarily carry over into another. When famous athletes, for example, "sell" themselves—transfer their ethos—by advertising commercial products, they should ask themselves whether they want their personas to be identified with a product and thereby encourage people to make purchases on irrelevant grounds.

The higher the communicator's ethos with audiences, the greater their responsibility to live up to it. The wisest and most compassionate have said for centuries that to whom much has been given, much shall be expected. Audiences should not be let down.

Communicator Shrinkage

In dyadic interchanges, one person may inappropriately dominate, and in a small group discussion, one or two people may do most of the talking. Organizational communication networks may have one or a very few individuals who dominate, in part because of their powerful positions or their strong personalities. In public speaking contexts, the format by definition gives the podium to one person, and few in the audience have an adequate opportunity to raise questions or voice views. Those in the role of communicator in any context should aim to give others the opportunity to be communicators, and thus to enrich the communicative transaction.

The area of mass communication presents troubling ethical concerns about the shrinkage in the number of communicators; that is, the ownership of radio and television stations, newspapers, and magazines is falling into the hands of a few organizations and individuals. Cunningham (1992) lamented that "a minuscule number of corporate bodies, dominated in turn by a handful of individuals, exercise inordinate power over what we see, hear, and read" (p. 242). We are witnessing breathtaking mergers, such as Turner Broadcasting System, Tele-Communications Inc., and Time Warner; Westinghouse Electric and CBS; Walt Disney Company and Capital Cities/ABC; and NBC and General Electric. The *New York Times* has purchased the prestigious and profitable Boston *Globe*. Some observers predict that by the year 2000 less than 10 corporations will control all of the world's mass communciation systems. Many think that this shrinkage of competing voices and interests will have a serious negative impact on democratic societies. Other analysts highlight the positive aspects in such amalgamations; The communication industry will be run more efficiently, higher quality will result, and multiple views will not necessarily be excluded. But whatever benefits may accrue, most observers are uneasy, and assert that the shrinking number of communicators will have a detrimental effect on the health of society. The underlying premise is that a democratic society is enriched and strengthened when multiple voices are heard.

Noncommunicators

People usually focus on contexts in which a communicator acts, and on the attendant ethical concerns— sins of *commission*. But we ought not overlook that communicators might also commit sins of *omission*, in which low ethical communication results from not communicating. The truism that people cannot *not* communicate is important from an ethical viewpoint. By not engaging in a verbal or even nonverbal transaction, people may do significant injustice to neglected communicatees, and sometimes to themselves, to the larger society, and to the unuttered subject.

This observation is manifested in a host of informal communicative contexts. For instance, we often fail to make an effort to talk with a stranger at an informal gathering, with new people in our organizations, or with newcomers to our circle of acquaintances. We do not seize the opportunity to introduce people to others who we know share a common interest and who might deeply appreciate the contact. We often fail to converse with people of different ethnic or racial backgrounds. People from minority backgrounds often report their loneliness at work or in social gatherings where people look past them as if they were not there. Many people are unaware of this subtle racism. Even when it is the result of social awkwardness, immaturity, or provincialism rather than of hostility, the silence is painful to those who are ignored. These people are in solitary confinement, which is one of the most terrifying and dehumanizing experiences, often more searing than actually being alone. Women are often excluded from male-dominated communication networks, and vice versa. Older or very young people are often excluded from conversations. We often look past the people with little power. Widows and widowers are gradually omitted from former communication circles. We must become more caring and confident when communicating with people of varying disabilities, who often report that they are forced to initiate conversations to make others feel comfortable— surely a reversal of responsibility. We must not shy away from people with terminal illnesses, which, with the mushrooming of AIDS, stalks all ages. To shut people out of communicative interactions gives a depressing message to those who desperately need human contact.

A simple greeting can make a world of difference in the lives of others. For example, an acquaintance told me that when he had moved into a new city, a clerk said as he was leaving a grocery store, "Have a good day, sir." He was startled; in the large metropolis he had lived in, he would seldom if ever hear such a friendly expression. Although the comment might sound mundane, trite, and routine, it gave the receiver a warm feeling that he (normally not very effusive) enthusiastically reported to people. The wide ripple effect of that clerk's courteous remark illustrates how much would have been lost if that comment had not been made.

Those who have traveled to a foreign country and have experienced the terrifying loneliness of having no one with whom to communicate should understand the plight of foreign students and immigrants. At a time when increased numbers of immigrants from non-English speaking countries seek to participate in the American dream, and when U.S. colleges and universities proudly announce the increased internationalizing of their campuses, we need to make sure we are adequately communicating with these foreign students and new arrivals to our shores.

We often have neglected to thank people who have done helpful deeds large or small for us. Some people send thank-you cards for Thanksgiving Day to express their appreciation to others who have enriched their lives. We often have not bothered to congratulate someone on an accomplishment. A child's success goes unacknowledged, an employee's efficiency elicits no praise, a student's creative endeavor encounters only silence. Indeed, as communicators our sins of omission are legion.

Employees in certain service roles, such as custodians, maids, and laborers, may be overlooked as if they did not exist. The democratic, egalitarian values of U.S. culture help us limit that oversight to some extent compared to countries in which the ostracism of people in service roles is more institutionalized and severe. But we too have much to improve. With increasing unemployment and mobile part-time employment, we are in danger of weakening workforce interaction. When people leave a company voluntarily or involuntarily, company officials or co-workers often offer no meaningful exit communciation to ease the pain of severance. (Exit communication is discussed more fully in chapter 5.)

An example of noncommunication in the academic world is the occasional attempt to boycott scholars from, or academic conferences in, countries deemed to have reprehensible political and academic climates, such as Serbia, apartheid South Africa, or Communist dictatorships. The term *boycott* comes from Charles Boycott, a despised 19th-century land agent in Ireland who was ostracized by his tenants. In economic and political boycotts in international affairs and in consumer boycotts against agricultural produce or manufactured products, we abstain from dealing with a person, group, institution, or country and thereby seek to exert pressure and to achieve behavior modification. Academic boycotts are aimed at denying academics access to scholarly materials and outlets for publishing their work. Some critics contend that such efforts are merely unfair, ineffective, irritating inconveniences rather than real weapons and that more behavior modification would be accomplished by maintaining contacts. Defenders counter that a boycott is at least a symbolic gesture, a statement of deep moral outrage, and thus another example of noncommunication as a communicative act. Alexander (1995) warned academics that they need to make sure that "the boycott does not become the proverbial cure worse than the disease" (p. 7).

Effects on Communicators

We generally think of the ill effects of low quality ethical communication in relation to the harm it causes an audience. When we try to be expansive, we look to long-range as well as short-range effects on a specific audience and on society in general, but we seldom dwell on the effect on the communicator. We seldom discuss whether a rhetor is likely to be diminished or enhanced in the process. We worry, for example, about the effects of obscenity, violence, and lying, on audiences, but not about the dehumanizing effects on the rhetors themselves. Some Eastern religions stress the ill effects of low ethical quality communication on the communicator more than Western traditions do. Throughout this book, I constantly emphasize the need to recognize that low ethical quality communication reduces the rhetor's humanity while working ill on the audience.

DATA GATHERING AND PROCESSING

Securing and processing information are early steps in communication whereby a would-be communicator strives to obtain and process data and ideas forming the substance of a subsequent message. To the early Greeks this focus on the substance of rhetoric— inventio— was of major concern.

Students

Coming from a Latin term meaning to "kidnap," plagiarizing occurs when a communicator sends a message to someone (e.g., a student submitting a paper to a teacher) using (kidnapping) another's material as if it were the communicator's own. To do so intentionally with the desire to deceive in hope of winning a reward (good grade, praise) merits the lowest rating on the Ethical Quality (EQ) Scale. Such intentional theft, such misrepresentation, is usually cause for severe punishment, including the possibility of expulsion, by educational institutions. Familiar student excuses, such as being under pressure of time (the paper was due tomorrow), or "everyone does it," hardly justify the act. Occasionally, students may be guilty of inept intellectual processes, for instance, not footnoting material properly, rather than the moral failing of intentionally deceiving. In such a case, this shortcoming needs to be ascertained and corrected— or prevented beforehand. In academic contexts, in which a person is being evaluated for a certification, passing off someone else's work as one's own seriously undermines the academic process and jeopardizes the academic rights of other students. The institution's role is thwarted and society and future "consumers" may be misled or injured (e.g., people assuming that a doctor or an electrician is genuinely certified).

Reporters

The job description of reporters, especially investigative reporters, calls for vigorous and effective pursuit of information, and ethical concerns become central. Reporters are faced, for instance, with an ethically sensitive dilemma in honoring confidentiality to their sources. Such confidentiality may often be necessary when reporters expose serious social problems, such as drug trafficking in a community. Not to give confidentiality to an informer would dry up that and other sources for the future and might endanger the giver of information. Such situations have generated the question of whether reporters have the right and power to promise confidentiality to anyone, or whether confidentiality can be granted only by the editorial office of the news-gathering agency.

Critics question the ethicality of obtaining data under false pretenses; for example, a reporter's taking a job in a nursing home to expose suspected shoddy care and inhumane conditions. A newspaper might harbor a legitimate moral outrage at what it believes are despicable practices in a given nursing home which cannot be verified without inside information. Their righteous indignation (and their desire for a scoop and increased sales) might lead reporters to use highly questionable means. In exposing poor health conditions in a particular restaurant, the media could put it out of business or seriously damage it before it could adequately correct itself. Critics questioned the ethicality when two well-known television reporters visited Rumania in disguises, to investigate the suspected scandal about child adoption. The pair posed as husband and wife who were tourists, and used a supposedly innocuous home video camera. Their "take" of those who were allegedly selling children for adoption to foreigners was aired on their widely viewed U.S. television network station. Believing that it had to use such subterfuge to expose a serious social scandal, the news-gathering agency thought its means were justified. Critics disagreed and thought that showing on national television the people involved in the transactions was prejudging them as guilty without a fair trial.

Data secured secretly through such means as telescopic cameras that record the activities of people like celebrities, political incumbents, or candidates in private activities—at a beach, on a golf course, or otherwise relaxing—are often ethically questionable. Investigative reporters have commonly recorded the activities of sitting judges or other public officials relaxing during working hours to bolster the case that these individuals were not conscientious public servants. This practice may be an unfair intrusion into a person's life and may portray an incomplete and biased picture of that person's behavior.

Securing information openly by being a participant observer of a community event—for example, a reporter who is also an official in a parent-teacher association (PTA) and writes a newspaper account of some PTA proposals— traditionally raises difficult questions about the objectivity and fairness of the reporting. Dual roles can, but need not, distort a reporter's account or at least raise doubts in the minds of some readers about the reporter's skill in balancing the two commitments.

Private interests who pay newspaper reporters to go on trips to secure information or to observe events that they subsequently report on are acting with questionable ethics. For example, critics might question the ethicality of a power industry's paying for reporters to visit a distant facility to attempt to prove that such a facility does not have ill effects on people living nearby. Presumably such acts are helpful and enable reporters to gain information and insights that they would normally not. Others, however, assert that these gifts manipulate the reporters into writing favorable accounts for their hosts. Free lunches and other perks given to reporters, who are, after all, professional data collectors and dispensers, may bring direct or indirect benefits to the contributors, but unduly influence the objectivity of the reporters, to the detriment of society.

Another context in which data is made available too easily is the flood of public relations handouts given by government and private sector organizations, profit and nonprofit alike, to reporters and news agencies. The temptation for news communicators to take this pre-prepared information at face value without exploring the subject more thoroughly is great, especially when deadlines swiftly approach. Regularly relying on uncritical and hastily presented public relations material is a highly questionable practice that may weaken a communicator's professional behavior and moral fiber, and work to the detriment of readers.

Experienced journalists often use clever tactics to deceive a naive interviewee and to extract information not normally given. Critics (Borden, 1996; Christians, 1995; D. Elliott, 1995a) noted that CBS's Connie Chung brazenly "seduced" Newt Gingrich's mother into revealing private information on the air. Although television interviewers commendably seek to put their interviewees at ease, the latter should not be taken advantage of when they are relaxed. Journalists might send potential subjects a list of noncontroversial questions to increase the likelihood of getting an interview, but during the interview itself, reporters might unexpectedly ask some additional highly sensitive and controversial questions. Borden (1993) catalogued the ways journalists routinely use empathic listening (feigned or real) to lull an interviewee into giving richer information. For instance, reporters might deceptively agree, act interested and attentive, use flattery, communicate encouragement, and show reassuring gestures and facial expressions. Borden (1993) suggested five guidelines for journalists:

> deception should be considered only in the service of the ideal community to which the journalist owes ultimate loyalty; the potential harm to individuals must be proportionate to the potential benefit for the community; deception should be a last resort; the journalist should not reach the decision to deceive alone; if the decision to deceive is made, a full accounting must be made to the source and the public. (p. 225)

Other ways of generating trust should be used with great sensitivity and caution; for example, reporters might plan for multiple sessions with the subjects, win more and more trust and obtain information that would not have been forthcoming in a single interview. Sometimes reporters conduct hasty interviews and hope that the respondents will unthinkingly reveal material. In all these situations, data gatherers carry a great burden of ethical responsibility to the respondents, to their public, and to the profession.

In extracting information from guests, all too many radio or television interviewers do not employ the conscientious care of a Ray Christensen, one of the nation's most professional radio announcers for the last four decades. In his memoirs (Christensen with Thornley, 1993) he summarized his philosophy of interviewing: "My basic approach to a guest is one of preparation: know a lot about your guest and about the subject, but, on the air, let that information come from the guest, not from you. The most important thing an interviewer can do is *listen*. I've always felt that if I learn something from an interview, my listeners will learn, too" (p. 205). Christensen praised one of his colleagues, Charlie Boone, as one who had "a special ability to make people he's interviewing feel a little better about themselves than they did before the conversation began" (p. 195). How we all would benefit if more electronic and print media interviewers had that skill and demeanor!

Some parts of society are gradually opening their doors wider to journalists. For example, hospitals are granting journalists access to areas formerly off limits, like operating and emergency rooms and intensive care units; but permission from patients and supervision by medical personnel are required. Reporters therefore can help the public see and appreciate more clearly and fully the complexities and professionalism of caregiving, and can expose deficiencies in need of correction. Reporters need to use such opportunities with skill and compassion.

Poll taking is an established technique for gathering data, whether it is an informal effort by reporters or a sophisticated, formal, and systematic process by an established polling organization. Those involved in taking a poll should represent a wide political spectrum, and the questions should be fairly chosen and worded. The process should be public so that observers know the means by which the material was gathered and interpreted, the size and description of the sample of respondents, and the time and conditions under which the answers were secured. The accuracy of the poll results over time—the track record—generates trust; once trust is undermined, poll taking has little significant value.

Legislative Bodies

Local, state, and national legislative bodies have the task of gathering information to pass the wisest possible laws. But sometimes their efforts to gain data are highly suspect. For example, Congressional delegations frequently travel abroad to secure firsthand information on a pending foreign policy issue. Perhaps several people are necessary to gather a range of observations and viewpoints, but after a point a large delegation becomes redundant and needlessly costly to taxpayers. Furthermore, these travelers sometimes increase the taxpayers' bill by bringing spouses, taking side tourist trips, and enjoying entertainments. It is illegal for foreign trips to be subsidized by foreign governments, but domestic fact-finding is sometimes privately paid for directly or indirectly by U. S. companies who stand to gain in some way. The legislators involved should secure a broad and representative number of people from whom to gather testimony and should be sure that the public' s interest is being served as efficiently and as fairly as possible.

Academic Researchers

Academic researchers must consider a host of ethical concerns in carrying out their mission of finding and reporting "new" information, of expanding knowledge, of learning about people, society, or the natural world. Some reseachers secretly observe their subjects' behavior, perhaps through a one-way viewing glass. Researchers might claim that to gather information otherwise would contaminate the data: The subjects would not behave normally and the experiment would be of little value. Some critics may disagree. Observing subjects not only in controlled experimental contexts, but in natural settings might raise ethical concerns. The use of hidden microphones to study such activity as childrens' language interaction and development as they play also gives rise to ethical questions, as does researchers observing family groups in shopping areas. Such secrecy is sometimes claimed to be necessary to obtain the "truth" about people's thoughts or behavior. Researchers sometimes claim that they need to lie about their purposes. In addition to the familiar problem of accuracy of perception when a researcher is a participant– observer, there are additional ethical concerns when a researcher plays this role secretly, and keeps others in the group unaware of that fact.

Ethical concerns may arise in the entire process of selecting and handling subjects. Sometimes there are complaints that professors too often use their classes as guinea pigs for research projects. Students may "volunteer" only because a teacher, with considerable power differential, subtly or not so subtly expects them to, and non-volunteers may behvae quite differently from volunteers. In some instances, it would be necessary to pay subjects in order to secure enough participants and to compensate them fairly for their time and effort. But financial reward might influence subjects to behave so that a researcher looks good. When the subjects are children, or people who are ill or troubled, some think that third parties should be present to aid or observe the proceedings. Some observers contend that the subjects should be told of the nature and purpose of the study beforehand. The questions should be phrased simply, clearly, and fairly. The material the researcher seeks to gather from the subjects might be embarrassingly personal and intimate, so privacy and confidentiality need to be protected. Researchers, as Labitzky (1995) warned, should not let the excitement of possible new discoveries lead them to treat subjects in a demeaning fashion. The data sometimes are inserted into predetermined categories, a procedure that can force and distort the results. When subjects have given informed consent, the meaning of informed consent may vary considerably. Projects should be appropriately sanctioned by a committee designated to oversee the use of human subjects. Care should be taken to ensure that no harm—physical, mental, social, immediate and long range—comes to subjects. Subjects might be unduly disturbed by the use of tape or video recorders or by the investigator's note-taking. The researcher's rough field notes are sometimes kept to check the accuracy of the final report and to refute a possible future legal claim. The notes might endanger the respondents or the researcher by being later misread or misunderstood—even by the person who wrote them! In most cases, the subjects should be properly debriefed at the end. Finally, the findings should be published accurately and fairly, not distorted to make the results look good for the researcher.

In cross-cultural research projects, investigators have additional skills to master and other ethical dimensions to consider. For instance, a researcher endeavoring to learn about the living habits of Hmong immigrants from Southeast Asia should engage in frequent, personal, empathic interchanges with them and especially with their leaders. Trust between the interviewers and interviewees is necessary even more than in other projects, and there is a great need to schedule enough time for the overall enterprise to discover problems in the procedure and to adust to them. How one researcher behaves may determine whether following researchers with the same group will be treated with cooperation or with sullen reticence. Groups interviewed by different researchers might perceive researchers as part of one intrusive and overwhelming effort and not as separate, small, and distinct research projects. Fieldwork in foreign countries sometimes produces a legacy of disdain and distrust among local people who feel used by those with something to gain. For instance, in one African country, the closest synonym for *journalist* is "white man who comes to ask us questions and then goes away." Researchers have an ethical obligation not only to their subjects but to their profession.

Professors sometimes have research assistants who might not be properly acknowledged in professional publications. Some observers, however, would consider paid research assistants to be rewarded by their salaries and thus not need other mention, but their employment should not be kept a secret. A few professors have been known to incorporate into their own work information and ideas from students' papers without proper citation. The hours and months of help from a professor' s spouse might often receive no proper acknowledgement.

As the data gatherer nears the publication stage, some additional ethical concerns arise. To share preliminary findings with colleagues may allow helpful feedback, but interfere with the nature of the final report. Peer reviewers may sometimes unfairly use a submitted work before its publication. In order to lend prestige to their publication, some researchers have listed famous co-authors who had little or no input to the project. The latter thus artificially puff up their list of publications. In situations like medical research, the question of when the findings should be communicated to the general public might arise: when the experiment is completed, when an article is submitted to a journal, or when the article is published. Waiting too long before making a public announcement might slow down the delivery of new medical insights. But announcing too soon might have other unfortunate results. Occasionally some researchers have withheld negative results or have even used fraudulent data or engaged in questionable procedures to rush into publication, to show results, to gain prestige, to justify years of effort, or to secure more grant money. Such behavior, fortunately atypical, is completely off the ethical chart, and those responsible ought to pay a heavy price.

In contrast to the researchers who rush prematurely into publication, some data gatherers hesitate inappropriately to publish their results. Professors with offices full of research data that remain unpublished contribute little to public knowledge. Indeed, information gathering might carry with it an ethical obligation to communicate it eventually, in an appropriate form, to others.

Many research artifacts unearthed by anthropologists or archeologists remain in universities or museums, to be used as teaching objects for a college class or the general public. Some critics have questioned the ethics of gathering these artifacts. National museums, like the British Museum in London, have accumulated historic items gained by military conquest or other less-than-ethical means. They attempt to refute the complaints of the countries of origin by asserting that the museum is actually saving valuable artifacts for all of humanity by ensuring that the objects are not destroyed, lost, or undocumented. Some nations, especially developing countries, weary of foreigners carting away valuable artifacts, explicitly state in their visa applications that exporting antiques and archeological items is strictly forbidden. Sensitive to this phenomenon, the American Association of Museums (1978) prepared a comprehensive document setting forth its ethical guidelines. Messenger (1989) and others have given some challenging insights on this sensitive subject of museum ethics.

Government Agencies

Research is carried on not only in academia but also by government agencies. History occasionally brings to light horrendous examples of experimentation carried on by governments with the most serious ethical implications. For instance, in Hitler's Germany doctors in concentration camps experimented on Jews and other war prisoners to discover answers by inhuman means. What is the effect of hypothermia on human beings? Experiment: Submerge them in ice cold water and find out. What is the effect of certain treatments on certain wounds? Experiment: Wound people in the particular manner desired and apply the selected treatments. From 1932 to 1972 the U.S. Public Health Service, in trying to understand the nature and effects of syphilis, studied about 400 Black men who were unknowingly infected with syphilis. The health effects of radon were partly ascertained by studying Navajo miners who were not informed that they had been exposed to the dangerous gas. Revelations that U.S. military personnel were exposed to radiation after World War II without their clear, informed consent have come to light.

The Watergate affair revealed the Administration's extensive use of tape recordings, known only to President Nixon and very few others; some trusted advisers were unaware of the practice. Nixon's justification was that such recordings permitted a verification of what was said, were such information needed in the future. (Jaksa and Pritchard (1994) devoted a chapter to discussing the case of Jeb Magruder, an initmate insider). People who believe that the telephones in their homes or offices are tapped (ambassadors, political dissidents) often speak as if they *were* being recorded and hence must dispatch their real messages in other circumstances. A tape recording is a valuable tool for gathering information; its vocal dimension can add much to a message, catch nuances lost on a printed page, be replayed often, and be analyzed in detail. Its very importance highlights the significance of the ethical dimension of such intrusion.

Totalitarian governments have extensive means by which to secure information on their citizenry. For example, Colonel Muammar Gadafy in Libya set up numerous purge committees to inform on citizens.

Law Enforcement Agencies

Law enforcement agencies of government units have the task of trying to secure information about the activities and plans of individuals and groups suspected of illegal behavior. Since 1992 there has been a dramatic increase in the U.S. of the use of federally sanctioned wire tapping and other sophisticated electronic surveillance equipment mainly to secure information on suspected narcotics dealers (McGee, 1996). Telemarketing con artists who telephone those who are vulnerable, especially older people, to ask them for money for products and causes have been successfully prosecuted only because the Federal Bureau of Investigation (FBI) gathered evidence by taping the telephone conversations.

Some critics, however, have questioned the ethics of such data gathering procedures as well as the ethicality of law enforcement agencies paying a gang member to inform on other gang members or paying an informer to infiltrate a gang or other groups suspected of past or impending illegal acts. An informant's life may be placed in extreme danger, and the reliability of the person's report might be in doubt. The ethicality of electronic surveillance of suspected criminals has also been questioned. The Waco, Texas, episode and the Ruby Ridge, Idaho, investigation are recent, highly publicized instances of law enforcement agencies engaging in flawed and ethically suspect procedures to gather information. On the national level, governments secure information about other countries' potential threat, and carry out highly secret, complex, and dangerous missions through their spy agencies. Countries accuse each other of spying but depict their own efforts as gathering information. Highly sophisticated spy planes secure detailed information about ground sites. Public safety and national security need to be protected but such protection should not be a blanket justification for whatever means law enforcement agencies employ to gather information. In early 1996, Baltimore instituted a pilot project to have video surveillance of a certain street area, with the objectives of deterring crime and making merchants and citizens feel safer. The video tape was to be destroyed after a few days unless needed for verification purposes. But critics said that this effort was too much like Big Brother watching.

Business and Professional Groups

Other segments of society also engage in data gathering as a preliminary stage in communicating. Businesses and corporations, for example, allocate considerable resources to research divisions that seek out new products or new and better ways of doing existing things. They likewise spy on competitors and seek to keep secret their own procedures and plans. Some companies have instituted surveillance mechanisms to monitor the effectiveness of production processes and the efficiency and dependability of employees. S. Bryant (1995) described an ideal situation:

> Workers must be informed about what surveillance tools are currently being used in their workplace and be provided with intelligible information as to what management does with the data. Employees should be invited to participate fully in decisions regarding how and when electronic monitoring takes place. And ... employees must be permitted to inspect,

challenge, and, when appropriate, have corrected the data gathered about them or their performance. (p. 518)

Eavesdropping devices in the workplace are supposedly illegal, but an Illinois law signed in December 1995 permits employers to monitor their employees' telephone conversations and creates the dilemma of the employer's right to know what is going on versus the employee's right to privacy. Monitoring has been justified to ensure employee courtesy, accuracy, and efficiency, but the Illinois law expanded that justification to include "educational, training or research purposes" (Smolowe, 1996, p. 56), an expansion beyond other state or federal laws. Critics assert that modern "electronic sweatshops" are being created. For security purposes, surveillance cameras are commonplace in banks, convenience stores, many institutions, and school buses. Lawyers, counselors, doctors, and clergy who seek information from their clients sometimes get unwanted data that they must keep confidential. Medical tests can now reveal that a person has a disease for which there is no known treatment. Should the patient be told? People might not wish to know that they carry a gene for an incurable disease that might develop in the future. When gathered information suggests that the general public might be in danger, for example, from unstable people who give every indication of harming a person, a building or an institution, the ethical concern may demand that such information not be kept secret.

Family

The means employed by parents to obtain information about their children's activities or associates might be ethically questionable: Loving concern can lead parents to use some dubious tactics. Listening on a telephone extension to the conversations of children or eavesdropping in other possible contexts suggests low ethical quality. Pressuring one child to inform on a sibling might result in broken trust between parents and children. Tempting, with a tangible or intangible reward, a child to pass on neighborhood gossip might be ethically suspect.

All of these seekers after data must sensitize themselves to the ethical dimensions of their acts. Desire for expanding horizons of knowledge, concern for safety of society, righteous indignation over misdeeds, desire to minister to people's needs, desire to help fulfill the people's right to know, concern for the welfare of children—excellent motives all—may so energize communicators that their means to secure the information become ethically blurred. Data gathering and processing, initial steps for communicators, need to be at the highest possible level of ethical quality.

Initiators

The power of an initiator in a communication transaction can be great, perhaps inordinately so. Interviewers have the power to determine when, where, and under what conditions the interaction occurs. They choose the subject, know its history, have a purpose in mind, phrase the query, and create a tone for the exchange. The questioner is often experienced, well prepared, and fluent; the respondent might lack those elements and could be experiencing considerable anxiety. A job applicant, for example, when being interviewed by a company' s human resources manager, can hope for employment if the interview is successful. How interviewers use their power differential as they initiate exchanges can have important ethical implications.

Experienced participants in small group discussions often manipulate the flow of discussion toward subjects of their choosing by making sure that they initiate the exchange not only at the outset but at subsequent transition points. The conversation thus is disproportionately directed toward them and their interests (unless other experienced members sense such attempts and blunt them), and information is elicited accordingly. The role of initiator, of course, has its positive aspects; such a person gets the dynamics started and does not let unhealthy lulls occur. But the ethical dimension is present in these initiating endeavors in small group contexts.

When initiators act as accusers, they have an even greater tactical advantage over the respondents. The former know and prepare their charges and can shift their focus at will, whereas the respondents have to make impromptu replies and hold to their fixed position on each of the charges or face the additional charge of being inconsistent. In political rhetoric there are often accusers who quickly capture the headlines and appear to be authoritative and damaging, whereas the accused candidate, office holder, or public figure has to reply quickly and often inadequately. By the time a strong defense is constructed, the accusers may have moved to another issue, and the media's attention may have shifted to other events. In law enforcement contexts, the police have great power as they initiate conversations or interrogate suspects. Consider the great power of the Soviet prison authority interrogating Nicholas Daniloff in a Moscow prison on a trumped-up charge of espionage during the Cold War. Daniloff (1988) wrote: "I felt at a terrible disadvantage, standing in front of my well-dressed adversary, hands behind my back, trousers falling down, shoes half laced. The stubble on my chin itched, and I reeked of sweat" (p. 88). The nonverbal factors, seemingly insignificant by themselves, added to the power of the interrogator' s questioning and the vulnerability of the respondent.

When salespeople initiate conversations with us as we browse, they sometimes hope to create a desire in us to purchase products. They might intrude on us by telephoning us at home or by knocking on our front door, and force an immediate response on our part. We might receive questionnaires by mail that require our responses to certain merchandise or services. The ethics of these intrusions are highly questionable: They invade our privacy and inappropriately demand our attention, time, and effort.

Many people are thrust into sensitive situations in which they have to determine whether it is appropriate to intervene, to initiate communication. For example, family members or friends might be troubled by alcoholism, drugs, or anorexia. Not to intervene permits a harmful habit to continue and worsen, but to initiate discussion on the subject might sever a relationship.

EXERCISES

1. Write a paper in which you analyze the strengths and weaknesses of some common metaphors used to discuss freedom of expression, such as the *chilling* effect or the *marketplace of ideas*. Suggest a new metaphor and clarify why you think it would be appropriate.

2. Write a paper in which you discuss the dilemma faced by the owner of a newspaper who must balance the desire for economic profit for the paper to survive and the desire to inform the populace.

3. Discuss a recent case that you have observed or read about in which obvious *gatetending* was taking place. Applying various ethical guidelines, evaluate the ethical quality of the proceedings.

4. Evaluate the ways some contemporary public speakers (in campaign presentations when an election campaign is underway) seem to be manipulating their ethos on a low ethical quality level. Discuss the subject in small groups in class or give individual speeches.

5. Discuss in class various instances in which you think some *noncommunication* episodes had immediate or long range adverse effects on one or more people. How serious do you think this sin of omission is? Why?

6. Write a paper in which you discuss the ethical dimensions of plagiarism. Apply the consequentialist approach, among others, in your analysis. If appropriate, give personal examples from high school or previous classes in college of which you are aware.

7. If you were a reporter, are there times when you would refuse to reveal the source of your information? Are there times when you would refuse free trips, lunches, and so on, from people about whom you might be writing? Why?

8. Interview some professors about their research processes. Ask them whether they encountered any ethical dilemmas. If so, how did they deal with them?

9. Read about some episodes in which government agencies or law enforcement agencies seeking to secure information engaged in practices involvong ethically suspect activities. Write a paper in which you evaluate the actions of these agencies.

10. Think about instances of family interactions in which parents or siblings engaged in ethically suspect acts to secure information from each other.

4

Ethical Issues Revolving Around the Communicator: Specific Agents

In this chapter I discuss ethical concerns as related to three roles in which communicators operate: as ghostwriters, hemispheric communicators, and whistle-blowers. I explore the positive and negative considerations for people who are ghostwriters. I define hemispheric communicators as those who speak to only one side of a subject—one hemisphere—such as advertisers, lobbyists, public relations personnel, lawyers, and deprogrammers, surrogates, demagogues, and those who consider themselves voices for the voiceless. Whistle-blowing as a communicative act is surveyed, as are the characteristics of whistle-blowers. Finally, I analyze procedural and substantive ethical tension points in whistle-blowing.

GHOSTWRITERS

When communicators present their messages, audiences not unreasonably assume the communicators have created them. If the speaker is not the creator and if this fact is not known or publicized, then the audience is to a considerable degree deceived and may feel cheated. Report-ers simply carry messages from point A to point B; they transmit, or deliver them (hopefully accurately, completely, and in timely fashion). In advanced societies, professional report-ers have come into being; Reporters get paid for their work; many win prizes, praise, and prestige. As messengers they say, "Do not blame me, I am only reporting what occurred." Theologians say they are only the messengers of God (but sometimes immodestly take on the aura of their source by claiming to be chosen for their work). Servant economies flourish despite their inequalities; servants get instant prestige from being associated with their employer, who has chosen them from among all other possible applicants. A scientist says, "Do not blame me; I am just reporting the results of the laboratory experiments." A secretary says, "Do not blame me, I am merely telling you what my boss said." The committee chairperson simply reports the committee's conclusions. A teacher says, "I am merely reporting what the author of your textbook says, these are not necessarily my ideas." Experienced teachers of course usually go on to indicate what their ideas are—shifting from reporter to creator. The dividing line between a reporter and a creator (composer) is not entirely clear. The messengers just described might select, omit, highlight, and massage the original message. In short, some creative action has probably taken place.

The term ghost is, of course, a loaded word, which may do an injustice to those who assist at speech writing. The term suggests something not only unseen and secret but also harmful and diabolical and might be more fairly replaced by *speechwriter* or *speech assistant*. Scholars are divided on the ethicality of ghostwriting. The speech communication profession has long had a keen interest in the issue. Several decades ago, Bormann (1961) published a strong denunciation of the growing reliance on ghostwriters in the *Quarterly Journal of Speech*, and at the 1982 Speech Communication Association national convention in Louisville he and Auer debated the issue con and pro respectively before a heavily attended forum program. Numerous convention papers on ghostwriting have been presented through the years, and a special conference on presidential speechwriting was held in March 1996 at Texas A and M University.

In our shrinking world, ghostwriting is needed more and more by national leaders who prepare speeches aimed at the citizens of a foreign country. Robert T. Oliver (1962), an adviser and speechwriter for Syngman Rhee, president of the Republic of Korea during the 1950s, defended the need for such transnational assistance, and his expertise and knowledge of U.S. culture and attitudes helped President Rhee enormously. Oliver (1993) recently summarized and again defended his practice of writing speeches for Rhee and other Korean statesmen, and concluded that the ethical test is "Do what you do in a manner that permits you to sleep well at night" (p. 80)! U.S. public relations firms have helped to prepare speeches for foreign national leaders who planned speaking tours in the United States. For instance, Dei (1989) documented how former prime minister of Japan, Yasuhiro Nakasone, used such assistance during the 1980s. One of President Reagan's speech writers, Peggy Noonan (1990), lamented the lack of knowlege about

Chinese culture when preparing Reagan's 1984 speech to be given at Fudan University in Shanghai.

With such widespread need for assistance in writing speeches, it is not surprising that some speech communication departments across the nation help to train students to become speechwriters and that a few college catalogs list courses explicitly geared for such a job. Private ghostwriter agencies advertise in newspapers that they can help train people for this work. Not a few people have made an impressive career and accumulated considerable wealth as speechwriters or successful assistants of famous people who are writing their memoirs. William Novak, for example, has become a successful memoir writer for Lee Iacocca, Tip O' Neil, Nancy Reagan, and Earvin (Magic) Johnson (E. Johnson, 1992; Smilgis, 1989).

Many have defended this practice by asserting that busy people obviously need assistance, and getting help to prepare messages is not different from obtaining assistance in other endeavors. Bricklayers and carpenters have laborers to help them in building a structure. Nurses, technicians, and interns assist surgeons in the operating room. Pressure of time, multiplicity of tasks, and desire for excellence all encourage employing assistants. When a person is expected to speak often and on a wide range of subjects, help is mandatory, especially when a thorough, meaningful speech is demanded. Public personages are expected to present highly complex and detailed messages that require assistants to gather and synthesize data, to generate ideas, to write early drafts of the speech (or article, report, book), and to refine the final version. Assistance can be extended to help the speakers rehearse their delivery to achieve a polished final presentation.

Defenders of these practices have emphasized that communicators take responsibility for their messages, and hence ethical qualms can be put to rest. There is no deception about who takes the responsibility for what is said, and praise or blame is forthcoming from the audience on that premise. Surgeons perform and take responsibility for operations even though they had many helping hands. The surgeon, not the helpers, gets sued! Executives, public officials, and other highly placed members of society take responsibility for the content and style of their speeches, even when they have relied heavily on the assistance of others. Because speech assistants are usually closely attuned to the ideas and style of their employer, they can reflect the speaker's thinking and manner; if they fail, they are likely to be replaced. President Ford used to complain that some of his speechwriters did not follow his simple, direct style, and that policies not yet finalized sometimes appeared in speech drafts as if the policy were carved in stone. Not surprisingly, these writers were replaced.

Many voices in and out of the speech communication profession have strongly condemned ghostwriting. Audiences do not understand the role of speech assistants at the moment of presentation, and might be misled into thinking that the presenter is indeed the creator; thus they do not gain a true insight into the mind, character, and capability of the communicator. Speakers might have had only a minor role in constructing a speech. Speakers might have paraded content and style different from and superior to their own. Speakers might have used helpers to create an impression that they possess qualities such as wit, intelligence, clarity, and sincerity, that they do not possess, at least not to such a great degree.

Opponents claim that ghostwriters are able to slip misleading ideas and style into messages. Ideologues on the staff can bend statements toward their positions, sometimes with a key term or phrase, or with a vivid metaphor. Ever so slightly, but powerfully, a speaker might be nudged in an undesired direction. Noonan (1990) admitted that she could become very defensive in her writing speeches for Reagan; she rebuffed the intrusions by those in other government departments, especially the Harvard graduates in the State Department, who wanted to tone down her colorful metaphors or other phrasing she thought appropriate. Speechwriters need to realize that government policies, not their pet phrases, are at stake.

Deprecators of ghostwriting emphasize that the practice demeans the essence and importance of public speaking, by suggesting that the task can be assigned to an assistant. Personhood and a public speech are so intimately intertwined that speechwriting demands the creative hand of the presenter; the audience is entitled to see the real speechwriter. But the reverse could be claimed, that is, that having assistance ennobles the enterprise, by indicating that expert complementary help can make a better quality product.

A rhetorical critic's task is complicated in today's world: For many public speeches, multiple "ghosts" provided input. Newscasts, television programs, newspaper and magazine articles often have multiple authors and more unnamed contributors behind the scenes. It is difficult indeed to find *the* author, when judging a rhetorical product. In massive bureaucracies, especially in government but also in business, industry, and academia, many people have a hand in crafting messages. Noonan (1990) gave a vivid, somewhat cynical portrayal of the group authorship of President Reagan's speeches: "Think of a bunch of wonderful, clean, shining, perfectly shaped and delicious vegetables. Then think of one of those old-fashioned metal meat grinders. Imagine the beautiful vegetables being forced through the grinder and being rendered into a smooth, dull, textureless puree" (p. 72). Spontaneity and liveliness are lost through re-workings by many people in isolated places and times. But picture the workings of Franklin D. Roosevelt's group of speech assistants, as reported by one of them, William O. Douglas (1974), before he was appointed to the Supreme Court:

> I often was with FDR on weekends as well as at other times when speeches had to be written. . . . For speechwriting he usually sat facing a ring of a few of us: Lauchlin Currie, Steve Early, Tommy Corcoran, Robert Sherwood, Ben Cohen, Isadore Lubin, and Harry Hopkins. The anchor man was Samuel I. Rosenman, a New York judge whose quiet presence was FDR's mainstay, for Sam stayed on after everyone else left. It would be announced before we met that the speech was to be given at a certain place and on a certain subject. FDR would begin by reading aloud a rough draft, and would then call on the people in the room for suggestions. Each of us had a partial draft we would hand up, and FDR read each aloud. He might say, "Well, I don' t think I ought to get into that," or "Use that, Sam." Then he would dictate a paragraph or so to a secretary and resume the out-loud reading of other morsels that various people had sent in. Thus a speech was built, section by section. By 11:00 P.M. or so the first draft of the finished product was ready. Each of us had a copy and would approve or disapprove. These speech-writing sessions usually took place in the Oval Room, as FDR slept next door. He was in shirt sleeves, relaxed, and in good humor. Speech-writing to him was like a house-raising "bee" on the frontier. These sessions were intense and fast, usually over in less than an hour. At the end of the meeting the notes would be turned over to Sam Rosenman, who would work up a final draft. (p. 335)

Regardless of the methodology or atmosphere, multiple people constructing a speech leaves a critic with a difficult task of evaluation. The critic might also be misled by ghostwriters who at that time, or later, exaggerated their role.

Evaluating historical speeches by famous people introduces another problem for the critic; the extant version of a speech might be the polished work of a reporter in the audience who has given it to posterity. In eighteenth century England, for example, such literary figures as Samuel Johnson and Samuel Taylor Coleridge had, in their youth, written up parliamentary debates of leading members and proudly asserted that they could write better speeches than the famous parliamentarians. Critics of public address who are ethically obligated to fulfill their roles with care, must be sensitive detectives, and ferret out the "footprints" usually left by speechwriters.

Some observers question the ethicality of speechwriters who remain anonymous or, conversely, publicize their roles. Some ghostwriters have made it a code of honor to keep their anonymity, at least until they have retired (Benson, 1974; Devlin, 1974). Some agree that speech assistants should indeed be unseen and unnamed, unknown ghosts. To publicize their roles is inappropriately self-serving. Their reward is their salary and the personal satisfaction of being close to center stage and to a figure of power. Their employers should ensure speechwriters get their perks within the organizations so they will not feel the need to publicize themselves for self-gratification and income. But in the last several decades, especially since Ted Sorenson's publicized speechwriting role with President Kennedy, speech writers have become much more visible. Greater openness would seem to be a healthy development, in part to fulfill the public's right to know whose efforts are contributing to public statements by people in high positions in society. At the conclusion of television programs, a listing of those who contributed is a helpful summary that fulfills at least to some degree the answer to the question Who created this public discourse? The initials at the bottom of letters make known the typist who might have had a role in composing the letter along with the person signing it. We can rightfully expect public speakers to inform us about who helped to create their messages.

Sometimes, however, even when the assistant is acknowledged, we conveniently overlook it. For instance, those who help famous people write their memoirs, or help celebrities write novels are named on the title page but are not asked to appear on television talk shows or to sign books. Only the famous person, the celebrity, is paraded by the publisher to boost sales, and usually the public does not complain.

Of course, in training situations, such as in a speech class where the context implies that what students present is indeed their creation on which they are judged, there is no more room for ghostwriting than for plagiarism. As students stand before the class, their metamessage is: "What I am presenting is what I have created, upon which you will grade me." For students to present something not created by them would be cheating not only their classmates but also themselves, the academic institution, and the well-being of society. Society depends on educational institutions to maintain academic standards and to certify that graduates have been evaluated on their own work, that they have done the research, the analysis, and the composition, as well as the delivery of the speech.

HEMISPHERIC COMMUNICATORS

Advertisers, Lobbyists, Public Relations Personnel, Lawyers

We live in a sea of hemispheric communicators. By this idiosyncratic term, I mean people who because of their defined roles in society, such as lawyers, advertisers, lobbyists, and public relations practitioners, express messages that speak to only half the landscape. Like the shining moon, they present only the bright side and leave the dark side hidden. Lawyers by definition are advocates for their clients only, and thus present only one side of an issue. Advertisers, lobbyists, and public relations personnel produce messages about the strengths and virtues, of their product, service, institution, or enterprise. Working for a big corporation, a small business, a government agency, an educational institution, a profit or nonprofit organization, they seek to put the best possible light on their client to impress not only customers, but also stockholders, government agencies, potential donors, stakeholders, and the general public. They must carefully select only favorable information, presented as appealingly and understandably as possible. To perform such a one-sided communicative task without being incomplete, simplistic, misleading, deceptive, and unfair to an audience indeed needs ethical scrutiny. Solicitors for donations to worthy causes, such as cancer research, ought not to dwell inappropriately on emotional appeals, such as fear of contracting a disease. Maintaining credibility and integrity can be extremely difficult for hemispheric communicators. As mentioned in chapter 1 in the section on the ethical landscape, our field of speech communication seems to aim only at training students to be effective and successful hemispheric communicators, to convince audiences, to convert skeptics, to win debates. We need to train our students to be fully rounded, highly ethical communicators, able to see, appreciate, and communicate both sides of the moon.

There is, of course, a justification for hemispheric communicators. They are an important informational engine for society and let people know of the existence and nature of those things that would otherwise not be known. Advertisers can hardly be expected to fill billboards or newspaper and magazine ads with an equal amount of favorable and unfavorable information. University catalogs aimed at prospective students can scarcely be expected to devote space to negative aspects of their institutions. Colleges and universities send self-report data to compilers of guidebooks designed to aid undergraduate or graduate students' choices. These data are obviously skewed, so that rankings of the institutions have questionable validity. Academic administrators have obligations to their faculty, staff, trustees, students, and alumni, but even more to truth and fairness. (Cahn [1990] has edited a book of essays on ethical concerns about institutions of higher education in their advertising and other behaviors; Arnett [1992] discussed honesty in college advertising [pp. 193–196]; and Elliott [1995b] edited a collection of essays on ethical dilemmas in higher-education fund raising). Spokespeople for a government program can hardly be expected to deprecate as well as praise their program, and political campaigners can hardly be expected to parade their weaknesses as well as their strengths.

The messages of competing universities, companies, and candidates contain information that balances the whole picture. Objective analysts also help maintain balance. Indeed, critics abound in an open democratic society to challenge assertions and to present other data and views. Help is also given by people such as high school counselors who give both strengths and weaknesses of various colleges and universities to help students make their choices and political analysts who dwell on both strengths and weaknesses of various political figures.

Furthermore, in certain contexts, receivers expect these hemispheric messages, and are on their guard. Their critical capabilities are aroused when they know what to expect and understand that college brochures show only positive images of campus life, that advertisers highlight only the appealing aspects of their product or service, that lobbyists speak only for their masters, that a public relations release portrays a company only in a favorable light, that a political campaign speech communicates only the candidate's positive characteristics, and that lawyers speak only for their clients. But when audience's do not expect such half-messages, such as when students expect a teacher to give all sides of an issue, and not a one-sided "pitch," serious ethical problems are present. Even when audiences understand that a messenger is presenting only the attractive, bright half of the moon, serious ethical concerns still emerge.

Receivers have a right to expect hemispheric communicators to present messages that measure up to high ethical standards. Although these messages are incomplete, they must be truthful as far as they go. Listings of ingredients in food products, of safety features on automobiles, of prices on products and services ought to be accurate and not deceptive. The public should not have to grapple constantly with misleading and fraudulent claims. The call for truth in advertising is a central demand of consumers and government. A list of ethical obligations would include the avoidance of unsubstantiated claims and distortions, of weakening the opportunity for consumers to choose rationally, and of excessively stimulating the grossest levels of emotional appeals to vanity, power, fear, and self-indulgence. Needs, not unbridled desires, should be targeted. Superlatives, exaggerations, embellishments, vagueness, tastelessness, puffery, and inappropriate use of testimonials should be rigorously monitored. Even if advertising deserves the poetic license that some claim for it, the use of imagination, feeling, ambiguity, suggestiveness, and arresting symbols should show care and concern. As has already been said, the ends do not justify the means, particularly when we are bombarded by the claims of hemispheric communicators with their bright-side-of-the-moon-messages.

The objectives of hemispheric communicators then, are to intrude into people's agendas by creating an awareness of a product, to hold attention, and to provide information and views in a simple, under-standable, attractive and compelling manner, to make the receivers do or think as the communicators want. Whether messengers represent profit or nonprofit entities, their ultimate goal is to survive. They can hardly be expected to spend their resources presenting self-destructing mes-sages—to commit suicide. But in fulfilling their mission they have definite ethical obligations. They should fulfill their obligations not only to their organizations, but also to the public and to their own personal integrity. They need to uphold the ethical principles of their profession.

Programmers and Deprogrammers

Increasingly today we witness programmers brainwashing young people until they commit acts of violence or take their own lives, for a cause. When people have succumbed to a siren song of a charismatic individual or group, be it a tightly structured gang or a religious, political, or social group, a counterthrust to rescue the people, to neutralize the persuasion, sometimes results. *Deprogramming* is an attempt, usually by a relative or a hired professional, to counteract brainwashing, often by strongly persuasive means. Here again questionable means are used to achieve good ends. The attempt to counteract unhealthy "conversions," to rescue people who have been "captured" or "kidnapped," by an authoritarian figure or organization may lead well-intentioned people to use highly unethical means.

Surrogates

The use of surrogate communicators is a familiar part of the rhetorical landscape. During political campaigns, for instance, especially on the presidential level, incumbent presidents have been heavily criticized by opponents, the media, and scholars for not discussing issues themselves, instead of sending cabinet officials or others in the administration as substitutes. Incumbents usually justify such action by claiming that they are too busy conscientiously tending to the duties of the office to campaign. To rely excessively (but when does reliance become excessive?) on surrogates would seem to deserve a low ethical quality rating; such behavior forestalls a direct clash between the candidates and does not give the voters a clear comparison and contrast between the individuals and their positions on issues. Democracy needs and deserves a fuller and clearer view of the contenders. Incumbents have a tremendous advantage; they get news coverage just by going about their normal routines, whereas a challenger has to create a dramatic episode, like a debate with the incumbent, to catch the media's attention.

Suppose a senator cannot fulfill a speaking engagement and sends a staff member instead. Suppose a corporation president cannot fulfill a speaking engagement and sends a vice president instead. These may be merely questionable ploys to avoid meeting the public or to avoid a time-consuming task. Audiences may feel cheated by coming to a meeting and not hearing the speaker thay expected. Sometimes those arranging a program use a well known name to draw a large audience although the arrangers know that the prominent figure will not be able to appear. Futhermore, audiences may also share in the problem. That is, psychologically they want the actual presence of the authority figure, who makes them feel important. At parties, for example, people might feed their egos by sharing a place and time with important personages even when nothing is said by or to them.

In some contexts, everyone understands that a spokesperson will be a surrogate for a high official or an agency, and an ethical dimension is absent. For example, when a press secretary for the president makes a statement and takes questions at a press conference, the person is known to be a substitute voice.

The press often claims to be a surrogate for the people. Reporters ask questions they think the public would want to ask. They are watchdogs, who monitor the power-full. Reporters might be aggressive, abrasive, and brash, but, they say, it is all in the public's behalf. Those who carry out such surrogate enterprises should nevertheless consider the ethics of their acts.

In medical situations, where relatives and doctors have to make decisions for an incapacitated patient, acting as a surrogate decision maker can be agonizing. To decide what treatments, or even whether a loved one is to live or die, is a horrendous decision. Journals devoted to medical ethics, such as the *Hastings Center Reports*, are full of articles about the ethical dimensions of these surrogate decision making events, which are increasing in number because of sophisticated medical technology.

Demagogues

The term *demagogue* had an honorific connotation in ancient Greece; it referred to a champion of the people's interests. But today its connotation is decidedly negative and usually refers to an oral communicator seeking to appeal to the masses by speaking with excessive zeal, strong and often irrelevant emotional appeal, arrogant bluntness, intentional use of innuendo, irrationality, a lack of fixed beliefs, and the use of a current social problem for personal gain and a crude pursuit of power. This label must be used with caution, not to unfairly tar all public speakers, who almost inevitably might show one or more of those characteristics. The habitual use of most of those characteristics, however, permits an appropriate designation of demagogue, and an appropriately low ethical quality rating.

Voices for the Voiceless

Many public communicators pride themselves on being voices for the voiceless, who speak in behalf of those perceived to have no ability, power, or circumstance enabling them to speak for themselves. Such communicators willingly respond to the admonition: "Open thy mouth for the dumb" (Prov. 31:8). Rhetors speak on behalf of children, people who are mentally disabled, unborn children, people at the poverty level, and homeless people. They speak in behalf of abstractions—Justice, Equality, God. They are the spokespeople for the wilderness and defend animal rights. Is the ego of such public advocates unduly inflated by their roles? Again, these people must recall that the ends do not justify the means. They must guard against a mind-set giving them license to run with the wind, to think that with such a commitment they can do no wrong. When vanity takes over, people assume a split set of values and see themselves as heroes, and those who oppose them as villains. At a state political convention dominated by pro-life delegates, a clergyman who gave the opening prayer on the final day slipped in some pro-choice statements because that view was not presented in the sessions (Whereatt, 1992). His "words fell like hot ashes on startled delegates" (Grow, 1992), who loudly booed him and stopped him from finishing. He was hustled off the platform by those in charge of the program and accused of giving a political harangue rather than a religious invocation. Although accused of improperly and deceptively misusing his assigned role, the clergyman thought he had been a righteous spokesperson for a silent minority. When presuming to speak for the voiceless, public communicators must be wary of letting one's personal commitments push them along without thinking about all their ethical obligations in such situations. Compassion and righteous indignation, like all other noble motivations, need to be properly harnessed.

WHISTLE-BLOWERS

The phenomenon of whistle-blowers in our society makes the role extremely important to probe for its ethical dimensions.[1] Cases are increasingly reported in newspapers, magazines, books, and on radio and televison. Engineers might reveal to the public that faulty brakes are being installed in automobilies at their plant; members of a senator's staff might publicize their employer's wrong-doings, accountants might accuse their superiors of mismanaging funds, employees might accuse their company of illegally selling weapon-related products to a foreign country; athletes might accuse their coaches of receiving payments from sporting goods companies to push their products. In this section, I define whistle-blowing as a communicative act, clarify the characteristics of whistle-blowers, and discuss the ethical tension points in whistleblowing.

---

[1]This section draws on my 1987 and 1989 articles: Ethical tension points in whistleblowing. *Journal of Business Ethics, 6,* 321–328. Copyright by D. Reidel Publishing Company, reprinted by permission of Kluwer Academic Publishers; The communicative act of whistleblowing. In C. A. B. Osigweh, Yg. (Ed.), *Managing employee rights and responsibilities* (pp. 187–198). New York: Quorum Books, an imprint of Greenwood Publishing Group, Inc., Westport, CT. Used by permission of the editor and the publisher.

Whistle-blowing as a Communicative Act

Whistle-blowing is an *intentional* communicative act. For example, photocopied documents were intentionally taken and published; an employee intentionally told a newspaper reporter the story of a superior's mismanagement; a former high official in a tobacco company intentionally revealed that the company knew their product to be harmfully addictive. Although there might be degrees of intentionality and some parts of the message might have unintentionally become known, intentionality is at the core of the process.

Whistle-blowing is a *responsive* act. Whistle-blowers respond to a condition they think is badly in need of correction; otherwise, there would be no need for their message. Whistle-blowing occurs when an institution has not taken adequate corrective measures; because corrections are not forthcoming, a response is necessary.

Whistle-blowing presents an *accusatory* message; it is an example of the genre of *kategoria,* "accusation." The group, or a portion thereof, is accused of a specific wrongdoing; the accused might be a single person, a small group of people, or the whole organization. The public is being informed of a specific, significant, willful wrongdoing. Whistle-blowing thus differs from leaking information. Both refer to transmitting information from inside an organization to the outside, but whistle-blowers are transmitting accusatory information (S. Bok, 1982). Whistle-blowing also differs from a confession, which is a first-person accusation: "*I* did something wrong." Whistle-blowing is a third-person accusation: "They did something wrong."

Whistle-blowing is a public act. Whistle-blowers go public. Because those inside a group would not listen, the rhetor delivers the message to an outside audience.

In so doing, whistle-blowers use *varying mediums*: a reporter who writes an article in a newspaper or magazine, a public official, a candidate for public office, law enforcement officers, even an autobiographical exposé (Eveland, 1980; Wright, 1987).

Whistle-blowing is *refutational.* An initial accusation is almost certainly followed by denials and counteraccusations, by demands for evidence and sources of evidence, by charges of self-serving motivation. Indeed, a whistle-blower's initial charges might include counterrefutation of points anticipated to be refuted by the accused. The conflict might end up in court.

Such charges and countercharges might continue for *a long time,* usually for years. Thus, "long-range commitment is perhaps the first requirement of successful whistle-blowing" (Peters & Branch, 1972, p. 76). A person does not make a single accusation and expect that to be the end of it.

The objective of whistle-blowers is to enlist support from a large outside audience. Correcting the wrongdoing cannot be accomplished by the whistle-blowers themselves, and when corrections by the accused group are not forthcoming, whistle-blowers seek outside allies. They want not only to inform, but to arouse an outside audience, one that is probably initially uninformed and apathetic. Thus, the message has to be clear, credible, and compelling. Finally, the act of whistle-blowing *strains contractual agreements*, written or understood. This topic is discussed later, in the section on substantive tension points.

Characteristics of Whistle-Blowers

To these rhetorical facets of whistle-blowing I now add the characteristics of whistle-blowers to give a full view of the communicative event.

Whistle-blowers usually *act alone*, although occasionally two or more might be involved. Generally, a single person has made an intensely personal decision to blow the whistle. As an individual, a whistle-blower takes on what can be a lonely task. It is one against a whole group, one against many. The group has enormous resources on which to draw—a large treasury, a fleet of lawyers and aides, a huge supportive clientele, and the power to punish. Whistle-blowers have only their information, talent, and credibility. In this underdog role, whistle-blowers have an uphill struggle. The public serves as a potential power balancer when it rallies behind a whistle-blower.

Whistle-blowers are usually *subordinate* to those they accuse. After all, people need not go outside a group to accuse someone lower in the hierarchial structure; that usually can be accomplished within an organization. When parents need to reprimand their children, they can do so within the family structure, but it would be extremely difficult for a child to reprimand an abusive parent without going outside the family. Occasionally children have been driven to report to authorities the illegal, harmful behavior of their parents. A whistle-blower, then, is not only outnumbered but is usually in a subordinate relationship. Sometimes, of course, the accuser and the defendant might be equal. For example, an employee might charge a co-worker with sexual harassment. Doctors might consider reporting an incompetent and irresponsible colleague. Recently the British National Health Service has written into doctors' contracts language that requires them to report substandard performances of their colleagues (Wintour, 1995). Cases of horizontal whistleblowing have increasingly surfaced, a fact highlighted by the title of an article, "Am I my brother's warden? Responding to the unethical or incompetent colleague" (Morreim, 1993).

A whistle-blower is an *inside* person, one who is or was a regular member of a group, who speaks from the point of view of one who has actually experienced the inner workings. A whistle-blower has firsthand, specific knowledge that outsiders cannot possibly have. A member of a college sorority or fraternity, for example, has experienced it from the inside. Any member of a family is an insider to that circle and knows about it in a way that a next-door neighbor or any other outsider cannot possibly know. A whistle-blower has usually been a member of the group for a long time, has accumulated a sizable amount of key information, has developed a close relationship with at least some members, and has become immersed in the culture of the group.

Whistle-blowers are *well-informed*. If not, they would have little significance, and their message would go unnoticed. They possess something others do not possess—valuable inside information—which makes them potentially powerful communicators. A strategically placed engineer might have technical knowledge about the dangerous aspects of machinery that others do not, or a member of a military unit might know the details of the unit's inhuman behavior. Obviously, a long-tenured, highly respected group member has more credibility than a shunned chronic complainer, but the dimension of expertness gives even the latter's ethos a powerful quality. Being well-informed, of course, goes beyond having a sizable amount of data: It means meeting the qualitative tests of accuracy, completeness, relevance, objectivity, and currency, together with proper analysis of the evidence.

Whistle-blowers not only possess facts but are *morally agitated* about those facts. Facts in and of themselves are not necessarily problems, unless they violate a value. Whistle-blowers think that one or more values have been violated. Their peace of mind, their conscience, is disturbed, and their frustration is compounded when an organization has not made sufficient efforts to correct the situation. Whistle-blowers are morally and intellectually convinced that there are "actions or conditions within a firm that are either illegal or harmful to the public or to consumers of the firm's product"(De George, 1985, p. 15).

Whistle-blowers are *motivated by laudatory ideals*, at least from their viewpoint. Holding an altrustic concern for the public, they challenge the assumption that what is good for the organization is good for society. They are dissenters in the public interest, as the subtitle of the Peters and Branch (1972) book on whistle-blowers labeled them. They perceive themselves to be servants of lofty values, but frequently those they accuse perceive them to be motivated by personal vendettas, disgruntlement, hunger for notoriety and prestige, or a chronic need to vent complaints. It is of course difficult to know when a person's motives are chiefly self-serving and when they are altruistic. As in most social situations, both high and not-so-high motivations probably prompt whistle-blowers.

Whistle-blowers are viewed by many in their group as *traitors* and by many of the public as *heroes,* and the ensuing rhetoric is cast in this two-valued framework. The etymology of *traitor* refers to one who has betrayed a trust or has *handed over* something. Critics contend that whistle-blowers have indeed handed over inside information and have betrayed a trust. Whistle-blowers, they charge, have not heeded the Confucian warning against "those who mistake insubordination for courage… [and]… those who mistake talebearing for honesty" (Confucius, 1938, p. 216). On the other hand, the public is often genuinely grateful to whistle-blowers for exposing dangerous inefficiency in a governmental agency, obsessive priority of scheduling over safety in a corporation, or insensitive care in a nursing home. There are no guarantees that whistle-blowers will be applauded for their efforts, and it is best for them not to expect it. Some who actually viewed themselves as heroes have been shocked to be considered traitors (Greenwald, 1995b). Whistle-blowers who expose surface problems can be honored as heroes, but those whistle-blowers who expose deep faults in a system can face great hostility.

Ethical Tension Points in Whistle-Blowing

The rhetorical characteristics of whistle-blowing and of whistle-blowers raise ethical concerns, and illuminate ethical tension points (ETPs). The accumulated ETPs build to a complex and agonizing ethical struggle for a potential whistle-blower and for society in general. In exploring these ETPs, I divide them into procedural and substantive.

Procedural Tension Points (ETPs).   A number of ETPs may be looked upon as procedural. First, *how serious is the problem*? It might be an exaggeration by an irritating problem-monger. A person might simply have a low tolerance level for shortcomings, and prematurely claim serious problems, much like neurotic parents who react too quickly and strongly to minor misbehavior of their children. The problem might be temporary, and predictions of dire consequences might be unrealistic.

Second, *how carefully has a whistle-blower handled the information?* The facts might not have been carefully checked and rechecked for accuracy, completeness, and relevance. The data might not warrant the charges. The sources of the information need to be documented and up-to-date. The case needs to be presented as clearly as possible, with a minimum of ambiguity and innuendo. The values that are supposedly endangered need to be clearly identified. The whistle-blower needs to see the whole picture so that bias does not color the selection and treatment of the data. How proper were the procedures in securing the information in the first place? How ethical is it, for example, to remove and photograph files?

Third, *have whistle-blower's motives been carefully explored and aired?* Is a desire for notoriety operating? The whistle-blower might be engaging in a personal vendetta, desiring to get even with a supervisor, colleague or group. A secret agenda might be kept from the public. The whistle-blower might be too rigidly or surreptitiously applying standards of a religious or other allegiance.

Fourth, *has the whistle-blower tried to have the situation corrected internally* through established channels? The whistle-blower should first have gone to the immediate supervisor and to other appropriate personnel up the ladder. An adequate attempt should have been made to reason with the wrongdoer(s), who in turn should have been given enough time to improve the situation. The whistle-blower should have demonstrated a positive, nonthreatening attitude, a genuine desire to correct the problem from within. In short, the whistle-blower should have tried to keep the problem "in the family" as long as it was possible and wise.

Fifth, *when should whistle-blowing occur?* There is some dispute over the ethical nature of whistle-blowing when a person is still an employee rather than when the person has resigned, been fired, or retired. Literature on whistle-blowing usually labels whistle-blowing while still on the job as *pure*, and courageous. Whistle-blowing after leaving is described as *alumnus* and carries a connotation of being less *pure*, and less credible, presumably because the whistle-blower makes accusations at a distance, and is not brave enough to face the full consequences of the act. Peters and Branch (1972) posed the dilemma:

> Does one leave the organization to become an alumnus whistle-blower, containing some maneuvering room but sacrificing the drama and immediacy of an inside exposure? Or does one stay inside, where the battle will draw more press coverage, but where there is great danger of being neutralized by a confusing barrage of emotion-filled loyalty and motive charges? (p. 295)

A former tobacco industry lobbyist, dying of lung cancer himself, admitted on the CBS television program *60 Minutes* that he had been lying thoughout his career, but now that he was terminally ill, he wanted to confess to the dangers of smoking although his act would be considered disloyal by those in his industry.

Sixth, *should whistle-blowing be anonymous*? Public whistle-blowers would create greater credibility by exhibiting courage in exposing themselves to considerable punishment from the organizations concerned. Keeping their identity secret would offer whistle-blowers more protection, at least initially, and might embolden them to be more comprehensive and incisive, and to get to the heart of the case more quickly and effectively. Sooner or later their identity would probably be revealed, and in the meantime their credibility might be somewhat suspect. How fair is it to an organization or to the public not to know the source of the charges?

Seventh, *with what intensity and how often should whistle-blowing occur*? The manner and frequency of the act might have ethical considerations: Whether a person is strident or composed, circumspect or not; whether the intensity is unfair, misleading, and creating a fearful atmosphere.

Eighth, *what is the proper audience for the whistle-blower*? Whether to channel a case to a newspaper reporter, to a political candidate, or to a government official, who might use the information for other purposes and thereby distort the case, needs to be carefully thought through. When publishing charges through a letter to the editor, in a public speech, or in written memoirs, ethical dimensions also need consideration.

Ninth, *how right is it for the person to shift from participant to judge*? The whistle-blower might be unilaterally and presumptuously undertaking an inappropriate role. *Whistle-blowing* is an apt metaphor. In basketball, for instance, a trained person is paid to blow a whistle to signal a rule violation. Blowing the whistle momentarily stops the action, the referee identifies the violator and the rule infraction, the violater is punished, and the team is penalized by giving the victim a free throw at the basket. Players, coaches, fans, and sportswriters might grumble about these whistle-blowers, but the authority of such referees is unquestioned, and the game depends on them. Without a designated whistle-blower, anarchy would rule. But the whistle-blower is a third party, a nonparticipant who is fulfilling previously agreed-on functions. An indignant player might insist that he did not foul an opponent, but the referee, not the player, makes that judgment. A person either plays the game or judges it. In nonsport whistle-blowing, an employee takes on the role of referee, and therein lies the ethical tension.

Finally, *how ethical is it to undertake an effort expensive* both to the whistle-blower and the accused, in terms of time, money, effort, and mental and emotional involvement? Similar costs might be borne by other parties called in to investigate or testify, or by those associated with the whistle-blower. In short, a whistle-blowing act is usually expensive, and its worth needs careful consideration. Perhaps those resources could be channeled into more productive, more ethical endeavors.

Substantive Tension Points.   Perhaps more difficult than the procedural ethical questions are substantive tension points. The overarching ethical dilemma in whistle-blowing grows out of trying to determine how to balance multiple loyalties, obligations, values, *goods*. Nurses, for example, agonize over whether to blow the whistle on what they think are seriously inadequate practices in their unit of the hospital. They realize obligations to the patients, to their peers, to their supervisors, to the medical profession, to the hospital administration, to their own self-esteem, to the public, and to the truth. Balancing all these conflicting loyalties and commitments is indeed difficult. For example, which takes precedence in a whistle-blowing situation: loyalty or the duty to inform? Some obligations might have to be sacrificed, deemphasized, or temporarily set aside. Whistle-blowers often find themselves in a "purgatory" as McDowell (1991, pp. 87–98) put it.

First, *what is the obligation to the organization*? As noted earlier, a contractual arrangement, written or understood, exists. In a commercial context, an employee agrees to give talent, effort, time, cooperation and harmony in relations with colleagues, and loyalty to the organization and its enterprise. On the other side of the contract, the company agrees to give the employee wages, an opportunity to use skills, decent facilities and conditions for working, and various stipulated items, such as promotions, pensions, parking. The company does not, however, own the employee; loyalty freely and thoughtfully given is different from blind and coercive subservience. A corporation is a "body" (*corpus*) of people granted legal rights, recognition, and economic advantages and thus can be expected to go beyond maximizing profits to showing a sense of obligation to employees and society.

Loyalty often involves confidentiality, and for an employee to spread key inside information to an outside audience is a direct violation of the contractual understanding. Organizations have trade secrets that must be kept from competitors, and any revelation of these secrets is a gross violation of contractual expectations. Was a pledge of secrecy valid or reasonable in the first place? Perhaps not, when a group's behavior was so improper and dangerous that violation of secrecy would be a small offense by comparison. Perhaps a pledge of secrecy was valid when revelations would be unfairly damaging to the organization, to its functioning, its profits, its internal harmony, and its credibility.

Whistle-blowers challenge the assumption that what is good for the organization is good for the larger public. Whistle-blowers have decided that the value of loyalty to the group is superseded by other values, such as the dignity of life, fairness, and efficiency. Nonconformity is a laudable value when the group's norms or activities are of an extremely low ethical quality, but the whistle-blower has to prove this. As Bormann (1975) wrote: "The participant in a group must make choices relating to his allegiance to his group when he finds their norms and ends in conflict with the larger purposes and norms of his society" (p. 65). The whistle-blower might, of course believe that the public revelations will actually help the organization in the long run. Once cleansed of its sins, its errors corrected, its financial accounting straightened out, its safety measures installed, its new leadership in place, the organization will go forward to greater accomplishments, greater profits, and greater credibillity.

The degree of loyalty to the group varies in different cultures. For example, in Japan an employee is usually linked to an organization for life (although less commonly than in the past), and whistle-blowing would be highly unusual. In the United States, with its transient population, its strong unions and its individualism, employees are less secure, less committed to a company, and are often in a confrontational stance with an employer. Hence whistle-blowing is more common.

Second, *what are the moral obligations to colleagues in the organization?* Their financial security might be damaged if the company's business declines. Their jobs might be threatened, and their lives made miserable by the increased tension and the probing of reporters. They might feel betrayed by a colleague, and friendships might be frayed or severed. Ties of mutual respect with immediate superiors are broken. Co-workers might feel guilty that they did not come forward with the information themselves or might feel relieved that someone else had the courage to publicize the problem. They might be relieved that the company can correct itself and move on to a more secure future. Thus, colleagues might have their morale lowered, raised, or unaffected. Whatever the case, whistle-blowers must be aware of a moral obligation to them.

Third, *what are the ethical obligations to a person's profession?* Whistle-blowers must somehow balance a commitment to a profession with an obligation to help the company make a profit. For example, when a research doctor in a pharmaceutical company permits insufficiently tested drugs to be sold on the market, serious ethical and perhaps legal issues are raised. Not to blow the whistle might result in a lowering of the profession's credibility if the deficiency is discovered in the future. A young researcher might face a struggle about blowing the whistle on higher ranking colleagues engaging in fraudulent scientific research practices (Sarasohn, 1993). Publicizing serious shortcomings of fellow scientists, engineers, doctors, or teachers might weaken the public's faith and trust. Not to do so might harm society. McDowell (1991) articulated a meaningful challenge to professionalism: "If the profession seriously wants to impose a duty of reporting improper professional activity and to develop a reporting mechanism that works, it must go beyond the negative one of protecting whistle-blowers against retaliation to a positive one of support and appreciation, while at the same time avoiding the appearance of 'buying' informers" (p. 92). Upholding the standards of a profession is upholding ourselves, for we largely define ourselves by our professional affiliation.

Fourth, *will whistle-blowing adversely affect a person's family and other close associates?* The family is no doubt subjected to much publicity and probably experiences financial insecurity, psychological agony, loss of friends, and social ostracism. A whistle-blower's children might encounter cruel taunts at school and on the playground. One whistle-blower (Glazer, 1983) indicated that "the impact on his children (was) comparable to radiation—difficult to measure but potentially very damaging" (p. 39). Other primary groups, such as a club, or a religious affiliation, might likewise be adversely affected by association with the whistle-blower. To balance moral obligations against the intimate relationships is indeed an agonizing exericise.

Fifth, *what about the moral obligations whistle-blowers have toward themselves?* Potential punishments are many and devastating. Although supervisors might focus on the message, all too often they focus on the messenger and bring chaos to that person's life. Whistle-blowers have experienced loss of jobs, loss of financial security, loss of mutual respect and trust from peers and superiors, loss of friendships, much psychological stress, social ostracism, and even loss of the confidence of family and loved ones. Threatening phone calls, being followed by suspicious cars, and other unnerving harassments might lead a person to fear being assaulted or worse (Greenwald, 1993). When applying for another job, positive references are hard to secure; whistle-blowers are labeled as untrustworthy employees. Imprisonment might even result. A person could remain with the company but be shunted to a less desirable position, with little chance of job satisfaction, promotion, and salary increases. Initial support of colleagues might wither away as they get promotions and wage inceases and grow weary of the whistle-blower's plight. A whistle-blower might be forced into early retirement, or made to take psychiatric tests to show fitness for service, at least until in 1984 when the government forbade supervisors from requiring such stressful tests of employees (Baldwin, 1985). Whistle-blowers might be subjected to silent treatment or to vocal harassment; their motives might be impugned, and their personal life invaded. A person might come to feel inwardly torn and fragmented, as expressed in the *Bhagavad Gita*, one of the Hindu scriptures, which described one who felt "like a broken cloud, having severed its allegiance, and yet having failed to gain a new one, come to nothing and melted away to nothingness" (Bhagavad Gita, 1935, p. 78).

On the other hand, could people live with themselves if they did not publicize damaging information? Integrity and self-worth are at stake: ethical standards are no doubt significantly altered for better or worse by actions. Whatever the situation, "Almost always," Westin (1981) concluded, whistle-blowers' "experiences are traumatic, and their careers and lives are profoundly affected" (p. 1). Glazer (1983) was more optimistic and concluded his study of 10 whistle-blowers by pointing out that virtually all of them were "able to rebuild their careers and belief in their competence and integrity. They found an escape hatch in private practice, consulting, and the media. Ironically, perhaps the diversity of American economic and social institutions provides opportunities to those who have dared defy the authority of the established ones" (p. 40).

Sixth, *what is the ethical obligation toward the general public*, those outsiders to whom the message is addressed? The whistle-blower is ostensibly their knowledgeable protector, warning them of potential dangers. The public might be greatly heartened by the exposé, or might feel unduly apprehensive or fearful. The short-range and long-range effects might be quite different. For example, the public might temporarily lack a supply of energy when an atomic energy plant is forced to close down for prolonged inspection; in the long run, however, greater safety and efficiency and alternative energy supplies might result. Not to warn the public might be difficult to live with if harm resulted.

Finally, *what is the effect on bedrock values?* Whistle-blowers might strengthen the value of freedom of expression by speaking out. If the remarks are irresponsible and false, the value is shaken, and the rights of the accused violated. Whistle-blowers might strengthen or weaken such values as independent judgment, courage, fairness, human dignity, safety, economy, efficiency, cooperativeness, justice, and loyalty. Without whistle-blowers, truth is hidden, unknown, unserved. Some values, such as friendship, might be subordinated to other values. Whistle-blowers must make hard choices about which values take precedence. Whistle-blowers might use an a priori ranking of values, as did Werhane (1983) when she vigorously asserted that individual moral rights take precedence over utilitarianism:

> If the notion of moral right makes any sense, one must recognize that persons have such rights, if they do, just because they are persons, that is, just because they are rational, autonomous individuals. They cannot have such rights as the right to life or to liberty because, and only so long as, acknowledging these rights promotes the general welfare.... . The existence of such fundamental rights cannot depend on whether collective interests are enhanced ... . The moral rights of the individual "trump" utilitarian calculations, both outside and inside the workplace. (p. 116)

Whatever the priority of values or the circumstances, we can conclude, as Peters and Branch (1972) did, that "every whistle-blower who is right contributes to a kind of education by example for the country, even if he [sic] is widely regarded as a failure or as an important martyr for his [sic] particular cause" (p. 297). To that statement I might add that every whistle-blower who is wrong weakens the fabric of society. Even then, undertaking such a daunting task against formidable odds arouses respect for such courageous people.

Recent Developments

Keeping abreast of recent developments in whistle-blowing can be daunting. Miceli and Near (1992) provided a detailed summary discussion of legal developments relative to whistle-blowing (pp. 232– 279) and a useful bibliography (pp. 309– 328). Three highly publicized whistle-blowing cases illustrated many of the points discussed in this section. Mark Whitacre, close to the throne in the Archer Daniel Midland company, acted as a mole gathering data for the Federal Bureau of Investigation (FBI) on price-fixing and other questionable activities (Henkoff, 1995; Whitacre, 1995). Jeffrey Wigand, former vice president at Brown & Williamson Tobacco Corporation (third-largest tobacco company in the United States), has blown sky high the claims that the company (and hence other tobacco companies) did not know of the harmful addictive qualities of nicotine (Gleick, 1996a, 1996b). A few states have filed lawsuits against the tobacco industry to recoup medical costs that taxpayers pay through Medicaid for treating health problems related to smoking. George Galatis and George Betancourt, senior engineers, charged lack of safety at a nuclear power plant in Waterford, Connecticut, and claimed that the federal government failed to enforce its own safety rules (Pooley, 1996). Readers particularly interested in whisleblowing issues will want to keep informed about developments in these and other contemporary cases.

EXERCISES

1. Write an essay on the interrelatedness of the functions of *creator* and *reporter* in human communicative acts.

2. Read about the experiences of some ghostwriters (e.g., Peggy Noonan, Robert Oliver, Sam Rosenman, Ted Sorenson) and evaluate in a paper both the positive and negative aspects of their contributions.

3. Develop and support a case either for or against ghostwriting. Present your material in a paper or a speech. The class may divide on this assignment and have a debate on the issue, with emphasis on the ethical aspects involved.

4. Interview a "hemispheric" communicator in the community (e.g., a lawyer, lobbyist, advertiser, public relations person), and ask the person how he or she views the profession, and whether any ethical dimensions are involved.

5. Analyze a series of advertisements in newspapers, or magazines, on billboards, on television or radio; explain where you would place them on the Ethical Quality Scale and why.

6. Write an essay evaluating the ethical dimensions involved in surrogates or demagogues. Include contemporary examples.

7. Discuss the ethical aspects involved when people take it upon themselves to speak for the voiceless. Include specific contemporary examples.

8. Read about the efforts of a contemporary whistle-blower and evaluate that person's struggle in light of the ethical dimensions involved.

9. Write a paper evaluating the activities of contemporary whistle-blower(s), and focus on one or more of the procedural ethical tension points.

10. Write an essay evaluating the importance of one or more of the substantive ethical tension points involved in whistle-blowing. Bring into your discussion some contemporary examples of whistle-blowing.

5

Ethical Issues Revolving Around the Message

In this chapter I focus on truth-telling, promises, reason, emotion, propaganda, exit messages, and withholding and releasing messages.

TRUTH-TELLING

We have seen at the beginning of chapter 1 how ancient religious literature honored truth-telling. So did some ancient secular literature. For instance, the 5th century B.C.E. Greek historian Herodotus (trans. 1947) wrote that Persian youths "are carefully instructed . . . in three things alone—to ride, to draw the bow, and to speak the truth" (p. 76), and that "the most disgraceful thing in the world . . . is to tell a lie" (p. 77). Moral philosophers through the centuries, and contemporary books and articles, have urged a commitment to truth.

Intentionality is at the heart of lying. The vast landscape of truth, the perceived realities around and within us, is represented by written, oral, or nonverbal symbols when we communicate with one another. When we *intentionally* misrepresent these realities, we seek to deceive our communicatees, and thus we exhibit low ethical quality. Here, then, we are concerned with the deception that is "a deliberate intention to mislead" (Christians, Rotzell, & Fackler, 1995, p. 51).

A message that is truthful, full of truth—implies that a communicative act is either fully truthful or fully untruthful. The terminology sets up a two-valued image of polarized options. But there are degrees of truthfulness, twilight zones of truth, gray areas that some call near lies.

Furthermore, truth can be divided into two components: *accuracy* and *completeness*. In answering her parents' question about where she had been the night before, a daughter might mention two places but omit a third. Her reply was accurate but incomplete. As has been said, a statement can be completely true, but not truly complete. If the daughter

87

had named two places she had not been, her statement would have been inaccurate. Sins of omission and commission, of concealment and falsification, are both at the core of lying. In the first instance we *keep* people in the dark, and in the second, we *put* them in the dark; whether a passive or active act, deception is the intent. The light–dark metaphor is instructive here, for we try to keep people from *seeing* the truth by not *throwing light on the subject*. Both "deliberate falsification or omission of information" (Miller, 1983, p. 92) concerns us. As Ekman (1986) wrote, "When there is a choice about *how* to lie, liars usually prefer concealing to falsifying" (p. 29); concealing doesn't seem so reprehensible.

True completeness is usually impossible, unrealistic, and at times even undesirable in human communicative transactions. When someone asks in the evening what I did during the day, I cannot report every act and thought, minute by minute, so I select and summarize. When I tell someone about my two-week vacation, I soon lose my audience with a full day-by-day account. The mass media, faced with severe constraints of time and space, select, summarize, and highlight the day's news. In the process of selection, omissions might be ethically suspect, but at times completeness is undesirable. For example, Dietrich Bonhoeffer (1972), wrote from a German prison to a close friend: "After all, 'truthfulness' does not mean uncovering everything that exists... . [M]any things in human life ought to remain covered" (p. 158). The severe inner tension no doubt experienced by conscientious communicators when intentionally withholding truth was expressed by Dag Hammarskjold (1964), former secretary general of the United Nations: "The most dangerous of all moral dilemmas: when we are obliged to conceal truth in order to help the truth to be victorious" (p. 147).

The great harms that lying can cause the deceived, the deceiver, and the larger society are many and significant. Lying is demeaning and disrespectful to an audience and gives unfair power to a deceiver. It weakens the trust between the two and sharply lowers the liar's credibility if the truth is later discovered. A major punishment for liars has always been that nobody believes them once the truth is known. Rebuilding trust and credibility can be a slow and painful process. When not discovered, a liar might repeat lies in the future, especially if the rewards are large and detection unlikely. A liar, however, might have to tell additional cover-up lies to keep the original one from being discovered. Thus liars severely restrict their own freedom in their future statements, for they have to remember what they said to whom in the past. Close associates might lie when they learn that lies are successful.

A liar's self-respect might be shaken, and a nagging internal conflict could ensue. Hample (1980) concluded his study of lying by noting that liars were "substantially more satisfied with the lie than with themselves" and that a seemingly successful lie "had little power to raise self-satisfaction" (p. 45). As these fabrics of interaction are weakened and multiplied, society in general can suffer. It is a familiar axiom that a democracy depends on its citizenry's being truthfully informed by the government, by public officials, and by the media, to be contributing, responsible citizens. When witnesses lie to Congressional committees, those decision makers are deprived of necessary information, and the democratic process can be in severe danger. For members of Congress and members of the British Parliament to lie in their sessions is one of the severest sins imaginable, a sin that shakes the very foundations of democracy. When a young mother murdered her two children by drowning them, and for at least a week tearfully blamed a Black man (thus slandering African-Americans), her lying came to be considered almost as reprehensible as the murders. These lies involved both concealment of the truth and creation of a falsehood.

This consequentialist emphasis on the harmful effects of lying is joined by the nonconsequentialist assertion, as noted in chapter 2, that in principle lying is a moral failing of great significance and ought to be shunned on those grounds. This fact brought S. Bok (1979) to coin her "principle of veracity", a phrase used frequently ever since. By this term, building on Aristotle, she meant:

> Truthful statements are preferable to lies in the absence of special considerations. This premise gives an initial negative weight to lies. It holds that... lying requires explanation, whereas truth ordinarily does not....
> .And it places the burden of proof squarely on those who assume the liar's perspective....[The] "principle of veracity" [is] an expression of this initial imbalance in our weighing of truthfulness and lying. (p. 32)

In investigative reporting, Hodges (1989) wrote: "Deception is sometimes right but most of the time wrong. That means every decision to use deceptive tactics must be jusjtified" (p. 49). Liars have to operate in a world where, fortunately, there is, as Vaclav Havel (1992) put it, "the human predisposition to truth" (p. 148).

But justifications, good reasons, are frequently given for lying, more so for concealment than for falsification. Perhaps lying saves lives, maintains harmony among people, spares people embarrassment, avoids pain, avoids rebukes, conflict, and hurt feelings, and softens sorrow.

Lying might preserve societal safety and orderliness. Other reasons are, for example, "No one will know anyway"; "I was just kidding" or "Everyone does it"; "It's not very important"; "It's necessary to cope with life." Students might claim that they "didn't have time" to check the accuracy of some material in a speech or paper, and hence inserted just anything. Print and electronic media likewise try to excuse shoddy deceptions by saying that they did not have time to check the sources.

The lie's degree of significance is an important variable when analyzing lies. When political campaigners say, "I went to Harvard," they imply that they graduated from Harvard but they might have attended only briefly. They probably hope that the audience assumes the first. When frozen food products are labeled "fresh," people question the ethicality. Although the federal government has prosecuted companies for such false claims, companies, and even some consumers, might claim that such a trivial item is not a problem, especially as this mislabeling has not caused serious harm. These suggestions suggest that the degree of triviality might be difficult to measure. Totalitarian regimes depend on lying to retain their power. In Hitler's Germany, propaganda was meant to make people believe lies, and Communist regimes have perpetrated similar practices. Dissidents in China and in the former Soviet Union have asserted that authorities are known to lie not only to others but also to themselves.

Hample's (1980) study concluded that most lies are told to superiors, and thus "that lies are a means of social or economic defense in a disadvantaged situation" (p. 45). The subjects of his research, however, were undergraduate college students. People in authority, for example, professors, supervisors, or public officials, might lie to maintain their power and illusion of superiority. Thus lies are usually employed to gain or maintain power. Hample also concluded that lies are usually told in response to a specific situation, and are usually told for personal gain.

What is probably the earliest recorded lie in human history—the story of Cain and Abel, the sons of Adam and Eve, in the Hebrew scriptures (Gen. 4:9)—illustrates some of Hample's findings. Jehovah accepted Abel's offering (a lamb, as he was a shepherd) but not Cain's (agricultural produce, as he was a farmer). In disappointment and jealousy, Cain killed Abel, his younger brother. When Jehovah asked Cain where his brother was, Cain answered, "I know not [and furthermore, why should I?]: am I my brother's keeper?" The biblical lie responded to a question, was directed to a superior, and endeavored to elude a painful moment.

How are lies detected—when they are? Ekman (1986) asserted: "Most lies succeed because no one goes through the work to figure out how to catch them ... . Lie checking isn't a simple task, quickly done" (p. 240). Sometimes a victim or another person stumbles on the truth. Sometimes vigorous questioning of an accused party flushes out the deception. Sometimes curious and energetic individuals expose the truth, like little Toto who pulled aside the curtain concealing the Wizard of Oz to expose the flustered "wizard" with his deceptive gadgetry. Sometimes professional probers, like investigative reporters, eventually piece together the lies and expose the fraud. Some people claim to possess great skill in reading nonverbal clues through long experience, like parents intimidating their children with the assertion that they know when the children are lying by looking into their eyes.

Then there is the polygraph. By measuring such things as perspiration, rates of respiration, and blood pressure, this technological device can supposedly be used to identify the liars. But its critics have ridiculed it as a machine that measures nervous tension, not lying. Ekman (1986) asserted that "there is very little scientific evidence about its accuracy" (p. 191), and he thought that trained observers of nonverbal body language provided a better, although not perfect, means of ferreting out liars. He noted: "The polygraph can only be used with a cooperative, consenting suspect. Behavioral clues can always be read, without permission, without advance notice, without the suspected liar knowing that he [sic] is under suspicion" (p. 237). Ekman's advice is: "*Never reach a final conclusion about whether a suspect is lying or truthful based solely on either the polygraph or behavioral clues to deceit*" [italics original] (p. 238). Since The Employee Polygraph Protection Act of 1988 was enacted, most polygraph testing has been banned, especially in pre-employment screening and in random use. Other studies describe attempts to use careful, systematic analysis of nonverbal clues for effective lie detection, but much more research needs to be done.

Despite all the human failings in truth-telling, we seem to accept the truth as a precious prize worth honoring and striving for. John Donne (1959), the early-17th-century English poet wrote:

On a huge hill,

Cragged, and steep,

Truth stands. (p. 376)

The climb to reach the truth is difficult indeed but worth the effort. It has been said that "science… depends on… the unmercenary love of truth" (Trueblood, 1944, p. 41). Would that we all could demonstrate that ideal.

PROMISES

Promises are intimately linked with truth-telling. "You promised to come last night and help with my homework, but you didn't show up. You lied." When a promise is not fulfilled, it is assumed that the promise-maker is a liar. A host of ethical concerns revolve around promises, and this section explores a number of them.

What is a promise? It is a first-person, intentional assertion, usually voluntary, tying the present to the future, committing a person to believe or act in a specified way. "I promise not to tell anyone." We can promise only for ourselves, not for anyone else. Although we can promise ourselves something (intra-promising), the act of promising is usually (and is considered so here) a public act, communicated to one or more people. Promises give continuity, form, and structure to the fluidity of life, to the uncertainties of the future. When we pledge to give a certain sum of money to a building program at our alma mater, we enable them to go ahead with their construction plans on the basis of their trust in us and in many others to follow through as promised. A promise sets up expectations and announces that the promise-maker owes someone something. We voluntarily make ourselves debtors, but as S. Bok (1979) wrote: "We can properly promise only what is ours to give" (p. 160). When a promise is broken, a debt not paid, expectations are unfulfilled, great harm or at least inconvenience can come to the promisee (and often to an enlarged circle), and the credibility of the promise-maker is lessened.

A number of synonyms or near synonyms, refer to promises and promising. We speak of an oath, a pledge, a vow (an earnest or solemn promise), a covenant, a contract, an agreement, an assurance, or a commitment. We *swear* in certain contexts: Newly elected officials swear to uphold certain values and processes; witnesses in court take an oath to tell the truth, the whole truth, and nothing but the truth. Police officers can die in service while fulfilling their oath to protect society. We pledge allegiance to our country. In religious orders, members take a vow of chastity. Youth group members express an oath of honesty. The bank promises to pay a certain rate of interest on savings accounts.

Credit cards symbolize the holders' promise to pay in the future for a purchased item. A wedding vow expresses lifelong commitment to a spouse. The Constitution is in a sense a listing of promises that define our nation's behavior toward, and attitudes about, its citizenry. The Statue of Liberty stands as a promise to immigrants that they will find in the United States a new life of freedom and opportunity. Through the centuries, martyrs have given their lives to live up to their religious or political pledges. We live in a sea of such future-binding communicative acts, labeled variously depending on the formality of the context. The metaphor, a *broken* promise suggests that a promise is indeed a solid entity.

Nonverbal rituals are sometimes employed to reinforce a pledge, oath, vow, or promise: placing the left hand on the Bible while raising the right hand, placing the right hand over the heart; removing the hat; kneeling, bowing, shaking hands, or grasping forearms; "Let's shake on that," we say. These gestures cement the bond of trust and make the promise-making firmer and more reliable.

Ethical evaluation plays a role when we measure how well a promise was kept; values of fairness and justice are involved, and even when harm comes, a promise is a promise. Along with this nonconsequential emphasis is the consequential concern: How much harm is done to how many to what degree when a promise is not kept? Some people wonder how ethical it is to make a commitment that dictates the future. Do we hold ourselves hostage? When the future moment arrives, so many unforeseen circumstances might have arisen that more harm might be done by keeping the promise than by breaking it. Perhaps we cannot afford to pay a pledge to a designated charity. Perhaps it is no longer wise to keep a friend's secret. Some people question the ethicality, as well as the wisdom, of making lifetime vows. People might come to think that a vow of lifelong chastity no longer makes sense. Tightly knit groups, such as sororities, fraternities, underground gangs, or religious orders might expect lifetime loyalty from their members. Promises often imply *forever*. For example, the U.S. government promised timber industry families that if they moved into certain forested areas, they would be permitted to harvest the trees—presumably forever. But times and resources change, and environmental advocates now want these areas declared off limits to timber cutting. To be fair to all, perhaps terminal times should be set so that the situation can be reevaluated and re-promised. But some think that setting a time limit is unfair: Long-range planning must usually assume an open-ended time frame.

Some states demanded loyalty oaths for teachers to establish that they were not subversives. Some observers question the ethicality of having children as young as 13 make ceremonial religious promises, at an age when they are unlikely to understand completely the content and implications of their statements. At the same age, Communist Party practices required the Young Pioneers to pledge loyalty to the Party. Some might question the ethicality of parents exacting promises from their children to come home at a certain time or not to play with certain peers. Some question the ethicality of groups forcing (exerting subtle or not-so-subtle pressure) their members to promise to believe or act in certain ways. For individuals or groups to refuse to take oaths on religious, philosophical, or personal grounds draws both praise and condemnation from different people. Some question the ethicality of a society's using oaths based on the Bible or the Koran when individuals do not believe in the Bible or the Koran as divine authorities. Cultural variations are also worth noting: In Japan an oral commitment often does not require a written verification, but in Tonga promises are made mainly to put people at ease in the present moment.

Keeping promises can involve continua of intentionality and fulfillment. At one extreme is the promise made by a promiser with no intention of fulfilling the promise; perhaps it was made under duress of the moment, or the promiser misled the other party. In some instances a promiser's originally firm intent is weakened by subsequent circumstances. A promise to pay back a friend's loan by a certain date was perhaps made with no intention to follow through, or was made with a serious intent but when the financial picture changed, the debt could not be repaid. Furthermore, the degree of fulfillment varies. A debt might be partly paid at the designated time but an extension of time requested for repaying the rest. A person might promise to meet a friend at 7 P.M. but show up at 9 P.M. A loving vow given in the glow of a marriage ceremony and intended to be a lifetime commitment wavers as the flame of devotion begins to flicker. What are the ethical dimensions to these contexts of intentionality and fulfillment in promise-making? How much harm is done to whom? Not only the consequential but the nonconsequential, the religious, and other standards come into the equation. Confucianism, for example, emphasizes promise-keeping as perhaps the most important moral imperative (Yu & Kessel, 1995, pp. 12–13). A sensitive promise-maker has much to consider. We of course are all too familiar with political campaign promises often forgotten, not implemented, or greatly modified, when faced with the need for compromising to carry forward the public's business. Whatever the circumstances, we consider going back on a promise to be an act of low ethical quality.

Although most stated ethical concerns focus on *promise-keeping*, we need to stress the ethics and wisdom of *promise-making*. There is little virtue in keeping foolish promises. Hastily made promises prompted by momentary emotion, promises made in moments of ecstacy, in moments of impetuous generosity, of fear, of supreme self-confidence, promises made when drunk all lack careful consideration of potential costs. A promise can be too open-ended. The gruesome story of King Herod (Mark 6:14–29) illustrates these points. Impressed with his stepdaughter Salome's dancing at his birthday party, Herod, probably in a drunken state, promised her anything she asked for up to half of his kingdom. Her mother advised Salome to ask for the head of John the Baptist. "And the king was exceeding sorry; but for the sake of his oaths, … he would not reject her" (Mark 6:26). Confucius gave sound advice: "Be cautious in giving promises and punctual in keeping them" (Confucius, 1938, 1:6).

A contemporary example highlights the costs of promise-making and promise-keeping. A young woman and man, traveling companions "since their college days in Europe, had promised to exhaust all efforts to find the other if either ever disappeared during their journeys." The man's plane later crashed in desolate Greenland; the woman spent about $50,000 on the search effort and against great odds eventually succeeded in finding his body and bringing it back. She is reported to have said: "I'm not stupid. I know what the odds are… . But a promise is a promise, and I won't let Dominique down. He would not have let me down." (*Minneapolis Tribune*, Feb. 5, 1982, p. 11A). Although the episode inspires admiration, it also generates some of the questions discussed earlier. The promise was no doubt made at the height of their friendship. If that friendship had soured and new friendships had been established, this open-ended promise carried a potential cost that new friends would not have appreciated. But that's what promises are for—to risk a leap into the future based on a present feeling. We need to be sure that the *feeling* is based on a thoughtful, rational footing.

REASON, EMOTION, AND PROPAGANDA

Promise-making and promise-keeping require the appropriate balance of reason and emotion, as do virtually all forms of communication. What ethical considerations apply to reason and emotion? Both emotion and reason are natural to humanity, but reason is a distinguishing element in our *human* nature. Reason needs to be trained, disciplined, honed—and honed again. Many courses in logic, argumentation, and critical thinking appear in college and university curricula, compared to courses on using emotion. Scholarly and popular books describe the ways for people to use their reasoning abilities more effectively. All the emphasis on reason implies that we recognize its premier role and our deep desire to use it well. Drawing on the Aristotelian heritage of honoring reason, we seek to build communicative transactions on it. At the same time an increasing attention is being paid in scholarly and popular literature to understanding and controlling emotions.

Reason and emotion are difficult to separate and are normally intertwined. We all too often think of them as existing separately, one present and the other absent. Language usage entrenches this notion. For example, the electrical metaphor that emotion *short-circuits* reason perpetuates the two-valued idea that rationality is either completely present or completely absent. When a short circuit occurs, the light goes off, and total darkness results. Except in highly traumatic circumstances, reason is not totally absent. Perhaps a better image is the dimmer switch, that gradually brings more or less reason to a deliberation. The objective is not to eliminate emotion, but, as Nilsen (1974) put it, "keeping the subject in appropriate emotional perspective" (p. 32), and "not to dissociate emotion from reason, but to arouse appropriate emotion and integrate it with reason… . [We should aim at] bringing about a constructive balance between thought and feeling" (p. 58). Reason disciplines emotion, and emotion energizes reason. Key terms, then, are *balance*, *integration*, and *perspective*.

The ethical concern around the issue of reason and emotion is rooted in the ethical standard that whatever furthers our *humanness* is highly ethical. As discussed in chapter 2, the section on human nature enhancement, two characteristics of humanness are the ability to reason and the ability to use symbols for communication. Whatever furthers reasoning and symbol-using capabilities is more highly ethical than whatever lowers them. To permit emotion to override reason is to dehumanize and hence to be ethically low. Emotional content is occasionally appropriately present to portray the degree of intensity, the depth of feeling, in a communicator's message, but when emotional appeals substitute for sound reason and logically supported claims, ethical quality is likely to be low. Emotional arguments can intimidate audiences, reduce their ability to evaluate accurately the strengths of the claims, affect the likelihood of making free and wise decisions, and unfairly exploit human weaknesses.

We must acknowledge that on certain occasions complete dependence on reason might lead to low ethical quality behavior. For instance, lack of success in holding an audience's attention might cause them to turn to a more interesting, more emotional, less substantive communicator. Not hearing out a too-rational point of view, they reduce their choice options and give acceptance to a less worthy message. Brembeck and Howell (1976, pp. 237–238) emphasized that the "cult of reason" is on somewhat shaky ground. It is unrealistic, they wrote, to assume that listeners are more rational than they really are. Furthermore, perhaps we ought to ask ourselves whether we are unwisely and with low ethical quality urging our students and others to be cautious in rational deliberation, to wait until much more information is available before uttering public assertions; such cautions perhaps enable less informed, less ethical, more aggressive people to push to the front of the line to make their claims and to lead others astray. In addition, apathetic and insensitive receivers might need an emotional jolt to awaken them. Coaches harangue their players, parents prod their children, evangelists excite their listeners, student leaders shame their lethargic classmates, cheerleaders stimulate spectators, social reformers stir audiences, and military officers intimidate those under their command. All do so in the belief that their ends are *good*. Without accepting the notion that the ends justify the means, I acknowledge that such factors as compassion, will, energy, and commitment—nonrational, not irrational factors—play an important part in human decision making and decision implementation. The French Revolution was symbolized by the guillotine as well as by the Temple of Reason. But despite reason's shortcomings, it remains a precious human attribute; when combined with compassion and a sincere concern for the well-being of the communicatees, it is nurtured by those communicators who rank high on the Ethical Quality (EQ) scale.

The balancing of reason and emotion is also part of the ethical concerns relevant to messages labeled as propaganda. The term originated in the early 17th century when the Roman Catholic Church created the Sacred Congregation for the Propagation the Faith, and propaganda simply refers to "spreading." Missionary work might have an honorific connotation at least to those in the faith, but in the 1930's the term's use by Nazi Germany in connection with spreading their doctrines of Aryan purity and the master race, coupled with cruel military aggression, brought a strong negative connotation. In the

United States in an effort to understand and cope with the menace of propaganda, the Institute of Propaganda Analysis identified key devices like: name-calling, glittering generalities, testimonials, and card-stacking. Because the ends of Nazi propaganda were so evil, the means were initially discussed as if they were inherently evil. But after a few years, some people realized that the ethical quality of these devices depended on how they were used. For example, the testimonial of a famous person for a product or a social program might be irrelevant and meaningless, and thus low on the EQ Scale, but when relevant and meaningful, such a testimonial would rank higher. Some scholars, however, challenge the neutrality of propaganda devices.

What are the characteristics of propaganda? It has come to be associated with the mass media and hence is viewed as large-scale persuasion, directed to a large audience. It is intentional, systematic, manipulative, one-sided, and exaggerated. In an organizational framework (government, religious, political, commercial, social), a planned campaign is sustained over a considerable time and presents highly selective material in a self-serving effort. Propaganda relies heavily on emotional appeals rather than on thoughtful premises and reliable evidence. It adopts the stance of the closed-minded true believer, the hemispheric communicator discussed in chapter 4. Propaganda is competitive and is a means, not an end. It is coercive psychically, if not physically. It overwhelms the audiences so that they accept its message; it makes free choice difficult, if not impossible. As Hoffer (1951, pp. 98–99) pointed out in his analysis of the Nazi propaganda effort, German leaders acknowledged that for propaganda to be effective, it needed coercive force behind it. Propaganda is aimed at the frustrated, the disgruntled, the fearful, the maladjusted, in short, at the most vulnerable members of society; it plays on their insecurities. It is evasive, parades vague general values rather than specific substance, and clothes the message in attractive dress. Urgency is usually exaggerated to achieve quick acceptance. Repetition, sometimes cleverly indirect, sometimes bluntly straightforward, dulls the critical faculties of the receivers. Contemporary government propaganda has even been able to "transcend culture and impact audiences from differing societies . . . by focusing more on universal values" (Parry-Giles, 1994, p. 463).

After analyzing the characteristics of propaganda, Cunningham made clear his oppostion to the idea of propaganda as neutral. He concluded his study with a resounding unambiguous statement: "Propaganda is reprehensible" (1992, p. 244). Although some readers might see the problem somewhat less starkly, the ethical concerns are there for conscientious members of society to grapple with.

EXIT MESSAGES[1]

In the discussion in this section I stress the importance of maximizing the well-being of all participants (especially the person who leaves), of increasing the satisfaction and comfort of those involved, of creating warm memories, of not dehumanizing people, and of enriching the larger community. If literature in the communication field has dealt at all with exit communication, it has usually been concerned with effectiveness, not ethicality, except grossly insensitive instances of terminating employees. I examine exit messages in interpersonal communication, organizational communication, public speaking contexts, and mass communication.

Interpersonal Communication

Numerous verbal and nonverbal acts signal leave-taking in interpersonal contexts. We separate with such phrases as "See you soon," "Take care of yourself," "Have a good day," "Drive carefully," "All the best," "I love you." A handshake, a wave, a smile, a hug, a kiss all contribute to a friendly or loving parting. Many departure scenes at airports—the soft crying, the hesitant wave, the passionate kiss, the gentle touch of the arm, the firm handshake—all communicate the sadness in the parting. To "let go" can indeed be painful. To omit such appropriate nonverbal or verbal acts might leave a sensitive person with nagging regrets, a feeling that the bonding was not fully consummated. Both the leaver and the one remaining have an ethical obligation to affirm the other and to strengthen the bond between them. In sadness, we may find it difficult to express the right words or may turn our gaze away, not wanting to *see* the severance take place; but these may be interpreted by the other person as signs of not caring. Thus, the other's perception is as important as the intention of the signal giver.

In major, long-lasting, or permanent severances, the verbal and nonverbal acts are even more significant and carry with them a deep concern for the ethical dimension. For instance, parting statements or gestures

---

[1]An earlier version of this section was presented in a paper at the Fourth National Biennial Conference on Communication Ethics, May 1996, at Gull Lake, Michigan.

between parents and children when the latter leave home, for college, for distant employment, or for foreign travel, usually embed themselves in the memories of the participants and hence are deeply significant. For example, when a young German doctor left Leipzig in 1876 to teach and practice medicine in Tokyo, he wrote in his diary: "Very early this morning I said good-bye to my dear parents. The parting was painful. I shall always treasure my mother's farewell words" (Baelz, 1932, p. 5). Many immigrants have recorded similar expressions through the years, and those last words and gestures lived in their memories the rest of their lives. Even more poignant were the parting glances and expressions when Jewish parents and their children were going into the gas chambers during the Nazi Holocaust (Wiesel, 1990, pp. 102-103).

Deathbed communicative acts, as the final exit draws near, are likewise full of intense feelings. Simply touching a loved one, even if the ill person cannot respond, fulfills a bonding; when words cease to hold any meaning, the silent, loving touch says all. The ill person gets as much strength as possible from the touch, and the surviving person is left with a sense of appropriate closure, of completion of the relationship that can be a help to future healing. To omit such opportunities might leave a survivor with a lifelong sadness.

Communicating with those near death, on the "edge of life" as it has been described, is a special context in which compassionate lying might be justified. The medical profession grapples constantly with this dilemma. Some health care personnel think that omitting certain facts (misleading by omission) is not as reprehensible as telling a falsehood. On the other hand, doctors who have compassionately deceived their patients can lose integrity in the eyes of peers and of the patient's family. Furthermore, to deceive terminally ill persons denies them "the opportunity... to come to terms with their own mortality, to reflect on the character of their life in the light of their imminent death, and to take proper leave of friends and family" (Bakhurst, 1992, p. 66). In this connection, euthanasia and assisted suicide have ethical dilemmas. Living wills express a person's attitude about dying; they inform medical personnal that certain life support technologies are not to be used if they do not improve the quality of life. Nurses rather than doctors are likely to be present as death approaches, and they must be skilled in exit communicating. Expressing sympathy at the bedside of a terminally ill person ministers both to the patient and to the visitor, but visitors must be sure they are truly concerned with comforting the patient and not with a self-centered merit- gaining for themselves. When death comes, morticians are increasingly trained to communicate compassionately with the grieving family and the friends of the deceased.

A CNN special television program on the lingering, agonizing goodbye to a family member suffering from Alzheimer's disease was titled "The Long Goodbye." For a spouse and other family members to cope at home with this or another slowly deteriorating condition of a loved one calls for great strength, endurance, and compassion over a long time; caregivers often grow exhausted and become patients themselves. Thus, some goodbyes are unfulfilling because of their brevity, some because of their longevity.

Hospice facilities are dedicated to caring for people who are dying by trying to bring as much comfort and meaning as possible to the final days. The stressful tasks of health care personnel are balanced by the opportunities of communicating in a caring manner not only with the patient but with the family—to walk the final corridor of life with them in compassion and dignity.

So far I have discussed contexts in which loving communicative acts are expressed or omitted. But many exits in life are driven by anger, hatred, or other negative motivations. When anger is central in exit communication between parent and child, sibling and sibling, employer and employee, teacher and student, courtship partners, or friend and friend, a high ethical quality in communicating is likely to be absent. But these are the very moments when ethics should be excercised; the rupture can be extremely difficult to suture when verbal or nonverbal parting shots are too wounding. Invectives, harsh and cutting criticisms, demeaning, obscene language and gestures, and abrupt departures make rebuilding the relationship extremely difficult. When a divorce is impending, the parties are involved in such an agonizing, drawn-out leave-taking, a change from a state of oneness to a state of separation, that being fair and humane is a great challenge.

Less stressful contexts in interpersonal communication harbor challenges in ethical behavior. Trying tactfully to terminate transitory conversations at social gatherings without showing disinterest can be a real challenge. Terminating interviews as ethically as possible is an important tool for conscientious professionals. Usually the interviewer holds the power and should be sure that interviewees have ample opportunity to respond to questions and to present a full picture of their capabilities. Interviewees should give an accurate portayal of themselves, and the company representative should give a true account of the company and the job opening. Neither party should mislead the other, and each should respect the other. Terminating a phone conversation or closing a letter or memo with high ethical quality may be more difficult than one imagines. The choice of words, the degree of abruptness, formality, friendliness, and softness all may have ethical dimensions.

Intercultural differences need to be kept in mind in emphasizing the ethical dimension in leave-taking. For example, U.S. students typically bid goodbye to a foreign student acquaintance with a cheery "I'll give you a call sometime... . " or "I'll see you soon." They usuually do not follow through, for in this culture such expressions are not taken at face value; a foreign student, however, is likely to take the expressins literally and feel slighted when the phone calls or meetings do not materialize. Rather than shaking hands to mark leave-taking, in India people bring the palms of their hands together; in Japan and Korea a graceful bow is a traditional, courteous *goodbye*. The Japanese *Sayonara* and the French *au revoir* have an untranslatable softness that lends grace to the parting. The English *goodbye* is of course a contraction of "God be with you," but this expression of religious goodwill is usually no longer meant literally. In the United States people use more casual expressions and gestures in leave-taking. Newspaper obituaries are looked on as a final acknowledgment and tribute to a person. In some cultures, such as some Native American groups, obituaries would not be published, and silence is the proper respectful acknowledgment (Gonzales & Bradley, 1990). We need to be more aware and appreciative of other cultures' leavetaking habits, not only to be more effective but to be more ethical.

The importance of exit messages in our society is highlighted by the goodbye and bon voyage cards on the market. These help us say farewell poetically, meaningfully, and sometimes humorously. Thank you cards can be an important closure for a kind deed or a gift, an expression of appreciation for another's kindness. Much potential pleasure is bypassed when a "thank you" is omitted. When someone leaves one job for another, gets a salary increase, or enters into a new station in life (marriage, parenthood), a congratulatory message can mark that important event. Exits after all are really transitions. When a card seems to depersonalize a farewell, a thank-you, or congratulations, a handwritten note can replace the ready-made exit message.

We also need to be sensitive to the importance of pre-exit messages in addition to the previously discussed living wills. Devoted spouses might say frequently, or at least occasionally, how much they love and are grateful for each other. When sudden separation or death comes, they feel they have said what they wanted to say to each other. Expressions of appreciation between teacher and student, employer and employee, and other such positive pre-exit messages can bring joy, satisfaction, and enrichment to people's lives.

Thus, we need to construct, verbally or nonverbally, graceful exit messages, much as actors learn to make graceful exits on the stage. We need to express ourselves with appropriateness, compassion, and with a high degree of ethical quality. We need to avoid sins of omission, and reduce sins of commission.

Oganizational Communication

When companies decide to lay off personnel, how ethically do they communicate this fact to the affected people? Many horror stories are reported about uncaring organizations dealing with this situation. One brokerage firm handled terminations immediately after the market crash in October 1987 in the following "efficient" manner. When employees arrived at work one morning, some "found cardboard cartons on their desks. Then, when everyone had arrived, an announcement *over the public address system* instructed all those with cartons on their desks to pack up and leave the premises at once" (Redding, 1990, p. 129). Redding mentioned additional insensitive examples of companies notifying employees of terminations. They remind one of the *New Yorker* cartoon in which a supervisor comes into a person's office and says, "As of noon today, you're fired. In the meantime, keep up the good work." Jaksa (1993), reporting on his research experiences, mentioned the following "ingenious" episode:

> I was told that a computer company in Florida held a fake fire drill as a strategy to get all of their employees out of the building. Once everyone was outside, management announced that they would permit persons back into the building who were not being laid off. A list of names was read of those who would be allowed [to] re-enter the building. Those who were laid off were told to leave the premises and that their personal belongings would be sent to them. Employees were told by management that the reason that this procedure was used was because they were concerned that there might be computer damage, theft, and other destructive acts by angry laid-off workers (p. 10).

What a high level of trust ! What a low ethical quality exit message !

Organizations vary in how much they help employees plan for and adjust to layoffs and retirements. Some more conscientious ones try to aid in the process by arranging exit interviews, making counselors available for individual guidance, and setting up group sessions. In cases of early retirement or layoffs, a special payment may be given, as well as retraining and job searching services. These exit messages tell those departing, and all employees, that the company values them; such messages may contribute to the overall morale of the workforce. Retirement receptions and gifts provide a suitable celebration of past services as well as pleasant memories far into the future.

Mandatory retirement set at a particular age is an exit message with pros and cons. Specifying an unambiguous departure time clarifies everyone's exit time far in advance, and hence is a message of high ethical quality, enabling the affected personnel to plan their futures. The organization can administer its workforce and operations more effectively. People whose energies, abilities, and interests may be subsiding will not be an embarrassment to themselves and to the company, and younger people have opportunities to get into the workforce. But mandatory retirement is also said to be unfair age discrimination that eliminates a person with a lifetime of experience whose skills and commitment are still intact. Setting mandatory term limits for public officials is likewise argued pro and con. The president of the United States is limited to two terms, and many advocates are calling for limiting the terms for senators, representatives, governors, and other public officials as well. Many citizens contend that term limits communicate unfairly a lack of trust in public servants, and eliminate experienced people just when they are the most knowledgeable and effective. Term limits turn the governing over to unelected staff without lessening the chances for graft and corruption. Advocates for term limits claim they reinforce the idea of citizen officals rather than professional politicians who stay in office far too long, to the detriment of the democratic ideal. Political and commercial organizations might have to come to a resolution of this exit issue in the future.

How ethical is it to have (or not to have) mandatory termination times for the completion of work sessions and meetings? For example, in some legislatures. "the clock is covered" as a playful way to ignore mandatory adjournment times. Many work sessions, committee meetings, and public forums function better with a clear termination time that creates a finite playing field and can stimulate participants to use the available time carefully and efficiently. On the other hand, such time limits might unduly rush the proceedings, cause important material to be excluded, reduce thoughtfulness, and result in unwise decisions.

Such temporal terminal exit signs bring to mind spatial exit signs, communicating the location of exits. Exit signs in buildings should be clear and easily seen in order to foster safety, security, and ease of movement. The color red has become a common nonverbal component in such signs. People who are confused and disoriented or who, in case of emergency, are in a state of panic need to find exits quickly. Airplane travelers are alerted before take-off to note the plane exits. Exit signs on freeways need to be large, clear, and frequent enough to enable swiftly traveling drivers to find the desired exit and avoid uncertainties and possible accidents. Clear exit signs are a matter not only of efficiency but of ethics.

Many business establishments have a sign above an exit door that reads, "Thank you, we value your business," or "Thank you, come again," Although these self-serving messages are designed to create repeat customers, they also show a sensitivity to customers not without merit. Japanese and Korean department stores station attractive women at the doors to bow to departing and entering customers. The parting words used by customers or workers in shops as they conclude their interactions can be more important than they realize. A brief compliment to people who have been courteous and helpful can encourage them to continue to be courteous and helpful to others. However minor they seem, pleasant exit messages linger on and play a larger role in organizations and in society than we think. A dessert at a restaurant is an exit message with which the establishment hopes to send diners away with literally a good taste in their mouth, a way of increasing the likelihood of a repeat visit.

Some organizations have built-in exit messages that tell their members that they *must leave* the organization or that they *cannot*. In churches that excommunicate wayward members, the members might wish to remain but are not permitted to. The Roman Catholic Church, for example, has wielded such excommunicating power for centuries, and excludes members from the fold during life and even after death. Dictatorial regimes force dissidents into permanent exile. Fraternities and other tightly knit organizations also exert the power to tell unwanted members that they must depart. On the other hand, people who choose to leave their religious affiliation are branded heretics or traitors, and are subject to severe psychological punishment. Some organizations like the Mafia, underground gangs, or religious cults force their members to remain within the group, which they leave at their peril. Organizations claiming such powers over their membership need to ask themselves how ethical it is to pronounce such devastating messages forcing or forbidding departure.

Organizations lose a valuable source for institution building when their human resources departments fail to take exit surveys of employees or interviews when they voluntarily leave. Such fact gathering of positive and negative comments could help the organization to correct its shortcomings and to strengthen its fabric. Surely institutions of higher education would profit by gathering such reactions from departing students.

Public Speaking

Farewell speeches are a common genre of public address, and some are preserved for centuries. Many speech anthologies and textbooks contain such addresses, which embody timeless values. They usually communicate a distinctive spirit that might be inspirational, defiant, apologetic, remorseful, challenging, adventurous, farsighted. Issuing warnings and charting directions, they play an important role in the life of a community or a country. General Douglas MacArthur's farewell speech to the cadets at the U.S. Military Academy at West Point after President Truman had dismissed him from his military position in 1951 has been frequently included in collections of speeches. Some resignation speeches by government officials leaving their posts under a cloud of suspicion might be ethically suspect charades, "aimed at misleading the public about actual events for the mutual benefit of survivor and resigner" (Martin, 1976, p. 257). On the other hand, resignation speeches in the British House of Commons have often been remembered as being highly principled and significant. When Senator Dole resigned from the Senate in 1996 to devote full time to running for President, his farewell speech was considered by many to be one of the finest speeches of his career. When a rhetor fails to seize the moment, he or she might well be judged lower not only on the effectiveness scale but also on the EQ scale. When a rhetor does seize the moment, the audience is prepared to absorb, accept, and affirm what the speaker has to say. This genre would also include the athletic coach retiring after many years or the athlete who has been in the national limelight but is now at the end of his or her career. Such farewell statements, given with poise and gratefulness perhaps at a press conference are an inspiring legacy for many younger athletes. The speaker who is charitable toward those who were strong opponents deserves a high mark on the ethical scale. When disagreement is expressed, a highly ethical communicator does so with dignity. A defeated candidate in a primary or general election may find it difficult to say goodbye (at least for the moment) to the hardworking supporters, but to do so with grace smooths the transition and contributes to a stable political party and to society.

Presidential farewell addresses have been a special genre in U.S. public address since the time of George Washington. In their study of presidential rhetoric, Campbell and Jamieson (1990) devoted a chapter to an analysis and synthesis of presidential farewell addresses. The authors stated that such addresses fulfilled a "ritual of departure" (p. 191), and attempted "to bequeath a legacy that will be enduring" (p. 198). Fields (1996) likewise devoted a chapter on "Executive Farewells" in which he presented a detailed analysis of Presidential farewells throughout U.S. history. On leaving office, a president might issue a warning, like Eisenhower's warning against the growing power of the military-industrial complex in which he called for a balance between military spending and domestic needs (Griffin, 1992; Litfin, 1974; Medhurst, 1994, 1995; Scott, 1990, 1995). Washington's warning against entangling alliances with other nations has remained a historical touchstone. In these moments, the speaker's ethos is perhaps at an all time high, as is the audience's readiness to accept the exit message. In this situation a speaker should be careful not to give exaggerated or false warnings or to pressure a successor to do something reckless and unwise. The ethical challenge to fulfill the demands and opportunities of such a moment is clear.

Valedictory addresses are given by other government officials too, especially if they have served for a long time. These farewell remarks can vary in formats, such as a newspaper interview rather than a public speech. For example, when the U.S. Ambassador to Japan left his post in 1993, he was interviewed by a reporter for *The Japan Times* (Pearce, 1993, February 8–14, p. 7) who invited him to reflect on his term in office and on the relationship between the United States and Japan. Such an opportunity allows departing officials to summarize accomplishments, set challenging goals, and build harmony between two nations. Surely the ethical component is present to a considerable degree.

Commencement addresses in academic institutions belong to the farewell genre. A wit has remarked that the audience at commencements is composed of relieved students, exhausted faculty, and proud and impoverished parents. The term *commencement* supposedly marks a "beginning", but is really a "farewell"; students realize they are leaving their institution, their teachers, their friends and classmates. Some might never return. Some might continue to be a part of the alumni structure. The speaker usually looks back, expresses gratefulness to teachers, parents, and others who have been partners in the accomplishments of the students, congratulates the students on their achievements, honors intellectual and other values, and looks into the future. Such addresses combine "ceremonial, educational, and deliberative purposes" (Loveridge-Sambonmatsu, 1993, p. 309). The speaker has an important ethical responsibility to rise to the occasion. The closing of a commencement program or academic ceremony with the playing and singing of the school song can be a moving leave-taking, which honors the school's history and commits the graduates to be worthy representatives of the school.

Public speakers who do not know when to stop, to exit, fail not only according to the effectiveness criterion but also according to the ethical dimension. They need to live up to the obligation they have toward the audience, the subject, and the occasion. Many excellent messages have been greatly weakened and many speakers' reputations have been lowered as speakers rambled on after the appropriate and expected termination time. Doing an injustice to the occasion and the subject is matched by the discourteous treatment of the audience, many of whom no doubt had tuned out and had even become antagonistic toward the long-winded speaker and the message. Conscientious public speakers prepare their closing sentences very carefully and keep their exit clearly in mind.

The closing portion of the speech, the peroration, has been recognized since the ancient Greeks as extremely important. Like the ending of a play, musical composition, or movie, conclusion of a public speech is likely to leave a disproportionate impression on the receivers. Hence the speaker has an ethical responsibility to construct and deliver an appropriate and effective ending. While leaving the listeners with heightened feelings, the speaker should avoid excessive and damaging emotionality. Concluding expressions in most religious services are benedictions, blessings for the audience. Ancient benedictions can provide a deeply moving linkage with earlier members of the faith. On the other hand, the frozen style of the benediction might bore contemporary audiences. Some hymns serve as benedictions, for example, "God Be With You Till We Meet Again," which can evoke a strong bond among the participants.

In central events in life, there is a leave-taking element, that when handled well greatly enriches the lives of those involved. For example, in a marriage ceremony, there is a "leaving" of parents and moving into a new life. Marriage marks a rite of passage, and lighting a unity candle symbolically expresses the departure of the bride and groom from their past individual identities to their new consubstantial relationship. A major departure might be marked by a formal speech or farewell statement. For example, when people in Sweden emigrated to the United States, their minister sent them abroad with "God's blessings" and with stern warnings to keep the faith when they arrived in the new land (Barton, 1975, pp. 139–140). The ethical quality of such sermons or farewell expressions would be viewed differently depending on a person's religious views. Clergy preach farewell sermons as they prepare to leave one congregation for another. Some clergy at funeral services use the occasion to further the faith more than to honor the deceased person. Deemphasizing a focus on the deceased, the clergy might do an injustice to the family and friends who desired an opportunity to honor that person's life and to cope with their grieving. Increasingly, family members and friends are delivering eulogies at funerals and memorial services. Sudden deaths, like the assassinations of prominent people, often generate eloquent speeches, even by those who traditionally were not noted for eloquence. For example, President John F. Kennedy's assassination brought forth many such expressions, a noteworthy one being by Senator Mansfield, normally a terse, colorless, unemotional speaker. His eulogy appears in Appendix B. The tragedy of such a sudden exit touches deep recesses in the human spirit.

State-sponsored deaths, at the scaffold, the guillotine, or the electric chair, have generated farewell speeches that sometimes have been recorded and have become historic utterances. A noteworthy example is Sir Walter Raleigh's speech from the scaffold in 1618, when he was put to death by King James I. Versions have been included in many anthologies, and a recent in-depth scholarly analysis by Parker and Johnson (1995) brings a high authenticity to what he actually must have said. He refuted the charges against him, defended himself for posterity, and insisted that when he was about to meet his God and Judge, he told the truth. In his anthology of speeches, William Safire (1992) collected a number of "Gallows and Farewell Speeches" (pp. 339–396). Aside from ethical questions of the justification of such state-sponsored deaths, or the guilt or innocence of a particular defendent, people assume that those about to die speak the truth, but cynics may still remain suspicious.

Mass Communication

A common exit message reported in the mass media is the exit poll during elections. People coming out of polling booths are interviewed by journalists or pollsters representing the print and electronic media, and are asked how they voted and why. The results are quickly collected and analyzed, and trends are immediately predicted and broadcast. Many observers contend that this has an inappropriate influence over those who have not yet voted, especially in a national election with its multiple time zones. The media justify exit polls as a means of getting the news out as soon as it develops. Critics say that the process is mainly a self-serving, money-making ploy, in the name of serving the public's right to know.

Other kinds of exit interviewing by mass media raise additional ethical questions. For example, electronic and print reporters interview and photograph exhausted and perspiring sports figures immediately following a contest on the baseball or football field, basketball court, or hockey rink, ostensibly to get athletes' reactions while they still feel strong joy or sadness. Reporters claim they need to record the emotion of the event, not just the sanitary, objective facts. Permitting male reporters into men's locker rooms unfairly excludes female reporters from equal access to the news.

Lawyers and jurors are usually quizzed by the media exiting a court-room trial, again to catch the emotion of the moment as well as the explanations for the verdict. Some observers contend that the media attention jeopardizes the jury system, and makes potential jurors hesitant to serve when they might get interviewed by the media and perhaps open themselves to threats and harassment from disgruntled members of the public.

The closing portions of television or radio programs, although not earthshaking in significance, are worthy of attention. Television news programs, say some critics, waste valuable time with closing chitchat, prepared or ad lib. The public would be better served, such observers contend, by solid news until the end of the program instead of inane attempts at entertainment. On the other hand, some observers praise Garrison Keillor's "benediction" closing his radio programs as a positive exit that leaves listeners amused and uplifted: "Be well, do good work, and keep in touch"

WITHHOLDING AND RELEASING MESSAGES

The dynamic of message flow creates important ethical considerations. Withholding information concerns secrecy, confidentiality, and censorship. Releasing information involves timing, leaking, rumors, and gossip. Much has been written on all of these, but S. Bok's book *Secrets: On the Ethics of Concealment and Revelation* (1982), is surely one of the best single volumes on this whole area of concern, and she brings the capabilities of a Renaissance scholar to her wide-ranging and penetrating analysis.

Withholding

Secrecy. S. Bok (1982, p. 9) defined *secrecy* as "intentional concealment," a phenomenon with both positive and negative aspects. Bollinger (1991) described this two-sidedness: "Sometimes secrecy is a cloak for bad motives or behavior; sometimes it is a necessary condition for the exercise of fair and good judgment" (p. 150).

Secrecy gives us a sense of control, of power, of protection from outside criticism, and of pleasure. It permits us to retain our individuality in the midst of community. It protects our thoughts, beliefs, and intimacies. Secrecy strengthens bonding between those who share a secret; groups cherish and protect *their* secrets that define their distinctiveness. Secrecy strengthens intimate friendships and family networks. At certain moments and in certain contexts it may be extremely kind to withhold unpleasant news from a loved one. Two erstwhile friends who develop friction do not reveal this to others, to protect their fragile relationship and to increase the chances for rapprochement. We say that we do not wash dirty linen in public. Secrecy protects plans, actions, and property (e.g., diaries, medical records). It is vital in professional counseling, in the business and corporate worlds, in investigative journalism, in diplomatic relations among nations, and in military and police operations. Insofar as these people and agencies work for the good of society, their secrecy is positive. In scholarly research, secrecy has its place; for instance, "blind" reviews of article or book manuscripts before conference presentation or publication and of grant applications help to ensure the necessary candid and objective evaluation. Secrecy helps to create an uninhibited atmosphere in which to deliberate and to make difficult decisions, in jury and board rooms and in other decision-making contexts. (With the increased television coverage of legislative proceedings, of city council meetings, of court sessions, people are surprised that they can deliberate in public more confidently and freely than they earlier had supposed.) For public safety, some emergency drills are kept secret prior to their exectution, to test people's readiness to react in the event of a real emergency. Secrecy deepens our understanding of such things as loyalty, betrayal, and discretion. "With no control over secrecy and openness," S. Bok (1982, p. 24) asserted, "human beings could not remain either sane or free."

But secrecy also holds dangers that highlight serious ethical concerns. By definition, secrecy excludes, and those outside the circle can be discriminated against. Secrecy generates suspicion, fear, intolerance, and even hatred. It stimulates others to keep secrets, limits information, and weakens judgments and decisions. Sunshine laws ensure the open and fair disussion of public affairs. Secrecy can generate strong inner tensions; a person might want to reveal a secret and yet to keep it at the same time. Secrecy can corrode our character, create feelings of guilt, embarrassment, and fear. People can become trapped in self-deception. Institutions with self-serving motives might keep important information from the public and affect the latter's well-being. For example, for many years the tobacco industry kept secret research findings that nicotine has a druglike habit-forming effect. In the workplace, failure to report health and safety dangers and to expose inefficiencies, drunkenness, or harassment of employees could have debilitating effects on an organization. With these potential dangers to self and society, secrecy needs to be examined conscientiously in the light of the ethical standards discussed throughout this book.

S. Bok (1982, p. 27) stated two moral premises: "Whatever control over secrecy and openness we conclude is legitimate for some individuals should, in the absence of special considerations, be legitimate for all", and there should be "*partial individual control* over the degree of secrecy and openness about personal matters." These principles of equality and personal control are helpful guides as we struggle with the ramifications of not sharing messages with others.

Developments such as freedom of information laws in the United States and in other countries and the fall of dictatorships in Eastern Europe and in the former Soviet Union have opened previously secret government files to public scrutiny. With these new resources and attitudes, and with powerful new electronic surveillance facilities, the future will be virtually transparent, with personal, organizational, and government secrets being difficult to keep. The transparent as well as the opaque has ethical agonies.

Confidentiality. As S. Bok (1982, p. 119) expressed it, "Confidentiality refers to the boundaries surrounding shared secrets and to the process of guarding these boundaries." Priests and ministers are expected to keep confidential the messages expressed to them in secret by their parishioners, and lawyers are expected to keep confidential their conversations with their clients. Medical professionals are expected to keep confidential the health records of their patients. Psychiatrists, psychotherapists, and social workers keep confidential their interactions with their counselees. This bond of understood confidentiality encourages people who need professional help to seek it without fear of the information becoming public and enables caregivers to render approporiate aid. Newspaper reporters and editors assert the right to keep confidential their sources of information, to protect the sources and to keep open lines of communication for future information. Do high-level executives privy to a corporation's secrets violate confidentiality when leaving to work for a competitor? Confidentiality is expected in many international diplomatic negotiations, in labor–management negotiations, and in a host of organizational decision-making contexts. The claim is that such confidentiality honored by the participants enables tentative positions to be modified in the dynamic process of seeking the best and most workable decisions, whereas public glare would make the participants take inflexible stances with accommodations to other positions extremely difficult.

When information gathered by professional counselors suggests that their clients could endanger the lives of others, public well-being takes precedence in most cases. If the medical records of a school bus driver reveal physical or mental conditions that might endanger the lives of school children, such information needs to be known. We again face the dilemma of trying to determine where an individual's right ends and the public's well-being begins.

Censorship.   A message might not be sent because someone censors it. As the Latin root *censere*, meaning "to judge," indicates, someone makes a judgment that a message should not go forth. The communicators themselves can engage in self-censorship. Virtually every day we all engage in self-censorship. We decide not to tell friends about plans that might hurt their feelings or cause us to alter our agenda. We hold our tongue from uttering profanity. Parents watch their language in front of their children, and many groups in society desire to protect children by eliminating certain programs on prime time television. The censor might be a government agency or a religious organization. Mass media are often accused of permitting powerful advertisers to censor material; for example, a newspaper or magazine might withhold news about the harmful effects of alcohol when the liquor industry is a heavy advertiser. In short, many individuals, groups, and agencies serve as censors, and we must question the ethicality of withholding messages when someone wields inordinate power. Some censors have their own selfish ends in mind.

Conscientious people try to determine how much harm is done to whom, and how serious the harm is. The price of censorship might be too high to pay, when benefits are considerably outweighed by liabilities.

Releasing

Leaking Information. In the communication context, *leaking* refers to the inappropriate releasing of information outside an understood boundary. For example, a member or a staff employee of a congressional committee can cause information to flow from that committee into the public domain, perhaps via an intermediary such as a news reporter. The unseen wall of the committee has been pierced, much as a pierced bucket allows its liquid contents to flow out. From that point on, frantic efforts might be made to plug the leak. The person—and it takes only one—who caused the information leakage could have done so with the purest of motives, for example, feeling that the information should be released for the public welfare. On the other hand, the leaker's motives could have been of low ethical quality, for instance, ill will toward a group, a desire to feel powerful, to maintain a sense of importance, or to keep a link to the press by befriending a reporter who eagerly seeks a sensational news story. A leak is secret, in contrast to a whistle-blower's open disclosure, and leakers are anonymous, at least initially.

Sometimes the results of polls, often incomplete and obviously favorable to the party disclosing them, are leaked to the press to seek an advantage in the competitive context of which the poll is part. Sometimes leaks are trial balloons sent aloft to gauge the attitudes of the public to an anticipated program proposal. Leaks from award-granting committees such as those who select winners of Nobel Prizes or receivers of academic honors can be disastrous; secrecy is necessary for frank evaluation of candidates. An employee of a famous household might leak information to the public, usually for monetary gain. A member of any family can leak family secrets to outsiders for a variety of reasons, some low and some high on the EQ Scale. Truthful messages would of course have a higher EQ than would false or misleading ones; but leakage affects the integrity of a group or process, and hence even truthful messages can have a deleterious effect and be low on the EQ Scale.

Gossiping. The message of gossip is personal, intimate, and informal, usually "idle," superficial, and trifling, often sensational, exaggerated, and distasteful, and virtually always negative, injurious, and demeaning. It is usually unconfirmed and thus of dubious accuracy or completeness. The absent person being gossiped about—the gossipee—is of some importance and is known to those participating in the gossip transaction; there would be little point in gossiping about an unknown, unimportant person. We speak of "small town," not large town, gossip, for the arena must one in which everyone knows the person(s) being talked about. In today's electronic global village, gossip might refer to someone thousands of miles away but well known, like Hollywood personalities, political leaders, business tycoons, or sports figures. The mass media are energetically engaged in selling gossip; gossip columnists have huge readerships, and many magazines are devoted to such material. An individual who habitually spreads gossip acquires the label of a *gossip*, and generally loses credibility and friendships. For centuries religious literature has deprecated "whisperings" (2 Cor. 12:20); "a whisperer separateth chief friends" (Prov. 16:28). Confucius said: "The gentleman calls attention to the good points in others; he does not call attention to their defects. The small man does just the reverse of this" (Confucius, 1938, 12:16).

But gossip has its virtues. After a long career, an ethically sensitive reporter concluded (Pippert, 1989): "A gossip is insatiably curious, a gossip is the world's best communicator" (p. 143). A mentally agile person can indeed discover inside information important for others to know. S. Bok (1982) wrote that "gossip may be an indispensable channel for public information" (p. 97). On a more mundane level, gossip that is not hurtful can bring pleasant interaction and humor into lives that would otherwise be drab and isolated. But the great capacity for hurtful, unfair, and untruthful messages delivered through gossip usually places such communication low on the EQ Scale.

Spreading Rumors.   Rumor reflects most of the same characteristics as gossip but is a larger category. Its subject is usually not an individual but a group, an organization, or an event. For example, Company X might be rumored to be moving to another state or the Research Division in Company Y might be rumored to be a candidate for elimination. Rumors spread the news that an enemy is going to attack in a certain location or that a riot is likely to occur in a neighboring city. There might be rumors of an impending flood or tornado, of a dangerous epidemic, or of a stock market crash. Rumor tends to focus on the future, gossip on the past. Rumor asserts that something is going to happen, or that some group, organization, institution, or agency is going to do something, and gossip spreads the message that someone has done something. In colloquial usage, *gossip* and *rumor* are often used interchangeably.

In a free society the press has the obligation to show restraint in publishing gossip and *rumor* and when such news is found to be untruthful, to be quick to publish that fact. In totalitarian states where mass communication is in the hands of the government, underground rumor networks have played a crucial positive role in keeping independent thinking alive and in communicating the true state of affairs to a news-hungry populace.

Flooding.   In the contemporary world we are drowning in a sea of messages. Via electronic means humans are sending and receiving a quantity of information incomprehensible to earlier generations and are doing so at breathtaking speed. On the Internet we are experiencing the worldwide spread of all kinds of messages, including pornography, hate pronouncements, and questionable advertising. Can this flood be controlled without infringing on freedom of expression? Telephone-answering machines, faxes, and E-mail spread messages before us as soon as we enter office and home. Organizations arrange for their members and sympathizers to flood elected officials with telephone calls, E-mail, faxes, and letters. Form letters are prepared for citizens to mail, and although these letters can be hailed as examples of democracy in action, they can also represent a horde of robots sending messages without investing any individual thought. The ethical dimensions of these phenomena are still embryonic and need to be sensitively explored with vigor and commitment, lest we be flooded with unwanted, insignificant, untrustworthy, and demeaning messages. "In trying to cope with this mishmash of stimuli," Zoglin (1996, p. 64) wrote, "people could react in two ways. They could throw up their hands and withdraw even further into their own interests. Or they could turn once again to traditional news outlets which help put the chaos in some kind of intelligent order."

EXERCISES

1. Write an essay in which you deal with the dual components of accuracy and incompleteness in some truth-telling episode(s). Under what circumstances would you tend to justify incompleteness and even inaccuracy? Include personal experiences, and illustrate by using Hample's findings.

2. In small groups, discuss how lies can be detected by nonverbal cues. Include personal and specific examples.

3. Write a paper in which you discuss the importance of wise promise-making and conscientious promise-keeping. Include examples of promises in relation to yourself and to those close to you.

4. Write a paper on the ethical dimensions of propaganda. Begin by carefully defining the term.

5. Write a paper on the ethical aspects of the exit messages in your interpersonal communication experiences through the years. Would you like to take back any remarks? Have you been the recipient of harsh, demeaning exit communication remarks?

6. Write an essay on exit communication in organizational contexts. Include your own experiences, as well as instances you have heard or read about, in which employees were terminated with unkind abruptness. Include some examples of high ethical quality communicative acts.

7. Write an essay in which you discuss the positive and negative aspects of secrecy and confidentiality. Weave in some personal experiences.

8. Write a paper either for or against censorship. Then examine your argument and proceed to attack it.

9. Write an essay in which you discuss the ethical dimensions of leaking information in government agencies or elsewhere. Apply the consequentialist guideline, and assess how much damage occurred.

10. Write an essay or give a speech in which you relate some experiences, of both high and low ethical levels, with gossip or rumor.

6

Ethical Issues Revolving Around the Medium

We employ a host of mediums to accomplish the act of communicating. We utilize a systematic series of sounds—languages—as a primary means of oral communicating. In January 1996 CNN reported that 6,628 languages were spoken in the world. Most of these have been put into written form. With our bodies we transmit nonverbal messages, and virtually all objects we encounter in our daily lives say something nonverbally if we but attune ourselves to them. We are flooded with print media and inundated with still and moving photographic images in printed materials and on television and movie screens. Daily our ears take in sounds through radio, television, and other sources. Our voices are amplified through microphones and carried thousands of miles via telephone. E-mail and fax machines astound us with their electronic medium capabilities. Photographic duplication permits us to pile high the copies of any given message. The artistically talented employ music, and all of us communicate frequently through the medium of silence. What of the ethical dimension in using these various mediums of communication? That is what this chapter explores.

LANGUAGE

We need to increase our sensitivity to the possible ethical concerns lurking in language usage.

People Oriented

A basic ethical premise is that we ought not to use this human capability, this gift, of language for the purpose of injuring others, just as boxers or other athletes should not use their physical powers to hurt others. *Defamation,* to injure people through language usage, has been deprecated for centuries; ancient religious literature included frequent warnings not to slander, defame, via speech. With the invention of printing, concern grew over defamation in printed, written, or pictorial form, that is, libel. In the presence of a third party we cannot orally or in writing make statements about someone else that are false, injurious, and intentional without being subject to court action resulting in fines or other punishments. Intentionality is difficult to establish in a court of law, and many cases have stumbled on that criterion. If mental distress has been intentionally caused, but not in the presence of a third party, the speaker can still be punished by court action. If statements are true and hence not defamatory (truth takes precedence even if it works a hardship on someone), the aggrieved can charge invasion of privacy and in some states can secure limited redress in court. In recent years libel cases against the media have grown in number and in the amount of money claimed, and in some cases paid. The Supreme Court has strengthened media claims that "erroneous statements are inevitable in the media if there is to be uninhibited and robust debate on public issues" (Hunsaker, 1979, p. 26), that "public officials" include "public figures", and that "right-of-reply" statutes (according to which the aggrieved has a right to reply, e.g., in the case of a newspaper charged with libel) "were unconstitutional... [because] it necessarily becomes a *compulsion to print*" (p. 28), which infringes on the media's First Amendment rights.

Racist Language.   One of the most grievous areas of ethical concern is racist language. Even if unintentional (as many offenders claim), it hurts, scars, and dehumanizes, and rates very low on the Ethical Quality Scale. Scholars like Van Dijk (1987), Bosmajian (1983), McPhail (1994a, 1996), and Nakayama and Krizek (1995) have explored it in depth, and McPhail (1994b) reviewed seven books on the subject. We are all familiar with the unkind terms applied to those of racial and ethnic origins different from our own, so I need not catalog them here.

The main problem in the United States is white racism, in which many White people express negative attitudes toward people who are non-white. Such attitudes are not new; in ancient cultures, expressions about light often connotated good and those about darkness connected evil. We speak of the dark ages. Many cultures and religions celebrate a festival of lights; how many have a festival of darkness? The everyday lexicon is filled with terms implying that white is good and black is bad: a knight on a white horse, whitewash, "mighty white of you", blackmail, blacklist, blackball. Black cats crossing a person's path bring bad luck: White lies are harmless. I suggest dropping *white* lies with its racial overtones, and replacing it with *compassionate* or *benevolent*. S. Bok (1979, pp. 60 –76) discussed white lies as being trivial, but I think that the issue is not the degree of triviality but the degree of beneficence. Although black has a few honorific connotations (the dignity of black robes of judges, professors, and clergy, the beauty of black limousines), we need to work harder to increase this connotation, as the slogan "Black is beautiful" has done since the 1960s. Derogatory terminology rigidifies unjust racial stereotypes, and unfairly injures the victims, in whom anger and distrust are generated.

Derogatory terminology is often used to refer to those of multiple heritages. People are described as being *pure* German, *pure* Japanese, *pure* Sioux, or *pure* Norwegian, as if having parents from more than one racial or ethnic heritage were somehow impure. Terms such as *half-breed*, common in early American history, implied that offspring of European and Native American parents were not fully human—and not because of the European parent. The term *mulatto*, offspring of White and Black parents, comes from a Spanish term meaning a young mule (a sterile hybrid of a male donkey and a female horse). In Hispanic American areas the term *mestizo* describing a person of European and American Indian ancestry and coming from the Latin verb *miscere*, "to mix", carries a strong negative connotation. In South Africa the term *Coloured* (British spelling) applies to those who have a White parent and a parent of darker color. Their social rank is below that of white people, although this ranking gradually might be modified now that the multi-racial government is in place.

It is virtually impossible to find an honorific term in widespread usage for offspring of multiple racial or ethnic heritages. I would suggest the term *blend*, which borrows an idea from linguistics in which blends are a way that any language grows and develops. For example, the term *motel* is a blend of *motor* and *hotel*, a place of lodging enabling travelers to drive to the door of the room. A *motel* is not an inappropriate hybrid but a new entity, a new idea. All people are, in varying degrees, *blends*; it is predicted that by the middle of the 21st century *pure* White people will be a minority in the United States, as they now are in the state of Hawaii. In our vocabulary we need to use terminology that reflects human decency and equality, and dignity.

The media have long been criticized for their unfair portrayal of people who are not White in reporting news and in fictional entertainment. Although the situation has improved, people who are not White are often absent from the news unless they have committed anti-social acts. The media usually portray news from Africa as negative occurrences, such as famine, tribal warfare, or social upheaval. The many positive accomplishments in that huge continent go largely unreported. Although improvements are being made, all too many fictional programs on television still present people who are not white in secondary roles, as inferior or as a negative figure in the plot, and seldom as professionals or members of the upper class. Such stereotypes perpetuate the unfair message of inequality of races and ethnic groups and demean and dehumanize everyone concerned.

The increasing instances of hate speech in contemporary society are cause for concern. Although certainly nothing new, the growing number of hate speeches and virulence in denigrating not only racial and ethnic targets but also religion, and sexual orientation have prompted some colleges and universities to create codes and regulations against them. But in turn, these institutions are criticized for violating freedom of expression. The media and the scholarly literature have grappled with this dilemma. *The Howard Journal of Communication* devoted its Summer 1995 issue to the subject. Some, like Simon (1994), emphasized that corrective action should go beyond controlling superficial language usage and should seek to develop an antiracist atmosphere throughout institutions and society in general.

Sexist Language.   The employment of *sexist language* likewise has unfairly demeaned and impoverished women, more than half the population of this planet. Omitted from ancient religious writings and from many history books until recently, women were invisible. When written about, they were usually in subservient, supportive roles compared to men, who *did* things. Women were, and still are in some parts of the world, looked on as keepers of the cave, largely excluded from professions, business, and other non-volunteer roles in society. The English language has often omitted them: *mankind* for "human beings," *mailman* for "mail carrier," *policeman* for "police officer," *chairman* for "presiding officer." Correctives to such oversights have included employing the plural (e.g., instead of "each student turned his paper in on time" "all students turned their papers in on time"), equalizing male and female examples, and equalizing titles (e.g., Dr. Robert Smith and Dr. Irene Kantar, not Dr. Smith and Mrs. Kantar). We are gradually omitting unnecessary adjectives, such as *woman doctor*, and are watching verbs (men *discuss* but women *chatter*), but we have a long way to go in achieving a humane equality in language. The circular mental process must be carefully monitored: We speak so we think, and as we think so we speak. We also need to be sensitive to the linear process, by which children pick up sexist nuances and stereotypes in the language around them, and perpetuate those terms and attitudes as they grow into adulthood. As the Fourth United Nations Conference on Women in Beijing in 1995 constantly emphasized, women's rights are human rights, and vice versa. Thus, it simply is elementary that gender equity ought to be entrenched in all language usage.

Ad Hominem Arguments.   A common practice with serious ethical dimensions is the use of ad hominem, arguments whereby communicators direct their language and arguments "to the man", to the person, rather than to the issues. For example, instead of discussing the stand that political opponents take on major campaign issues, we focus on their loose relationships with sex partners. Often this process is a diversionary tactic used to avoid dealing with ideas. Charges of moral failings or intellectual weaknesses are of course often relevant to the ethos factor in judging people who run for public office, but when used as unfair, irrelevant diversionary tactics, they are low on the ethical scale. Likewise, charges of a person's inconsistency need to be carefully handled; the fact that a person who opposed compulsory health insurance five years ago now favors it can show growth and courage, not necessarily weak opportunism. To dismiss an argument on the basis of a person's change of mind can be an irrelevant and unfair skirting of the issues involved.

Name-Calling.   Name-calling is attaching to a person, group, institution, or concept a label with a heavily derogatory connotation. It usually is an incomplete, unfair, and misleading characterization, which rigidly stereotypes the person so named. Once we have called someone "a tightwad," "a crook," "a troublemaker," "a terrorist," or "an egghead," we stop thinking further, dismiss the person, and overlook other dimensions in the individual's nature. Occasionally when later experiences permit us to see the person in a different light, we perceive additional sides to their character and feel embarrassed and apologetic for having applied such narrow, demeaning labels for so long. But by then it might be too late to right the wrong. The journalist, Alistair Cooke (1979) wrote: "Slang exists to boost the self-esteem of its users with the least possible effort. It is the handgun of the man who wants to put down his enemy in no time flat" (p. 23). Substituting *name-calling* for *slang* would be appropriate in this instance.

Flattery. Though seemingly at opposite ends of a continuum, name-calling and flattery are not far apart. Religious literature and moral writers through the centuries have warned against flatterers and flattering others. Flattery is excessive and insincere complimenting of someone, often for the purpose of winning an immediate reward. Exaggerated praise diverts attention from that individual's actual merits or faults and thus misleads the person and other receivers. It is often a cover-up for real feelings toward a person; to praise excessively a person's wisdom in a particular instance suggests that the individual is usually not very wise—hence the affinity to name-calling. The smooth language of the flatterer is indeed to be shunned.

Two-Valued

Another category of language usage with ethical dimensions is two-valued terminology. We often utilize "God" and "Devil" terms, which reflect what we highly value and what we strongly dislike. We treasure such things as "democracy," "liberty," "freedom," "justice," and "equality." We strongly dislike "dictatorship," "militarism," "inefficiency," "tyranny," and "selfishness." Our "God" terms are glittering generalities; we unashamedly espouse them, and think that they have inherent virtue and that society has tarnished their glitter. Two people might call one quality in a person obedience and subservience, caution and cowardice, obstinacy and firmness. One person's terrorist is another's freedom fighter. Such strongly loaded terms unnecessarily and erroneously create two polar positions, either all positive or all negative. They generate too much emotion, and thus become an impediment to thoughtful analysis and discussion. They can bring an unsophisticated audience to passively accept the claims. When a ripple effect occurs, loaded terminology stimulates others to use similarly strong language, and emotional and thoughtless behavior escalates. Readers will note that throughout this book I have warned against the two-valued mind-set and its resultant terminology.

Particularizing

Language creates qualifiers, quantifiers, and reservations, functions that might be called particularizing and that have ethical considerations. In the social sciences and the humanities, in contrast to the natural sciences, probabilities, not certainties are dealt with; qualifiers need to be employed to give an indication of the strength of the claims. We use terms such as *probably, perhaps, certainly, maybe, almost, virtually, possibly or sometimes.* Qualifiers can be used with a high degree of ethical quality to let communicatees know the amount of confidence or commitment of the rhetor, but with a low degree of ethical quality to hedge and obscure the real claims. Advertisers often make such statements as "Virtually all dentists recommend our toothpaste", a clever way of enticing the careless public to ignore the *virtually* and to accept the rest of the claim. (In fairness, such an ad can also be an honest attempt to make clear that not all dentists recommend the product.)

Responsible communicators also need to select their quantifiers with great care so as not to mislead or intentionally confuse communicatees. The use of the quantifier *all* produces an unlimited generalization, as in "All college students are intelligent." If we intend, however, to communicate a limited generalization, then we select quantifiers such as *some, many, a few, or a majority.* The absence of a quantifier when making a generalization tends to imply the unlimited *all.* For example, "Professors are disorganized," tends to imply that "All professors are disorganized," and thus might be unfair to the group being discussed and might mislead the audience. If the communicator intentionally meant to lead people astray, and lamely responds when accused that he or she did not mean *all,* then that person has an ethical lapse with which to contend. Choosing quantifiers carefully can reduce the likelihood of controversy; tempers often flare over an immoderate quantifier, even more than over the substance of a remark. Thus, quantifiers should be chosen with care, to fulfill both the intellectual and the moral criteria.

Reservations are dependent clauses indicating under what conditions a central claim does not operate. For example: "I will enroll at your University, *unless another university gives me better part-time job opportunities.*" Reservations can be honest attempts to let the communicatee know of contingency situations involved; they are not necessarily meant to weaken a claim but to narrow, specify, or make a claim more precise. But when reservations are evasive tactics to avoid making firm commitments, they may rank low on the ethical scale. Special concerns of ethics and fairness occur when reservations are unstated, but supposedly understood. For example, parents might say to their daughter, "We'll support you through college." After two years of their daughter's dismal academic performance, they announce that they are terminating support. Their daughter responds, "But you said you would support me through college." They reply, "Yes, but it was assumed that such support was on condition that you did well in your studies." In other words, they felt that they had said, "We'll support you, *if you do well in your studies.*" The daughter did not hear or understand that reservation, she did not get that message, and she thinks she is being treated unfairly. Reservations, expressed or unexpressed, present an ethical concern that must be taken seriously by any conscientious communicator.

Form

Language forms, the crucible in which expressions are uttered, play an important part not only in the degree of effectiveness but in the degree of ethicality. A number are surveyed in this section.

Figurative Language. We have a tendency to think in images, and figurative language is one vehicle that enables us to do so. Rather than being a stylistic gimmick, frosting on the cake, it is more like a drop of coloring placed in a cookie mix, pervading and coloring the whole message. Hence its ethical significance must be noted. In simile, two items (objects, concepts, actions, qualities, or situations) are compared by using an explicit linking term such as *like* or *as*. "Her pleasant personality is like a sunrise." An analogy is an extended simile, that develops the comparison more fully. A metaphor is a compressed simile, without the *like* or *as* but implying the comparison, for example, "her sunny disposition." The medical metaphor is often used in public discourse: Society's problems are spoken of as ills or as a cancer, and the speakers portray themselves as desiring to heal, or cure, the situation. Audiences might find it difficult to question the authoritative "doctor's" solution. Some military terminology masks the tragedies of war: smart bombs, the theater of operations, collateral damages, hitting targets, not people. Applying animal metaphors to enemies during wartime dehumanizes them and hence minimizes the act of killing or wounding.

Figurative language can have great power and attraction. It can capture attention, simplify the complex, make concrete the abstract, and foster visualization. It can provide a fresh way of looking at things and can create cohesion. Where once there were sticks and straw, now there is a meaningful structure. It can make the message interesting, understandable, and memorable. It can communicate judgments swiftly and subtly and can create a compelling mood or perspective.

But these positive features immediately suggest serious ethical concerns when figurative language is used inappropriately with little concern for the solid analysis of the subject and the well-being of the audience.

Its very power can obscure rather than clarify, and can lead audiences to assume they understand when they really do not. Figurative language can infiltrate the minds of receivers with the ease of subliminal advertising and subtly and firmly mold and control attitudes and outlook. Thinking can become rigidified, and we weaken the ability to see variations and additional options (Jensen, 1977). (Ethically irresponsible use of the American frontier metaphor in U.S. history is discussed by Carpenter [1990].) The conscientious communicator wants to be sensitive to the ethical nuances involved.

Slogans. The arranging of words into brief slogans to propagate a claim is a significant and familiar form that dates to ancient times. Contemporary social movements and protest groups rely heavily on slogans. In large demonstrations, slogans are used to crystallize and simplify claims, unify supporters, and energize gatherings and marches. Organizations depend on them in their public relations efforts, and commercial advertisers live on them. Short, succinct advertising slogans fill billboards, handbills, newspapers and magazines; space is at a premium. Bumper stickers and buttons are fixtures on the U.S. scene. Candidates for public office create slogans to catch the attention and win the vote of the citizenry. Terse, memorable, often witty, and easily repeated, slogans can be powerful for both good or ill. Nations at war, (*cold* or *hot*), rely on them to foster loyalty and to denigrate the enemy. But slogans can generate blind obedience, can be used for indoctrination, and can unfairly dehumanize enemies. All too often, simplistic and harsh assertions work against careful thoughtfulness and make resolution of differences difficult. Surely, then, the ethical dimension should be a central concern.

Fabricated Anecdotes. The telling of anecdotes, parables, and stories to illustrate a point or underscore a moral lesson is as old as humankind. Ancient oral traditions relied heavily on such tools, and contemporary communicators know their power to clarify, vivify, and personalize a message. But what of fabricated anecdotes? When the governor of California discussed apparently fictitious individuals in a speech to illustrate his understanding of the problems of unemployed people, his staff's defense when questioned was that the people were "symbolic representations," "composites," of people with whom the governor had talked (*Star Tribune,* 1992, January 18, p. 13A). Former President Reagan was severely criticized for his misuse of anecdotes (Johannesen, 1990, pp. 242 –245). We admire the inventiveness of storytellers in the realm of fiction. Former Supreme Court Justice William O. Douglas (1974) wrote about a shepherd friend of his who was a great storyteller: "[he] never ran in short supply [of stories] because he could invent his tales as he went along" (p. 239). We do not appreciate such inventiveness in elected officials; we expect to hear the facts from them to judge social issues and policies.

Statistics.   In the mid-20th century, Huff in his book, *How to Lie With Statistics* (1954/1993) discussed nine major ways that statistics can mislead and highlighted the suspicion and concern that people have long harbored toward statistics. His analysis has lived in the literature ever since. In her book Crossen, *Tainted Truth* (1994), continued to lament the potentially misleading quality of statistical information. Statistics are a compact numerical way to express information, either as raw data ("10 students in the class got A's on the test") or as percentages. If there were 50 students in the class, then 20% of the class got A's on the test. If a student in that class of 50 asked all the classmates whether they liked the class, and 30 said *No*, and the student reported that three-fifths disliked the class, the student would be using descriptive statistics. She would be employing inferential statistics when asking only 5 classmates, 3 of whom said *No*, and reporting that three-fifths disliked the class. Statistics can have a strong appeal because of their precision and scientific aura and their ability to support a claim in a clear and compelling fashion. An audience is likely to be strongly impressed when told that air travel is safer than road travel because there are 120 auto deaths each day but only 200 air deaths each *year*. But we often assign too much power to statistics; we let them do our thinking. We might feel overwhelmed, and unable to refute such facts.

The methods by which statistics are secured, the accuracy with which they are presented, the care with which they are interpreted, and the ethical commitment of the communicator are all of utmost importance. We need to remind ourselves that statistics can distort and conceal the truth, can oversimplify, and in their supposed clarity can actually make something unclear. We want to be assured that the statistics have been collected accurately. If the statistics are inferential, the sample should be representative of the group and large enough. The subject being analyzed should be clearly defined (e.g., when measuring unemployment, are the underemployed and the part-time employed included? The subjects being compared should be comparable, not apples and oranges. The base of the percentage should be reasonable and should remain constant. In many instances, the average should be clearly specified as the mean (arithmetic average), the median (midpoint of the list of numbers), or the mode (the number occurring most frequently). The average should be significant and meaningful, unlike the witticism about the statistician who was drowned fording a river that averaged three feet in depth. The subject should be quantifiable: Claiming that "wives who work outside the home are 20% happier than those who work only in the home," presumes that *happiness* can be mathematically measured. The statistics should cover a sufficiently long time. If the statistics are visually presented, the portrayal should accurately and fairly present the information. For example, on a bar graph, pictures of money bags instead of bars would add the dimension of width as well as height and hence distort the depiction. These questions suggest that statistics, for all their wonderful attributes, cause genuine concern as to whether their message is misleading, inaccurate, and unfair. Ethical commitment as well as scholarly commitment is needed.

Obscenity and Profanity.   The Latin root of obscenity means "repulsive," and other synonyms round out its nature: loathsome, lustful, offensive, and indecent. *Profanity* is coarse, degrading, abusive, and sacrilegious language that shows contempt for things held sacred. Although both are condemned widely, obscenity and profanity are difficult to define in any legal language, and court decisions have specified that they must be defined and considered in light of a particular community's standards of decency.

Many ethical standards apply. Democratic values are damaged: Offensive language harms thoughtful deliberation and increases controversy. According to consequentalism harmful effects to individuals and to society can result from the creation of an intensified combative atmosphere. Pornography, barnyard metaphors, and other such terminology and depiction are demeaning to human nature and keep communications at the lowest level. At the very least, such expressive behavior is tasteless. According to the religious standard, obscenity tarnishes the image of God, which humans are supposed to reflect, and profanity is a shameful treatment of things sacred.

People who defend or deemphasize the evils of obscenity and profanity claim that at times, such as when protesting a horrendous social evil uncorrected by an inattentive power structure, harsh language is needed to awaken people, to shock them into action. Language provides a catharsis, which keeps individuals and societies from exploding. The ends justify the means they say, an idea as I have frequently noted, is a weak reed. The omnipresent mass media, E-mail and international computer connections flood us with obscenity, profanity, and pornography (Elmer-Dewitt, 1994). Where in such an international setting is the community whose standards are supposed to be used to regulate these matters? Communicators committed to transmitting the highest possible ethical messages need to be concerned.

Humor.   Often obscenity and profanity are intertwined with humor, which tends to weaken the condemnation and heighten the appeal for some audiences. We tend to excuse exaggeration when it is humorous. Fabricated anecdotes and strident slogans combined with a humorous touch do not upset us quite so much. Humans enjoy humor, as a relief for sadness, worry, boredom, and loneliness; we like to be told humorous things, and we like the people who do so. Humorless people lack appeal, and jokesters at parties or as performers are popular. During funeral eulogies, a reference to the person's capacity for humor (no matter how miniscule it might have been) often is included. When we speak, we like to insert humor, for we know the audience will like it, and by extension, like us and our message. Humor bonds speaker and audience. Humor eases the pain of suffering, and even has a therapeutic effect in some illnesses.

But many public speakers go astray when they try to be funny, not only in a prepared speech but perhaps especially in ad hoc forums like a press conference or a question period after a speech. Humor often depends on the context, and rhetors can get in trouble when reporters or others take their remarks out of context. Jokes at the expense of an individual or a group usually provoke resentment. To the vulnerable object of a joke, the remark is not funny. "Oh, it was just a joke, why get so upset" hardly smoothes over the hurt. When an audience laughs, a speaker is often stimulated to make more humorous remarks that occasionally lead to trouble. A chastised speaker might offer the lame excuse, "The audience led me to do it." With humor's power to entertain, to heal, to hurt, and to enrage, the communicator who would be highly ethical needs to be exceedingly careful in its use.

NONVERBAL CUES

Much human communication is carried on nonverbally; people often seek to deceive, and mislead, by these cues that we should be quick to discern but slow to interpret.

Vocal Cues

Vocal cues include such things as the rate of speaking, the volume, and the tone. Some speakers speak rapidly and loudly to intimidate the audiences, to forestall the possibility of their thinking, and to create a pretension of having a command of the material. Higher volume does not equal greater truth, no more than the loudness of a telephone's ringing is related to the importance of the message. A rapid rate of speaking does not mean greater soundness. The loud voice and machine-gun delivery of a television salesperson does not mean the product is of good quality. Political campaign oratory is often delivered stridently and bombastically to impress audiences. A supercilious, arrogant, or domineering tone can cow and exhaust an audience into a state of non-reflective acceptance. A unique aspect of deceptive vocal cues is impersonation. A Canadian radio talk show personality impersonated the voice of the Canadian prime minister so well that he got through the security of Buckingham Palace in London and chatted for some time with Queen Elizabeth about serious political affairs before the hoax was discovered. Humor aside, impersonating can indeed generate a serious ethical concern.

Body Cues

Body cues add to the communicative repertoire. Obscene gestures are obvious acts of low ethical quality, and in other cultures foreigners need to be sensitive to potentially offensive gestures. The "Everything is O.K." gesture in the U.S. made with the thumb and forefinger coming together in a circle is obscene in Latin America, where the "thumbs up" gesture would be the common and accepted cue. Facial expressions indicating extreme disagreement can be demeaning and intimidating to another, and smirks can likewise hurt a communicatee. Repeated flirtatious winks can be offensive. Television reporters can exhibit subtle and unfair bias by facial expressions. A raised eyebrow and a shrug of the shoulders might be unkind reactions to a person's statement. When a patient relates symptoms to a doctor, the latter's frown and sad countenance might deceive the patient into thinking the condition is serious when the doctor was merely being solemn and thoughtful, "the way doctors are supposed to look." A person can lie by nodding the head, and feigning agreement. A weak handshake can make the other party feel inferior and unimportant. Hugging can have a negative connotation. For example, a woman took her clergyman-counselor to court for sexual aggression, and cited the "duration and firmness" of his hugs. The court, however, ruling against her, said that a hug is a form of affection, not sexual aggression. Although legal in this case, the hugs no doubt were at least of an inappropriate ethical quality but in other contexts could have warranted the highest possible ethical rating. An upraised clenched fist can have an affirming message to a particular group but to outsiders may connote an abrasive and intimidating demeanor. Posture, such as slouching by a member of an audience, can be discourteous to the communicator. People who put their feet on the desk might project a relaxed, friendly manner in some contexts, but in some cultures it would be extremely rude to display the bottom of the feet to someone else. As many, if not most, of these vocal and body cues might be unconscious, we might soften our ethical judgments, but we should sensitize ourselves to the presence and power of such nonverbal cues. Indeed, as our true feelings and attitudes are often expressed nonverbally, the ethical dimension needs to be employed rigorously.

Signing for those who are hearing impaired in the audience is used to enable them to enter into private and public communication readily and fully. Some churches have services for people who are hearing impaired, and at some universities signing is taught as an accredited second language. But society is still guilty of the ethical sin of omission in not making such a body code more available than it is.

Attire

Ethical considerations enter into our choice of clothing. Torn, untidy clothing, in a formal setting demeans the wearer and insults the communicatee; (in informal contexts such attire is relaxing). Neat grooming can be a positive attribute in most communicative contexts but ought not to be considered a substitute for substance. Men and women color their hair to look young; to discuss this as an ethical issue seems ridiculous, yet by thus trying to mislead potential employers or other audiences such an act can enter into the ethical domain. In cold climates with minimal central heating a person might appropriately wear a hat inside a building simply to keep warm; but in other contexts this behavior would insult others. In some cultures in warm climes, women may customarily leave their bodies uncovered above the waist; in other cultures they leave their legs uncovered. The wrong behavior in the wrong culture would be highly offensive. Women in some Islamic cultures are required to cover themselves totally when in public; not to do so is a serious religious offense. Such attire, as Reece (1996) discussed, communicates virtues of chastity, respectability, strength of character, obedience to religion, and modesty. To those outside that religious persuasion, such clothing demands seem to be a low ethical quality message denigrating women. Some religious rules dictate the wearing of certain articles of clothing; to adhere to those rules communicates commendable obedience to the in-group but can connote narrow, sanctimonious provincialism to an out-group. For a professor in a state university to wear religious attire in the classroom would seem an inappropriate intrusion, that could intimidate students, or at least create an unprofessional awkward atmosphere and convey a low ethical quality nonverbal message. Some university athletic coaches wear shoes and jerseys advertising athletic gear companies; when games are televised, the free advertising reaped by the companies can be enormous and questionable. Athletes, especially famous ones, command high fees for wearing certain brands of athletic gear. Professional garb —academic gowns, military uniforms, ecclesiastical attire, judicial robes, doctors's white coats—can carry great power in their nonverbal communication. These should be worn only by those who are certified to wear them and even then should not to be worn to generate excessive authority.

Other Objects Attached to the Body

Other objects attached to the body likewise can be important nonverbal cues. Jewelry can communicate elegance or ostentatious snobbery, an inappropriate attachment to material possessions or an appropriate appreciation for beauty. Rings on various fingers or attached to the ears or noses of men and women in various cultures and subcultures communicate a host of potentially different messages, and communicatees may read such situations in a host of various ways. Women can apply color to various parts of their face: in India a red dot in the center of the forehead and in other cultures a reddening of the lips, a darkening of the eyes, or a powdering of the skin. Again, many messages are thus conveyed and received, an enhancement of beauty or a prostitute's advertising. The cosmetic industry is a vast enterprise that rests mainly on the desire of people to be attractive. Other nonverbal cover ups used by men and women include deodorants, which communicate the deceptive message that bad odor does not exist. Think of the vast amount of money spent to transmit that message! A number of *false* items are worn: wigs, eyelashes, teeth, fingernails, breasts, shoulder pads. Their messages can be appropriate insofar as the items add beauty or may be deceptive. The practice in many gatherings to wear nametags facilitates communication and enriches interactions. Planners of gatherings who do not arrange for this body attachment could well be chastised not only for inefficiency but also for low ethical quality communication—a significant sin of omission.

Intangible Behavior

Intangible behaviors manifested by individuals also are important non-verbal cues. When people are habitually tardy for or absent from meetings, they signal a disrespect for those assembled and for the task at hand; and can generate considerable antagonism. Inattentiveness during meetings, displayed through a host of nonverbal means, likewise may be low ethical quality behavior; of course it can also be an appropriate wake-up call to the communicator(s) to be more effective and interesting! In committee meetings the unspoken overlaid meta-messages are often more important than the spoken words. A person's demeanor can say, "I'm lazy," "I'm a hard worker," "I'm dependable," or "I'm a fun person to be with." Public speakers try to communicate many meta-messages, that they are concerned, open, efficient, real problem-solvers, empathic, pleasant. A friend told me of her friend visiting from the Netherlands who had lost her return airflight ticket. They went to the airport, and her friend methodically walked up and down the long ticket counter, carefully scrutinizing each ticket seller. The one she chose proved to be very sympathetic and helpful. She explained her wise choice: during WWII people in her German-occupied country learned how to study people and carefully determine who would likely help and who would not. What people are speaks louder than what they say, and those behaviors thus need to be carefully monitored, not only for their degree of effectiveness but also for their ethicality.

Body Rhetoric

The use of the body, usually in concert with many others who share the same views, has increasingly become a part of public discourse. Mass demonstrations, marches, or silent vigils can communicate powerful messages. People picket outside their place of employment to express grievances or to protest policies, and usually carry signs to supplement their message. Picketers try to maximize the embarrassment of their employer and hope that television cameras will catch the message and spread it to thousands not present. Such "body rhetoric" may be fraught with ethical concerns. Employment of such body rhetoric usually solidifies those who adhere to that given view, and usually deepens the animosity of those who strongly oppose it, and what it does to those in the middle is the big question mark. But if it serves to reduce the likelihood of rational dialogue, to intimidate and to lead to violence, then it is low on the Ethical Quality Scale. However, adherents may insist that the evil against which they are protesting is so heinous, that their body rhetoric is high on the ethical quality scale. Obviously, each episode needs to be evaluated empathically on its particular merits or demerits. This medium of communication has great potential for stimulating needed societal reforms or for decreasing the possibility for a peaceful, humane, rational, dialogical society.

Personal Encountering

Another nonverbal medium of communication might be called personal encountering acts. During election times, candidates go door-to-door to deliver their campaign literature and to meet the voters. Such an act has been found very effective; voters, particularly those who are undecided, often are persuaded to vote for a candidate they have actually met, as irrational as that may be. Door-to-door selling, be it Girl Scout cookies or a host of other products for charitable or purely business ends, leads many to purchase things from or give money to organizations that they would otherwise not have patronized. Religious proselytizing door-to-door or in such places as shopping malls or airports, might win some adherents and make the rhetors feel good , but might also antagonize communicatees and invade their privacy.

Gift Giving

Gift-giving is a form of personal encountering even when the gift is not given in person. It is a person-to-person act, whose motivations range from the purest good will to the most crass hope for a favor more valuable than the gift itself. Journalists may have their egos stroked and their objectivity tarnished by gifts and perks from people about whom they report. Lobbyists give meals, vacation trips, tickets to sporting or other events, and other gifts to win the favor and vote of law makers. Although legislative efforts at the national and state levels are curbing these activities, such personal encountering will no doubt always take place. Gift-giving and bribery have always been difficult to distinguish. When a gift precedes an impending decision, it of course is more highly suspect. *Accepting* gifts is as ethically demanding as *giving* gifts. How ethical is it for company personnel to accept gifts from contractors seeking business connections? Non-profit organizations often worry about accepting gift offers. Speaking of those who solicit donations on behalf of institutions of higher education, Wentworth (1995) posed the dilemma: "Numerous ethical issues surround the accepting of gifts, because of the donor's character, reputation, or underlying motive; because of the character or source of the gift assets; or because of the donor's explicit or implicit conditions or expectations that accompany the gift" (p. 9). In some cultures, such as Japan, gift giving is a deeply embedded value and practice (with all its positive and negative connotations), and the principle of evenly reciprocating, of paying back, can extend to succeeding generations. Indeed, the nonverbal communicative act of gift giving and receiving has many dimensions, some of which have serious ethical considerations.

Artifacts

Virtually all artifacts around us communicate a message, but not always the same message to all communicatees. Architecture communicates various messages; some viewers see great beauty and exciting form, where others see ugliness. Skyscrapers have been the U.S.'s unique way of claiming excellence, and the city with the highest structure is superior. Now Malaysia's twin tower skyscraper in Kuala Lumpur is the highest structure in the world, soon to be surpassed by buildings in Shanghai, Hong Kong, and other cities. Some critics find that such buildings communicate misguided personal and national vanity and arrogance; other observers see more positive messages. Elaborate mortuary buildings can likewise communicate obscene ostentacion or peace and solace. Car styles communicate different messages to people. Golf courses might communicate openness, challenge, peacefulness, and exhilerating exericise to the golfer, but non-golfers might see wasted space catering to the wealthy, athletic few in society. Actions communicate messages. Half a century ago, smoking communicated being suave, macho, "chic". Today it communicates to most people (holdouts and the tobacco industry excepted) a life-threatening health hazard, environmental pollution, thoughtlessness and senselessness.

Flags

Flags communicate many things, and stimulate some people to insist that any descecration of a national flag is a serious social offense for which severe punishment should be meted out. The burning of a nation's flag in protest, wearing it as clothing, portraying the flag in a demeaning manner in art work, or using the flag to advertise commercial enterprises' locations is in the minds of many citizens a demeaning treatment of their nation's symbol. Some claim that having a nation's flag in a church or other place of worship weakens the separation of religion and state, as does having religious flags or other symbols in state buildings and in schools. In Bavaria, southern Germany, where religion and state have been traditionally intertwined, a court ruled that displaying crucifixes on the walls of the public schools was undemocratic and coercive, unfairly propagated one religion, and intimidated those with other religious views. Some Bavarian communities currently are challenging that ruling and refuse to remove the crucifixes as ordered.

Postage Stamps

Postage stamps likewise communicate a message about any given country: a famous person, a tourist attraction, a national treasure. When stamps are used to mail a letter to a foreign country, a special ethical question arises. When sending a letter to a friend in Japan, one would have great reticence to attach a stamp with a picture on it a WWII admiral instrumental in defeating Japanese forces. Some observers question the ethicality of stamps praising U.S. values when the recipient lives in a country where these freedoms do not exist. For example, a U.S. 3 cent stamp reads, "To cast a free ballot: a root of democracy," and a 10 cent stamp: "People's right to petition for redress". Although commendable public relations in behalf of cherished national values, such stamps can lead to charges of cultural imperialism and interference in another country's domestic affairs. Religious stamps at Christmas with angels and other Christian motifs may alienate many people and sharply reduce their options when purchasing stamps.

Mechanical Devices

Various mechanical devices might communicate nonverbal messages with ethical dimensions. We keep our houses lighted when we are gone, and use timers to turn lights on and off at set times for the purpose of deceiving would-be intruders. Apartment dwellers, especially women, might leave a radio on all day, to communicate the untrue message that someone is at home. We justify these deceptions by contending that protecting property and person overrules deception in this context. Roving police cars in a residential area communicate a sense of security, or intimidation, to residents and a warning to possible vandals. Unmarked police cars and plainclothes officers deceive people and encourage con artists to pose as police and rob the people they stop. Entrapment of law breakers by such means is both lauded and deprecated by the citizenry. Fog horns communicate warning and guidance to ships at sea but disturb the sleep and well being of nearby residents. Railway whistles warn people of an approaching train but also disturb people living in proximity.

VOICE EXTENSIONS

A third broad category of mediums of human communication is voice extensions, such as microphones, telephones, beepers, tape recordings, and radios.

Microphones

We have all attended public meetings in which no microphone was provided to amplify the speaker's voice to enable the audience to hear distinctly; such a situation is inevitably unsatisfying. Planners of meetings need to realize that providing an adequate public address system, and making sure it is in good working order, are not only a matter of efficiencey but also of a high ethical quality. Speakers likewise have an ethical obligation to use a microphone properly, to speak into it, to be close enough but not too close to it, not to wander away from it, and so on. Many speakers, some experienced ones, have an unwarranted fear of the microphone (understandable apprehension with such a new mechanism a half century ago but hardly defensible today) . They need to realize that the microphone is their friend, and helps them transmit their voice to the entire audience. To fear such a friend is strange indeed. The arrangers of public meetings in which audience participation is expected also need to make microphones (stationary or roving) available for members of the audience to ask questions and make comments. When no audience microphone is available, the speaker needs to repeat the question or comment for all to hear. In auditoriums or enclosed sports facilities, the authorities controlling the public address system need to make sure it is working properly, is not too loud, and does not pound ear drums. Microphone use can go beyond preference or good taste and become an ethical concern.

Telephones

The telephone has become an omnipresent part of developed societies and a mark of progress in developing ones. The value of such a convenient and life enriching instrument is difficult to measure. But it can have its disadvantages beyond expense. A family member may excessively tie up the phone. Advertisers can make a forced entry into the home (usually during dinner time!) selling their wares. Telephone marketing is a lucrative $400-billion-a-year industry (Peterson, 1993); state and federal laws have restricted commercial (not political or nonprofit) phone messages, especially taped solicitations, with no calls permitted before 9 A.M. or after 9 P.M. The national Telephone Consumer Protection Act specifies that companies must stop calling people for five years when they request to be put on a company's "no-call" list. Pollsters, some more legitimate than others, likewise barge into the living room. Going far beyond these irritating instances are threatening or harrassing calls, which can cause fear and distress. The telephone has also been accused of killing letter-writing. Cordless phones give enormous freedom of movement and location for communicating, but make people ever available to others. A cordless phone offers no right of privacy; others can legally eavesdrop, on what is technically similar to a radio transmission. Teleconference raise questions of fairness, in that the conferences can be arranged at a time when troublesome individuals cannot participate; they also intimidate less vocal people who do not contribute as much to the dialogue as they would face-to-face. Beepers now pervade society and sharply intrude wherever people may be, but they also keep people in necessary contact with others and suggest a person's importance.

Tape Recordings

Tape recordings of a person's voice enable us to carry that person to distant locales. Tape recordings are commonly used today to catch and preserve the human voice, but in earlier years wire spools were used to record. As a young college instructor, I used them as a device to train my debate students and to record our college president's brief message which could then be taken or sent to be played in alumni gatherings across the nation. Over the decades the advances in taping facilities make high quality recording easy and convenient. But such advances have of course created questionable uses, including their secret use in the Oval Office, the surreptitious recording of phone or other conversations, their use by law enforcement agents without proper warrant, their use by estranged spouses, by insecure employees, and by others who want to record secret information. Two 19-year-olds who thought that a hotel was unfairly refusing rooms to young people, carried a hidden microphone to record the hotel clerk's comments. A university newspaper reporter saw fit to resign when it was discovered that he had planted a hidden tape recorder in a closed meeting of the Board of Regents. Investigative reporters secretly record an interview and thus gather publishable evidence proving wrongdoing. But even the best of intentions (e.g., the desire to correct society's faults) might not justify secret recordings. With the flood of sophisticated recording facilities comes the tidal wave of ethical concerns.

Radios

For seven decades the radio has enriched our lives and brought voices of entertainers, newspeople, sports announcers, musicians, clergy, and political figures into our homes. What a wonderful medium to increase information, to bring laughter to our sad and boring moments, to reduce our loneliness, and to increase connectedness with a society, even the world. To use the public's air waves, radio stations must secure our permission, and have to meet certain requirements and standards to get and renew such permits. The 1934 Federal Communication Act gave radio broadcasting free and exclusive use of broadcast channels on the condition that they serve the public's interest. Legal and ethical dimensions are of central concern. Type of programming, amount of time allocated to commercials, use of profanity, and unfair balance of political material become the public's concern. We are justified in overseeing that the level of programming is not insultingly low, does not pander to baser instincts, does not overlook serious social issues, and does not damage the moral fabric of society. The mushrooming radio talk shows in recent years has won praise for enabling the public to express themselves on the air but has brought charges that bullies—loud, outlandish, intolerant, arrogant, profane—can impose their views. Far from generating a thoughtful public dialogue, such programs have often stifled the impulse for reasonableness.

VISUAL MEDIUMS

Photography

For well over a century photography has been a medium through which we have captured visual images, and spread them through secondary media, such as newspapers. Still photography, and later, motion pictures have both negative and positive effects. People have had their privacy invaded with hidden cameras or cameras with telephoto capabilities. Print media have used pictures out of context to fit their story line. For example, an anguished looking President Clinton in an otherwise jovial gathering in the Oval Office was shown on the cover of a newsmagazine, with the laughing staff members in the room cut out; the magazine wanted a photo to accompany their story on Clinton's troubles related to the Whitewater investigation. The picture had actually been taken four months earlier. On one occasion, London tabloids showed a sad-looking Prince Charles and Princess Diana to supplement a story on their estrangement; the photo really was taken at an earlier date when they were solemnly visiting a war memorial in South Korea. How ethical is it for print media to use photos in this fashion to supplement an unrelated story? Photography freezes the moment, then reproduces and frames it, and in its manipulation much injustice can be done. Photos can be edited, enhanced, doctored in various ways to fit a story line. Camera angles can show a person in an unfair pose or with an unflattering facial expression. Degree or angle of lighting can result in a distorted image. Cameras catch close-ups of people at moments of deep grief or great joy, supposedly reflecting the essence of the story, but the photos may do injustice, or at least cause unfair embarrassment, to the persons depicted. Surveillance planes have the capacity to photograph details from 75,000 feet in the air of great areas of the earth's surface. Camera people at public meetings usually position themselves in the front of the room, cause an intrusion into the setting, and obscure the view of others. When covering a court case, newspapers show the accused (often an unflattering picture, day after day, and usually on the front page) and implant a negative image in the minds of readers. If the person happens to be a member of a minority group, that negative image becomes unfairly extended to that group in the minds of readers and viewers. But many of us also use photo manipulation: In job applications or publicity material, we might distribute a younger, more flattering photo of ourselves. Pictures give the illusion of showing things as they *are*, but these factors and the process of selection sometimes mislead the viewers.

Motion Pictures

All the ethical factors in still photography are multiplied when applied to motion pictures. The ability to catch movement on film has indeed captured the communication scene in the 20th century and has brought entertainment to millions via home movies, public theaters, and especially television sets. Sports events, cultural programs, political proceedings, and everyday occurrences are brought into our living rooms. Families record their history with video cams and depict, in living color, the antics of their children and their growth to adulthood. Private citizens by chance can record the questionable behavior of police officers, other officials or other citizens; such records can end up as evidence in some future court proceedings. Video cams record people's entries into buildings, hallways, subways, and elevators, and capture people in banks and many other institutions. Although helpful for security purposes, such practices make people wonder whether Orwell's Big Brother is watching our every move and whether an undue invasion of privacy has occurred.

Motion pictures, especially as shown on television programs, worship many gods. By definition, moving pictures worship the *gods of motion and the visible.* Television cameras are drawn to the scuffling of a few rather than to some quiet assemblage, to marches and loud shouting rather than to quiet discussions, to the breathless thrills of skating and soccer rather than the quiet deliberations of chess. Parades, be they joyful celebrations or solemn funerals, attract motion picture cameras. Active animals, not stationary objects in nature, do likewise. When television news reporters and editors go about their work, the excitement of motion—car accidents, robberies, fires—is a top priority criterion in selecting and presenting; in other words, motion defines news, and suggests that motion equals significance. Furthermore, when only the visible is depicted, much unseen but significant material is lost to consideration.

The *gods of violence and conflict,* both in fact and in fiction, in news and in entertainment, dominate television and movies: The motion picture medium, violence, and conflict go hand in hand. Military conflicts with all their dramatic visual takes, their movement, violence, and confrontation get top billing, as do domestic confrontations. The media are quick to exploit underlying racial tensions in society. For example, the Stuart case in Boston (Cooper & Carey, 1996) where the white husbamd who murdered his wife spread the hoax that a black person did so; and the white mother in Georgia who drowned her two small children and accused a black man. The media, with all too much relish, fanned the flames of racial tensions prior to any verification. Television soap operas, situation comedies, and sporting events all draw from the appeals of conflict and violence. Negative campaign ads, tearing down an opponent (euphemistically called comparative ads), create a heightened atmosphere of conflict in which substantive issues are sidelined. Where friction is, where scandal lurks, there the cameras are drawn like a magnet. Polarity, conflict, and divisiveness are often exaggerated and sometimes invented. Studies keep documenting that television fare contains an enormous amount of violence of the type that encourages imitation and desensitizes viewers, especially children. Attempts by the federal government to mandate a "V-chip" to enable parents to guide the viewing fare in their homes is hailed by some as a long overdue step in the right direction, but others fear it is a step toward a form of censorhip. V-chips do not distinguish among the violence of war, fictional encounters, Shakespeare, and sleazy material. Television stimulates confrontation that otherwise might not occur; for example, stimulated by television coverage, Greece and Turkey almost came to armed conflict over a tiny uninhabited island they both claimed in the Aegean Sea. (Paraschos, 1996).

Besides worshiping the gods of visible movement and their cousins, violence and confrontation, the medium of moving pictures also tends to focus on other gods. It emphasizes *singularity.* It focuses on individuals, the speaker on the platform, the questioner in the audience, the actor on the stage, the football player carrying the ball, on any individual who at a given moment calls for attention. When 33 people died in a plane crash in Croatia, the media focused almost exclusively on one person, Ron Brown, a member of President Clinton's cabinet. It focuses on personalities, on individual heroes and villains. But it is also drawn to *magnitude*, to enormous demonstrations, a huge beached whale, and a raging forest fire, The magnificent cathedrals of this world, not the small edifices, appeal to the camera operator. Televison and movies gear their fare to the *masses*, to maximize profits; all too often the result appeals to the lowest possible intelligence, excites sexual appetites, panders to whatever sells, portrays action and violence ad nauseam. The bizarre, the outlandish, the outrageous, the atypical, the deviant are magnets for the television camera, and we thus are shown people with funny hats, nontraditional clothing, and provocative signs at sports events, political conventions, and other public gatherings. The sensational, and the spectacular are loved by the movie camera.

Television worships brevity: the quick view, the short phrase, the rapid image-building, the swift transition to the next item. Coherent in-depth analyses of society's issues will have to be dealt with elsewhere. Television impressively portrays, but does not analyze or interpret nearly as well. It loves simplification. Television worships the god of recency. Whatever has just occurred sneaks to the head of the line, however insignificant, incomplete, or inaccurate, however disturbing to viewers or listeners. A plane has crashed, some deer hunters have been killed, a building has burned; further details will come later, but meanwhile many people with loved ones involved might have to wait and worry, often needlessly. The speed of foreign news transmission by CNN, for all its virtues, makes it difficult for diplomats who often need time to gain a detailed view and who must let emotions subside before formulating decisions. The god of anticipation is worshiped, by looking forward to and advertising future events (even a station's own programming). But once the event is over, the contest decided, or the tragedy reported, the media do not stop to reflect, to evaluate, to consider implications; that approach would slow down the assembly line, which by now is ready to take on another story. Television provides an ideal stage for the god of humor; sitcoms and other programs give our 20th century court jesters (more highly paid than medieval court jesters) a wonderful opportunity to display their gifts. But news departments in television increasingly play second fiddle to entertainment and often feel pressured into becoming *infotainment*, to take on the show biz mentality.

Television and printed media are problem oriented, they focus on problems that are usually more dramatic than are solutions. The media are problem-mongers, that sell society's problems, much as fishmongers sell fish. The media in the world of free enterprise worship above all else the god of the Market. What sells determines what is depicted. But this problem in democratic countries is certainly to be preferred to the situation in totalitarian countries where the government determines what sells. At the same time extremely wealthy political candidates are able to buy media advertising denied to those with smaller bank accounts. The powerless in society are absent from the media, and when a program does present these fringe elements, we can rejoice as Christians (1986) did after a Bill Moyer's CBS report: "Moyers gave no moralistic preachments. He sought only to make the faces of the poor as distinct and their voices as clear as audiences typically hear and see from agents of the establishment. The result was redemptive media, mass communications honoring the cause of social justice—at least for a fleeting hour" (p. 124). These gods are not necessarily false gods, but they need to be kept in their place, for gods run amuck, like elephants, can be dangerous. Properly tamed, these gods can bring much enrichment to our lives.

The television medium introduces additional potential ethical concerns. The industry prides itself in protecting privacy of interviewees (undercover agents, informants, or others who desire not to be shown) by portraying only a darkened silhouette of the person. But all too often, anyone who knows the person and who studies the portrayal closely, can fairly easily identify the person; thus in many cases this dubious technique does not actually protect privacy. Another highly questionable procedure is to re-create a scene for visual portrayal. The practice of television stations inflating their ratings score by airing a highly dramatic program immediately before ratings is, according to some critics, an act of distortion, that misleads advertisers and the public. Representatives of minority groups are often portrayed unfairly, both in terms of frequency and in terms of positive contexts. Women are portrayed unfairly. For example, a study indicated that television coverage of women athletes, although improving, cannot match the coverage of men athletes; "networks both ignore and infantilize female athletes and women's sports" (Winegar, 1994, p. 1A), and there are fewer interviews with female athletes and coaches. In addition, the uphill struggle of women for equality with men in the journalism field is generally acknowledged. (Reddi, 1994).

Decisions made in the field and in the editor's office give the television medium an enormous power over the agenda of television fare and hence over what we encounter. By the age of 18, the average American has supposedly watched 2.6 years of television, a statistic that makes us vividly aware of this medium's great potential for good or ill. Critics contend that the medium ought to live up not only to its entertainment potential but also to its educational opportunity. Many would agree with Vice-President Gore (1992), when he wrote that in "the age of electronic image-making, reasoned discourse... plays less of a role than ever before... .Skillful 'visual rhetoric' has become as important as logic, knowledge, or experience in determining a candidate's success" (p. 168).

The VCR is a visual companion to millions, and complements, rather than competes with, watching television or going to the movies (McIntyre, 1995). Most of the ethical concerns voiced in connection with television would also apply to VCRs.

Cartoons

Another visual medium, incorporated into visual and print media, is the cartoon, an imaginatively created artifact, not a camera reproduction. In print and in electronic form, cartoons have been a significant medium of human communication, and reach a wide and diverse audience. They catch our attention easily. We tend to give cartoonists (or they tend to take!) considerable freedom, and we realize that their creations usually exaggerate physical characteristics, distort people's views, ventilate anger and other strong emotions, and stir a considerable depth of feeling in viewers. They sneak by our mental defenses. Cartoons can be ruthless and unfair, but they, together with their captions, can succinctly and arrestingly summarize the main point of a complex issue. Furthermore, they usually leave us laughing uproariously or at least chuckling softly, so we give them a long leash. They are memorable, and we find ourselves passing them on: "Say, did you see the cartoon in... ", or, "I remember a cartoon in *The New Yorker* a couple years ago that... ." Their simplicity, their quick messages, and their broad universal appeal make them a powerful medium. Because they deflate authority figures in government and society, it is understandable that there are no political cartoons in the People's Republic of China (Schnell, 1995). Their very appeal and power make us concerned about how well they measure up to ethical standards. Comic strips frequently draw readers before they turn to the front page news. Narratives in comic book form lengthen the message and deepen the impact and find readership in adults as well as children.

Cartoons in motion multiply the fun and the concern. Animation, breathing life into drawings of animals or people, amazes us with its creativity but also frequently leaves us despondent at its excessive violence. All too often the dominant theme is that problems are solved by the hero's violent acts. Citizen groups, worrying about imitative effects on youngsters, seek to have the television industry lessen the violence but with very limited success. Although cause and effect have been difficult to establish conclusively in scholarly studies, I see little enrichment in such fare, and do not hesitate to put many cartoon programs at the low end of the EQ Scale. Such talents and imagination should be used for more edifying productions.

Visual Aids

Other examples of the visual medium are visual aids used in public presentations. Overhead projections of charts, graphs, key terms, and outlines are common, as are slides. Their effective use is the aim of any communicator, but the many inept instances call for consideration of an ethical dimension. That is, a rhetor has the ethical obligation to be reasonably proficient in using visual aids. Often the material on the screen is too small to be seen, and too complicated to be understood. The speaker goes through the items too quickly, and seldom has a pointer to identify items. Sometimes the projection on a screen is so low that only a few people in the front can see, and other viewers distract the audience by stretching and shifting to see. The projections are not always in proper focus. Sometimes the visual aids seem more important that the lecture, and the voice becomes an audible aid to the projected material, the communicator a mere machine operator. The very impressiveness and beauty of the projected material, usually in color, leaves a feeling that the speaker is hiding behind technique, that form rather than substance is dominating, and that the speaker uses these aids as crutches. But even if this judgment is too harsh, the communicator has an ethical obligation to use these aids well, and not to let visual projections replace content and sound analysis of that content.

PRINTED AND ELECTRONIC MEDIUMS

In addition to visual media, voice extensions, nonverbal cues, and language, a fifth category is printed and electronic communication. In most countries the daily newspaper is an expected source of messages about life. Journalism, from the French *journal*, "daily," relies on people's belief that they need and want *daily* news. The profession worships the gods of recency, immediacy, excitement, and speed, for old happenings are not news. "What's new?" we ask, and the *news*paper proceeds to tell us. Thus newspaper reporters gather news items quickly and constantly, not only to feed the public but also to compete in the marketplace. Do we really want and need such frequent information? We—and the journalism profession—claim that we have not only a right to know but an obligation to know the news to make wise decisions in a democracy. But much of this rapidly acquired information might be incomplete and inaccurate. Would a weekly news version more complete and accurate be preferable? Newspapers often lack context for their stories, as well as multiple viewpoints. They fight time and space, and can report only so much. Deciding what to omit involves ethical reflection as does fairly presenting what is chosen. When we judge the ethics of what we see on the printed page, we judge the unseen people in the editorial offices. The highly respected *New York Times* has as its motto, "All the News That's Fit to Print," and the *Japan Times* proclaims, "All the news without fear or favor." Newspapers claim to live up to the highest standards, and like to admit that they *are* biased—in favor of good stories that are interesting, significant, fresh, and well written. Critics have long complained of the shortcomings of the press, and a respected journalist, James Fallows

(1996), in his *Breaking the News*, leveled a devastating critique at the press's coverage of the political landscape. The desire to make a profit, to best competitors, can result in the press seriously slipping from high professional and ethical pedestals. Alistair Cooke (1979), the English *Manchester Guardian*'s U.S. correspondent for many years, wrote of the Watergate hearings in 1973: "The flurry of charges is so serious that we should all take a deep breath, wait for all the indictments, wait for Senator Ervin's committee findings, wait for the trials, and then come to a conclusion. This self restraint is long overdue. It is not, I admit, a good recipe for selling newspapers" (p. 106). In totalitarian countries, of course, where the newspapers are simply an arm of the government, the desire to please superiors results in warped products from the start.

Ever since Gutenberg put a dent in the need for good handwriting, humans have spread information in printed forms: books, newsletters, pamphlets, and newspapers. As I have previously noted, ethical concerns of defamation existed from ancient times, and grew from religious admonitions not to use the gift of speech to slander others. These standards were applied to printed works through religous and secular laws against libel. Printing untrue and injurious statements about some-one, invading someone's privacy, and causing mental distress, can lead to harsh penalties for a writer. Libel suits today can involve enormous sums of money, and many contemporary cases have made headline news.

Today the printed word appears on posters—in buses and subways, for instance—advertising goods or services to a captive riding audience. Billboards rear up into the skylines to speak to rapidly passing travelers. These messages are attention-getting, terse, provocative, simple, and memorable. We need to be concerned with how accurate, fair, and ethical they are in their claims.

Private written works that find their way into public printed form are also important to consider. Many individuals have kept diaries or jour-nals, and these or rewritten versions might in the future be published as memoirs. Private letters might be published by scholars. These private communicative acts need to be evaluated carefully, for they generally put the composer in a good light and see life through only one pair of eyes, but they can also be enriching views of the experiences and thoughts of other human beings.

Electronic advances in communication in recent years leave us breath-less. Computer-mediated communication (CMC) enables millions to be in touch—friends, acquaintances, strangers, businesspeople, profes-sional colleagues, and those who are isolated by age or illness. Approximately 33% of U.S. homes now have computers; but how often and how well they are used is another story. E-mail and faxes have revolutionized, increased, and speeded up communicative interactions on electronic super highways. We find ourselves in a borderless world without national or geographical boundaries. Indeed, the global village, and the global neighborhood, exist in full measure. Internet, a network of networks composed of computers that talk to each other through telephone lines, cables, and satellites, boggles the mind. It is estimated that by the end of 1997, about 80 million people worldwide will use the Internet at least once a week, and that by the end of 1998 its content will exceed that of the Library of Congress (Glosserman, 1996). The technology is so stunning that we *reason* by the authority of the technology, a new cousin of reasoning from authority. People need to realize that just because something is on the Internet does not make it true or significant; Internet users are not necessarily superior beings. Goodman (1995) teasingly wrote that Internet users often "discover that the folks in their computerized chat groups have no more insight and wit than the people they talk to at the water cooler" (p. 18). Mendelson (1996) was more caustic: "Until now the Web's main social achievement has been to provide a cure for spare time." Whether the Internet is to be classified as a print medium (thus protected from government regulation) or a broadcast medium (thus subject to government regulation) is a puzzle. Cable television, like newspapers and magazines, has the advantage of a dual source of income: advertising and subscription fees, whereas commercial television has only advertising income. The Internet is moving toward some sort of user fee, and regulations may be forthcoming. Bollinger (1991) asserted: "A major question is whether public regulation of the electronic media should be continued or even extended" (p. 151). Where anonymity is possible, misuse of these astounding facilities increases, and hackers' willful damage and theft has already become notorious. Computer crime bills are being passed in some states, and some nations, like Japan, are devloping defenses against hackers. Traditional cautions become underlined: watch what you say, for you may not be sure who will see your message; document quotes and other borrowed material, and observe copyright laws scrupulously.

Electronic mediums of communication have both democratized human communication and widened the gap between the haves and the have nots. Most people, even in developing countries, now have access to radios (village or neighborhood radios if not personal sets), and in developed countries virtually all people have access to television. (During the last California earthquake, people commented frequently that the destruction of their televisions was a major loss.) A person who is economically disadvantaged and a wealthy individual hear and see the same messages and are part of the same communication interplay. But although millions can receive messages, only the very few—wealthy and powerful people in capitalistic societies, and a few government officials in totalitarian countries—determine what the messages are. Agenda-setting in the media is controlled by a very few, who can, for instance, spend millions to gain media access for political campaigns. Many developing countries complain about , and take actions to exclude, the dominating media fare thrust on them by more developed countries. In Southeast Asia, for example, people think that Western morality as depicted in movies and other media destroys the moral fiber of their society. Singapore is particularly aggresive in keeping out pollitical, religious, and other material deemed offensive (Halderness, 1996). Tracey and Redal (1995), however, documented that this unidirectional cultural imperialism is not as pronounced as has been claimed. But where it does occur, there is a classic clash between two rights, the right of freedom of expression and the right of a community to preserve its historic values.

The printed and electronic mass media, especially television, are our constant companions, whose strong influence needs to be carefully monitored. They are among the very few professionals today who make house calls! We open our doors wide to them. We need to make sure they do not take advantage of us.

ADDITIONAL MEDIUMS

Cutting across many of the above categories is the medium of music. "Clearly," Holmberg (1985, p. 81) has written, "music is a symbol system, which like language, may be analyzed for its effect." It combines sounds, words, visuals, voices, and instruments, and its rhythm, melody, and chords come together in ways that can strongly move an audience. That being so, the ethical dimension needs to be considered. We are familiar with the power of marching music to stir martial attitudes, patriotism, and blind cohesiveness. Naziism surged on the wings of stirring Wagnerian compositions. Hymnology stirs commitment to religious claims and values, and when a happy combination of uplifting lyrics and a beautiful tune occurs, a hymn can be enormously powerful. Country music lends itself to various campaigns, and the guitar blends prose and melody in a highly effective manner. Jazz, with its spontaneity and improvisation, generates a relaxing looseness of body and mind. Social movements have been given impetus, direction, and unity by a particular song: "We Shall Overcome" became an anthem for the civil rights struggle. Music can tip fencesitters to take a stand.

Educational institutions have school songs to express ideals and to strengthen a sense of unity. A few hospitals have creatively brought together interested doctors, nurses, administrators, clerical staff, and medical students to join an informal orchestra to entertain patients and their families. Surely such actions merit a high EQ rating, as does the utilization of music in therapeutic contexts such as helping people with Alzheimer's disease and other disorders. Spooky background music can create a crucial atmosphere for a radio, television or movie murder mystery. Supermarkets and department stores play carefully selected background music as subliminal persuasion designed to encourage customers into making more purchases. Clever advertising jingles on radio and television are integral to the persuasive pitch. Political gatherings are often bathed in music, and we immerse our individual selves in music with our stereos being such a firmly established part of our lives (Lind, 1995). "God Bless America," "America the Beautiful," and our national anthem have had and continue to have powerful roles in our society. "Dixie" has for over a century provided a strong rallying call for Southern regionalism, even though this was not its original intent (Holmberg, 1985).

The field of speech communication engages in rhetorical criticism of music and songs, and generates insightful observations and interpretations about the effects. Some critics claim that music, often grotesquely loud, supplemented by simplistic lyrics, excessively stimulates the emotions, and thus entrenches irrational behavior. Large audiences can be melded into a faceless unity, with independence and thoughtfulness expunged. People have been pushed into violent acts, and have been sustained in their violence by the tune and words of a song. We have been lulled into unthinking complacency with soft melodic strains. Thus, music may soothe or excite, inform or educate, and weaken the operation of the reasoning faculty; hence music's ethical dimension needs to be monitored.

Silence as a medium of communication also arouses ethical concerns. "For everything there is a season, and a time for every purpose under heaven ... a time to keep silence, and a time to speak" (Eccles. 3:1, 7). Our eternal task has been to ascertain the proper times! We also need to reflect on the words of a mid-20th century monk, Thomas Merton (1957): "The world... has forgotten the joys of silence, the peace of solitude which is necessary, to some extent, for the fullness of human living" (p. 143). Silence performs many communicative functions, as I have discussed elsewhere (Jensen, 1973), and we need to know the adverse and positive effects of keeping silent. Silence can warmly bind friends together, but can chillingly separate individuals. Holding our tongue can avoid hurting someone and maintain harmony but also devastate people with the "silent treatment". Silence can communicate scorn and hate as well as communicate kindness and acceptance. Silence can inappropriately hide something that ought to be made known. It can let ignorance or a bully take center stage. Silence may be taken for assent when such was not the intent. Sensitive communicators, then, monitor their silence for any potential hurtfulness or misleading messages it may bring to others.

EXERCISES

1. Be alert to racist language used in blatant or subtle ways around you and the media. Write a paper recording your observations, and place the episodes on the Ethical Quality Scale; use as many ethical guidelines as seem relevant.

2. Be alert to sexist language used in blatant or subtle ways around you and in the media. Write a paper recording your observations, and place the episodes on the Ethical Quality Scale; use as many ethical guidelines as seem relevant.

3. Be aware of the two-valued mind-set as revealed in the media, in public speeches, or in informal communicative contexts that you encounter. Notice the use of figurative language, name-calling, "God" and "Devil" terms, slogans, and so on. Write an essay summarizing your insights.

4. Write a paper in which you discuss the ethical concerns related to the use of humor in its various forms in interpersonal communication, public speaking, or the mass media.

5. Write an essay in which you discuss the potential ethical dimensions related to nonverbal communication. Weave in some personal experiences.

6. How has the use of tape recorders added a new area of ethical concern? Analyze some cases discussed in the media and also some instances that you are aware of from your own experience.

7. Write an essay in which you discuss the various gods that motion pictures worship, and relate these gods to specific instances of ethical concern.

8. Carefully keep a journal of your television watching over a period of a few days, and note all instances in which your ethical sensitivity is disturbed. Indicate the reasons for your evaluation and the ethical guidelines instrumental in bringing you to question the level of ethics in the programming.

9. Write a wide-ranging paper in which you discuss the potential ethical concerns related to the incredible advances in electronic communication. Weave in some specific examples.

10. Write a paper in which you discuss the relevance of ethics in the human communication modes of music or silence.

7

Ethical Issues Revolving Around the Context: Receivers and Situations

In this chapter I discuss a number of ethical issues revolving around the receivers and the situations, which are the broader context in a communicative transaction. In the circular process of communication, we have tended to focus too much on the sender and not enough on the receiver. Here I survey the rights and responsibilities of, and opportunities for, the receiver; ethical concerns stemming from the behaviors and characteristics of receivers; ethical dimensions dealing with the relationships between sender and receiver; and ethical nuances in audience adaptation. A host of situational variables affecting the ethical equation are discussed. The shifting situational variables give the unscrupulous a convenient excuse for avoiding the constraints of principles, and require the conscientious communicator to make difficult decisions in trying to fit guidelines to the specific demands of the context.

RECEIVERS

Rights, Responsibilities, and Opportunities

Rights belong to audiences in communicative events as well as to speakers. As already discussed, in a free society we enjoy freedom of *expression*. But we ignore a receiver's freedom of *im*pression, that is, the freedom not to attend or respond to a given message. This freedom can be thought of as analogous to explosion and implosion . People ought to have the right to refuse a flyer handed in their direction or to enter into a dialogue with an advocate, in a building entrance, in an airport, on the sidewalk, at our front door, or elsewhere. People seated next to us on the bus, subway, or airplane sometimes try to force us to be communicatees. We ought to feel free to ignore the "invitation" tactfully. We ought to be free to absent ourselves from communicative events like a company function, a fraternity or sorority party, or a public lecture (unless there is a compelling reason to be there) without incurring punishments of a material, social, or psychological nature. We ought not to be pressured at the office or in other settings to contribute to political, charitable, or other financial drives against our will. In a totalitarian country, freedom *not* to attend rallies, marches, and other government-organized functions is absent, and free societies ought not to create pressures perhaps less explicit but nonetheless uncomfortable and inhibiting.

We should not feel guilty about not reading the pile of junk mail that fills the mailbox. We should feel free not to respond to a reporter's questions. We ought to feel free not to enter into a conversation with an advertiser who intrudes into our home via telephone. We ought not to feel pressured to respond to tasteless questions, to antisocial requests, to inappropriate advances. We should be free from the aggressive and inquisitive intrusions of others. In many appropriate circumstances we might wish not to respond if it unfairly embarrasses us or others, needlessly prolongs a discussion, shifts the focus from the issue at hand, or merely oversimplifies or misleads. We should feel free to walk away from a communicative event if we desire and if doing so does not injure others. We should have the freedom not to be assaulted by messages from loudspeakers in open or enclosed gatherings or in passing vehicles. We need not be slaves to those who initiate communicative acts. This right of privacy stems from a respect for individuals, and includes a respect for their autonomy.

The freedom not to respond to certain inquiries in a court of law is protected in the Fifth Amendment to the Constitution. This right not to reply to possibly self-incriminating questions is a fundamental legal protection against the potential abuse of power by law enforcement agencies. Although the tortures practiced in earlier times are no longer the common means of obtaining information in many countries, unethical means of obtaining the truth are still practiced. "Taking the Fifth" has in too many instances unfairly implied that a witness hid something, or was guilty of something. Inquiries, legal or nonlegal, can all too often become virtual inquisitions.

In the case of well-known people or those in high office, the media claim that the public has the right to know, for instance, the medical condition of the personages; this claim sets up a classic tension between two *rights*. Tennis player Arthur Ashe had wished to keep his AIDS condition private, but the media thought it should be public knowledge. The publicity caused Ashe deep anquish. Hodges (1994) expressed a traditional journalistic stance: "In reporting on public figures, we should publish private information, even against their will, if their private activity might significantly affect their performance of duties to their publics" (p. 206). Many observers thought that Ashe had been unfairly invaded in this instance. About public officials, Hodges (1994) asserted that journalists "should publish private information even against their will, if their private activity might reasonably have a significant effect on their official performance" (p. 205). Although a public person relinquishes some freedom of self-government, before we go too far in that direction, we need to keep a sense of balance and fairness about the right to and need for privacy. Everyone should have at least a minimal right to a wish not to be a part of a communicative intrusion.

In public speaking situations, audiences should have some important rights. As I have discussed in chapter 1 in the section on key terms, receivers have the right to a significant choice, that is, to a free, informed, and rational choice. When a communicator in the substance or manner of the presentation eliminates or seriously impinges on that right, he or she is highly unethical, especially as at that moment the speaker is the only source of information. The audience has a right to know something about the speaker, and the chairperson of a public speaking event has the obligation to inform the audience, and not to present humorous anecdotes or other irrelevant comments, as all too many chairpersons do. The audience has a right to expect to have its time respected; a speaker who arrives late or who talks far beyond the set termination time is demonstrating a low ethical quality.

But as I discussed in chapter 1 in the section on "rightsabilities" and opportunities, rights and responsibilities are intricately related. Communicatees have an obligation to let communicators know that they are being listened to; otherwise the communicators might be tempted to be less truthful, to do less than their best. Just as speakers must have empathy for their audiences, so audiences must have empathy for the speakers. Listeners should truly listen with an open mind and give respectful, courteous attention, especially when opposing ideas are presented. An open mind does not mean an empty, gullible mind or an unthinking mind that too readily accepts contrary views. Listeners have an obligation to cherish and protect truth as they see it and to nurture their own integrity in the communicative transaction. Realizing that it is highly unethical to *accept* bribes as well as to *give* them, the receivers in any communicative event should beware of bewitching messages or flattery, mental bribes that offer ego satisfaction while snatching away the critical faculties. Receivers have a responsibility to be as prepared as possible to enter into the communicative transaction, and to see as clearly as possible the real intentions of the communicator. Audiences need to analyze and carefully evaluate all the substance that is presented, especially by hemispheric persuaders, and need to exhibit thoughtful and balanced skepticism. Critics have an obligation to apply their well-chosen evaluative criteria with as much precision, care, and thoroughness as possible. They need to become involved in the communicative transaction although not so involved as to lose fairness and objectivity.

Just as communicators should see that beyond rights and responsibilities are opportunities for them to be contributors to a richer life for all involved, so should receivers of messages realize that there are endless opportunities for them to enhance the life of others. For example, when receiving news of a great tragedy or splendid success (or somewhere in between) of a friend or acquaintance, we can seize the opportunity to express comfort or shower praise, to show that we are thinking of them and bonding with them. Such a reaction is not an obligation, but an opportunity. By direct or indirect feedback, audiences have always given public speakers confidence by showing appreciation. Sprinkled throughout this book are examples of situations in which a communicatee can go beyond responsibilty into the land of opportunity. This possibility is one reason why the Ethical Quality (EQ) Scale mind-set that I have been emphasizing is so helpful; It leads us to strive constantly for higher ethical performances, not just to avoid low ethical quality acts.

Behaviors

During or After a Speech.   Listeners who would be as highly ethical as possible need to reflect on specific behaviors during or after a communicative event. During a public speech, for instance, members of the audience ought to avoid making visible or audible distractions which could make the speaker feel ill at ease. They ought also to refrain from distracting conversations with neighbors, which reduce their listening opportunities, and they should discourage those who speak to them during the speech. A presentation should not be judged until it is finished. Listeners should not disengage from the presentation by exhibiting mannerisms readily picked up by the speaker—unless they can argue that the speaker deserves to be tuned out. Interrupting the speaker has varying degrees of ethical quality depending on the context. Some classroom or public lecturers might encourage and appreciate interruptive comments or questions from the audience, but otherwise a listener should refrain from such interjections. Meaningful comments or questions appropriately presented to add something positive to the proceedings would merit a higher ethical quality rating than would comments or questions aimed at unnerving or embarrassing the speaker or at making the questioner more visible and appearing to be important. Hissing, booing, and derisive laughter, except for a brief and reasonable show of disapproval, soon descends to the low end of the EQ Scale. Prolonged and abusive heckling aimed at disrupting the presentation merits little praise. There are cultural variables in this evaluation, of course: In the British House of Commons or at the Speakers' Corner in London's Hyde Park, vigorous audience involvement and even heckling are not considered inappropriate as they would be in the United States (Jensen, 1967).

Speakers might be aided if hecklers are seen by the rest of the audience as being "outsiders" (Beatty & Kruger, 1978), intent on injecting mischief into the proceedings. The speaker needs to honor the heckler's right to free speech and to respect the importance of the free flow of contrary views and yet to defuse the hecklers and retain control of the meeting. This task is difficult both in terms of skill and of high ethical demeanor. Besides coming to the meeting thoroughly prepared to respond fairly and effectively, the speaker should consider the concerns of hecklers, should repeat their questions in case others in the audience could not hear, and respond with as much courtesy, confidence, accuracy and relevance as possible.

Surreptitious Listening. What of surreptitious listening? Telephone calls to the Social Security Administration and other government and private agencies are openly monitored by supervisory personnel to ensure that the caller is getting accurate advice. In early days of telephones, party lines with several parties on one connection resulted in many people listening in as a matter of course, and talkers assumed that others were listening. Today, most people would consider such an intrusion to be highly unethical. In mass media contexts people are grappling with the legal and ethical dimensions of unauthorized receiving of programming via private antennas that intercept cable television without paying the fees.

Forum Period.   Frequently we complain that there is no opportunity for responding to a speaker, no opportunity to be an active participant in a communicative occasion. But often we do not enter into an exchange when invited to do so. For instance, in a designated forum period following a public speech or lecture, often the audience although urged to raise questions or make comments, seldom does so. The entire audience should not or could not ask questions, but reticent and silent receivers are hardly playing a significant role or enhancing the occasion. On the other hand, a member of the audience should not consume disproportionate time by making lengthy comments or asking multiple questions. In short, when we are members of an audience in these contexts, we have an ethical obligation to contribute appropriately. In small group dicussions where receivers are expected to enter into the exchange regularly, there is an even heavier ethical obligation to do so.

Feedback.   An audience likewise has an ethical obligation to give accurate and supportive feedback. Applause of appropriate intensity and duration is a common message of approval. (Some cultures do not, however, enjoy such noisy behavior; only in the late 19th century, for instance, did Japan import that strange U.S. custom.) An example of a memorable audience reaction was following Martin Luther King, Jr.'s August 1963 "I Have a Dream" address in Washington, D.C. His wife, Coretta Scott King, wrote in her memoirs (1969): "As Martin ended, there was the awed silence that is the greatest tribute an orator can be paid. And then a tremendous crash of sound as two hundred and fifty thousand people shouted in ecstatic accord with his words. The feeling that they had of oneness and unity was complete" (p. 240). Hubert Humphrey (1976) later wrote in his autobiography: "If I had to pick one day in public life when I was most encouraged that democracy would work, when my spirit soared on the wings of the American dream of social justice for everyone, it was that day [of King's speech]" (p. 271). In some public addresses, the ultimate nonverbal expression of approval is of course a standing ovation. For people to pretend to like something when they really do not is hardly high on the ethical scale; the pretense deceives the communicator and others in the audience. It is also demeaning to themselves for people to pretend to like something when they do not. In speech classes, it is helpful to encourage students to applaud appropriately their classmates' presentations, for all thus learn the satisfying feeling of such congratulatory feedback associated with the arduous task of preparing and presenting a public speech. Classmates thus can contribute to each other's encouragement.

At the termination of a public presentation, members of the audience have an ethical obligation and opportunity to interact with the speaker and express praise when it is warranted. Effective speakers are often left to themselves after their address, a lonely and deflating situation, as anyone knows who has experienced it. Such an omission on the part of the audience hardly contributes to speakers' well-being and hardly encourages them to make future speeches. A sensitive, highly ethical member of the audience will be among those who make an effort to approach the speaker with some words of thanks and praise. Those in charge of the meeting have the additional ethical obligation to give positive feedback (if warranted) and to meet the speakers' needs by ushering him or her to wherever the person must go after the meeting. Receivers can also be sensitive to letting people know after the event, for instance, by writing a note to the communicators, be they speakers, musicians, or artists, that although they now are gone from the scene they are not forgotten.

Receiver Characteristics

Varying characteristics of receivers can generate special concerns for the communicator who would be highly ethical. Included are such things as the audience's emotional condition, state of health, age, disability, and worthiness.

Intense Emotional Conditions.   Receivers should be considered in times of great emotional stress. Moments of sorrow, such as when selling a casket to a bereaved customer, calming a young child who has just experienced an important disappointment, or informing an ill person of a bleak prognosis, call for a communicator to possess a compassionate demeanor and in no way to take advantage of the receiver. Pharmaceutical companies and health care professionals should not make unsubstantiated claims for medicines and raise false hopes for those who are ill. Likewise, communicatees should not be taken advantage of when in a state of great joy; for instance, wedding dresses are often priced unusually high because the purchasers are euphoric and unlikely to consider cost carefully. People who have experienced moments of great fear , during bombings, hostage takings, rape, or natural disasters such as earthquakes or hurricanes, should be treated with special care and respect by news media and interrogators. Phone operators at 911 or other emergency centers need to deal carefully with the likely emotionally distraught callers, as should health care providers when anxious clients call about personal health problems.

Illness. Communicating with people who have a severe illness, especially people who are terminally ill, calls for highly sensitive and compassionate interaction. As S. Bok (1979) asserted, those professionals who "take care of the sick and the dying have to learn how to speak with them, even about dying" (p. 254). In her book *Lying*, S. Bok included a chapter titled "Lies to the Sick and Dying" and there concluded that "defending lies to patients stand(s) on much shakier ground as a counterweight to the right to be informed than is often thought" (1979, p. 251). She wrote: "Concealment, evasion, withholding of information may at times be necessary. But if someone contemplates lying to a patient or concealing the truth, the burden of proof must.....rest... on those who advocate it" (p. 252). Veatch (1989) expressed the following opinion: "In the case of what to tell the dying patient, a calculation of utility will have to give weight to happiness, anxiety, and hope" (p. 168). Much has been written about communicating with people with aquired immune deficiency syndrome (AIDS), for example, Cameron's 1993 book, *Living With AIDS: Experiencing Ethical Problems*. Not communicating with people who have AIDS is often more cruel than is talking to them awkwardly. Informed consent is a basic right of patients faced with treatment decisions, but when patients are insufficiently knowledgeable, *informed* is used loosely and cannot be equated with *educated* consent. Often patients are not fully aware of the situation, are depressed, confused, and paralyzed by apprehension. For doctors to engage in benevolent deception, even if deemed for the patient's own good, might be an inappropriate act of medical paternalism. In short, communicating with people who are trying to cope with serious health conditions calls for great sensitivity in respecting, and if possible strengthening, their dignity and self-esteem.

Age. The age of the receivers is an important concern. Very young and older people are both potentially vulnerable and hence should command special sensitivity. As a society we are concerned with the high amount of violence and other demeaning portrayals in the media and particularly fear its negative effect on the impressionable and immature minds of young people. Television programmers pride themselves on showing adult fare late at night when children are supposedly less likely to be exposed to it, but much more needs to be done to nurture the young. *Sesame Street* and other such programming seek to be positive forces, teaching youngsters sound values of cooperation, kindness, and respect for diversity. Only in 1990, with the Children's Television Act (CTA) that requires television stations to air some educational programs for children, did Congress recognize children as a special audience; of course, the law is generally ignored. The tobacco industry is accused of concentrating their ads in stores frequented by youth (Hilts, 1995). People often recoil at the practices of some religious groups, such as the Branch Davidians in Waco, Texas, and the Aum Shinrikyo group in Japan, where children's minds are manipulated. Some critics point out that social activists enlisting children to march in protest parades is inappropriate. Others question the practice of religious groups having teenagers publically affirm basic religious beliefs they might not yet understand. To be fair to youth, we need to nurture their rational and emotional capabilities and strengthen their moral fiber to enable them to later make sound decisions. We are not forever young, but some of us remain immature into adult years.

At the other end of the chronological spectrum, older people should be viewed more sensitively and fairly than they often are at present. The population of the planet is growing older, because of medical advances and economic gains. By the year 2007, about 20% of the population of Japan will be over 65 years of age, the oldest population in the world (Church 1993). The United States will not be far behind (Chin, 1993). In our youth-oriented culture, we in the United States segregate older people from the rest of society. Carmichael (1985) asserted what we all probably know, that "our culture has not shown concern for the communication needs of the elderly" (p. 140). In her book, *The Fountain of Age,* Betty Friedan (1993) moved on from her earlier focus on women to call for the empowerment of older people and lamented their absence from, or unfair treatment in, society and the media. She sought to correct the lingering stereotypes that people in their 60s and above are dependent, unattractive, inflexible, inactive, dysfunctional, deteriorating in mind, body, and spirit, and burdensome to family and society. The field of communication should join in presenting more realistic, complete, accurate, and fair images of older people, and should help to celebrate and affirm the positive aspects of aging. Older people rely more heavily on family communicative networks as friendship networks gradually disappear (Patterson, 1995). Unscrupulous con artists peddling questionable investment and other fraudulent schemes, target older people, many of whom may be uninformed and may possess considerable financial resources. The obviously low ethical quality of such communicative acts should not blind us to the numerous less blatant and more subtle practices demeaning older people in our midst.

Hopeful signs are the increasing number of courses, books, convention panels, and periodical articles focusing attention on the communicative needs of older people. Institutional centers such as the Sanders–Brown Center on Aging at the University of Kentucky are helping society facilitate high quality of life for older people, and are trying to assure that they are not marginalized. The United Nations has designated 1999 as the International Year of the Elderly, an act that should help to focus on the problems and opportunities connected with that segment of the population.

Disability.   There are about 500 million people who are disabled in the world. Among the many situations with which they have to cope is that others do not communicate with them or at best interact only perfunctorily and awkwardly. As society makes strides in accommodating people with disabilities, by means of entrance ramps, in addition to stairs, appropriate bathroom facilities, and sports opportunities, we in the field of communication need to make more progress than we have in making sure that these people are included in social interaction and that their self-worth is enhanced.

Unworthiness.   When we deem an audience to be unworthy, for example, hijackers, greedy landlords, con artists, drug addicts, kidnappers, thieves, dangerous national enemies, dictatorial leaders, and bullies of all sorts, we say they do not *deserve* the truth. As familiar instances, when a Nazi soldier knocks on a door and asks whether the inhabitants are harboring any Jews, saving the latters' lives takes precedence over truth-telling at that moment. Lying does not take place in a vacuum; numerous values are involved, and it is a question of which value takes precedence in a particular context.

Diversity.   The United States is sharing in the dynamic phenomenon of a diverse population on this planet; people are forced or spurred to move by wars, intranational ethnic and tribal killings, religious persecutions, and economic hardships. The mixture of racial, ethnic, and religious heritages presents a major challenge to the quality of human communication. Highly ethical communicators should be sensitive to the responsibilities and opportunities that need to be met when interacting with a diverse audience. We should go beyond *tolerating* to *celebrating* diversity. We need to remember that someone *different* is not *inferior*, and that we do not have to reach complete agreement with the *other*. We should seek to develop a mature mind-set enabling us to live confidently and comfortably with those outside our self-defined group. As Barbara Jordan (1993), wrote: "We are one, we Americans, and we must reject any intruder who seeks to divide us by race, gender, or class. We must honor cultural diversity" (p. 3). We are in this world as sojourners, once strangers to everyone; gradually we come to know, love, and trust members of our family and others close to us. This circle of respect must continually widen until we can embrace all the diverse peoples on this tiny globe.

To increase respect for diversity we can intentionally expose ourselves to varying *others*, and sustain that exposure. We can take the initiative to travel to other countries or to enter into different ethnic and racial population pockets in the United States, to experience how it feels to be in a minority. We can *travel* by reading novels, biographies, memoirs, and histories drawn from or about other cultural groups. The mind must travel, not necessarily the body. We can individualize our experiences with *others*, by making at least one friend or acquaintance. We can seek out common interests and concerns. A helpful technique is to list some things about the *others* which you like, and some things about your group which you do not. We usually reverse these procedures, but if members of different religious affiliations, for example, would look for positive aspects in other religious frameworks and for weaknesses in their own, they might reach some startling insights.

Relationships Between Receiver and Sender

Power Differential.   A *power differential* often exists between senders and receivers in the communicative act. Such power differences, usually arising from cultural, social, political, or economic factors, often separate and isolate the participants, and exploit the vulnerable. When the sender of messages holds considerably more power than the receiver in a given context, the highly ethical communicator must be careful not to use that advantage to the detriment of the audience. Parents often hold much power in relation to their children, as do professionals to their clients, teachers to their students, employers to their employees, and sometimes salespeople to their customers. The power-full in these contexts have the opportunity not to misuse their power and instead to demonstrate highly ethical communication contributing to the enhancement of the power-less. Such sensitivity usually works not only to the receivers' advantage, but also to the senders' enhancement and can often be a win-win situation. It is not a case of giving up power, but of sharing power. The greater the power possessed, the greater the responsibility to use it appropriately, and the greater the opportunity to enrich the lives of others. The more powerful usually are initiators of communicative transactions; for example, they extend greetings, introduce self and others, and in so doing set the agenda, especially in interpersonal and small group settings. Thus there is a need to use that initiator's role responsibly. When parents, teachers, and employers as part of their functions find it necessary to correct children, students, or employees, such "correction" can surely be communicated with courtesy and humaneness, with concern for the well-being and growth of the receivers.

Sometimes the power differential is such that the receivers are a virtual captive audience; in such contexts, the sender needs to be particularly sensitive. For instance, students in the classroom ought not to be subjected to the irrelevant political, social, or religious views of the instructor. Primary and secondary school pupils are in the audience by law; when students in higher education choose a class, they also become a captive audience, paying tuition and coming with expectations to learn about a subject, not to be confronted with the instructor's biases. Children, employees, and clients are also in many instances captive audiences of parents, employers, and professionals.

In some instances a power differential results when one party is an outsider in a communication transaction. For instance, newly arrived people, such as immigrants, first year college students, foreign students on a college campus, strangers in a new city, travelers in a foreign land, or new members of a small group invariably lack information about their new surroundings and are to some degree disoriented. Hence they are vulnerable in any communication transaction with the established in-siders, and the latter should thus be particularly sensitive in their interactions with the newcomers.

Two final observations should be made about power differential. One is that we live in an age witnessing a rapid shift from spectator to participant living. That is, women, people with low incomes, various ethnic and racial groups, people who are disabled—power-less people in the status quo—refuse to play only the role of supporters, of cheerers in the stands, who watch the privileged few perform and profit. All want their chance to be center stage. Second, we need to note that there is a problem not only for those who wield power but for those who are questing for power. The latter must be sensitive to the fact that low ethical quality questing can tarnish the prize.

Trust. One of the most important dimensions in the relationship between receivers and senders in any communication context, interpersonal, small group, organizational, public speaking, intercultural, or mass, is the degree of trust between them. Confucius asserted: "I do not see what use a man can be put to, whose word cannot be trusted" (Confucius, 1938, II:22). In Taoism and other Chinese philosophies (Lu, 1994), trust was also emphasized. Humans are social beings, and the cement of society, organizations, families, and interpersonal networks is trust. In an organizational context, for example, middle-range managers need to trust their supervisor to acknowledge mistakes or report other negative news; otherwise the mistakes are not corrected and the bad news is not counteracted. Those in a dominant position need to honor a subordinate's confession or criticism and receive bad news maturely, to enable the situations to be improved. But trust must be thoughtfully granted and developed gradually and carefully. It must be reciprocal and earned. It is delicate yet strong, like a thread that holds two entities together. The dialogical spirit, discussed in chapter 2, depends on trust. When people cannot trust the messenger, they cannot trust the message, a fact constantly illustrated in courtroom discourse where lawyers strive to discredit witnesses. As Bonhoeffer (1972) wrote during his imprisonment in Germany during World War II, "Trust will always be one of the greatest, rarest, and happiest blessings of our life in community... .Without trust, life is impoverished" (pp. 12, 29). Once broken, trust is extremely difficult to rebuild. Trust is a gamble, a risk that those who have suffered from misplaced trust know to their sorrow. Trust allows us to act with assurance, but there is no guarantee that the trust will be honored. Pellegrino (1991) crystallized the benefits and potential dangers of trust: "Trust is ineradicable in human relationships. Without it, we could not live in society or attain even the rudiments of a fulfilling life. Without trust, we could not anticipate the future and we would therefore be paralyzed into inaction. Yet to trust and entrust is to become vulnerable and dependent on the good will and motivations of those we trust" (p. 69). According to a common witicism, the trouble with the world is that half of the people do not know, and the other half does but nobody trusts them.

We are appropriately concerned about those who place blind trust in a leader, group, or organization that dehumanizes and eventually tears the fabric of society. This danger is present, for instance, in groupthink, where individuals place so much trust in and reliance on a group that individual critical thinking is ignored. Individuals irrationally accept conclusions they would not adopt without the group's dynamic. The group becomes so enamored with its wisdom, morality, invulnerability, power, and unanimity that it trusts itself to do the right thing without critical scrutiny of the decision-making process or of the decision. Unwarranted optimism and complacency are created, assumptions, evidence, and claims go unquestioned, and group loyalty becomes blind conformity. Adversaries are stereotyped as lacking in wisdom, power, and morality; opponents become enemies, and any action against them, however questionable, is justified. These attitudes have been confirmed in books by Robert McNamara (1995) and Colin Powell (1995) as operating at the highest levels in decision making about the Vietnam war, as many critics of that war had long claimed. Ethically sensitive receivers in a group context need to apply rigorously a critical analysis of all that is said by other group members and not let blind trust take over the proceedings.

Friendship and Prejudice.   A number of other communication contexts provoke ethical problems when the receivers are too friendly with, or too prejudiced against, the communicator. There is a danger when reporters become too friendly with public officials or other public figures whom a reporter interviews to secure information. Some sports reporters are criticized for becoming too chummy with famous athletes and coaches and producing laudatory writeups. The objectivity of movie and drama critics likewise can suffer when they become too friendly with the artists and performers about whom they write. As one experienced journalist put it, "[F]riendship with news sources make(s) it difficult to write critically" (Krauss, 1977, p. 350). Teachers would be hard pressed to evaluate objectively the exams of their own children if the latter were their students. When animosity or prejudice is present, objectivity is also likely to be questionable. Thus, the relationship between receivers and senders can raise a number of ethical concerns. The chemistry between the two might sometimes be difficult to ascertain, define and measure, but we must be sensitive to it.

Audience Adaptation

A central axiom of effective communication is that communicators must adapt their messages to their audiences by trying to meet the intellectual level, the desires, the mind-sets of the receivers. Not to reach an audience is a mark of failure. But there is a danger that the goal of effectiveness submerges the ethical dimension, and some communicators might justify highly questionable methods in the name of the need to adapt.

Inappropriate emotional appeals, weak substance, sloganizing, and catchy terms and phrases might dominate. Sometimes the communicator needs to say what alienates the audience—to say what needs to be said, to trouble them rather than to make them feel good. The voice of the prophet needs to afflict the comfortable as well as to comfort the afflicted. Communicators may hide their real position in order to win audience approval. Persons who would be highly ethical must somehow be true to their beliefs as they seek to adapt to receivers. Achieving that balance is admittedly not always easy.

The importance of audience adaptation is highlighted in presenting cases before a jury in a court of law. It is commonly asserted and believed that cases are won or lost in the process of jury selection; thus much care is given to that unique process where the individuals of an audience are chosen by the communicators. The lawyers then need to adapt carefully to that audience. Common folklore depicts lawyers as pandering to the jury, demonstrating rather low ethical quality in their presentations.

When communicators know that multiple audiences are taking in their messages, they might too readily justify the construction of an ambiguous and unclear message. Government leaders or candidates for public office, realizing that friends and foes, and people of varying backgrounds will compose their audiences, can convince themselves that innocuous statements are appropriate.

Some audiences cannot give sustained attention to a message, and in such situations communicators again too easily justify the use of exaggerations, emotionally loaded terms, or other eye- and ear-catching phrases, pictures, or sound bites. Billboard advertising is aimed at a moving audience, and advertising of most kinds, especially in the media, encounters receivers who are moving mentally if not physically. In these and similar contexts, communicators justify their dubious messages to capture attention.

SITUATIONAL VARIABLES

Ethical sensitivity in communicative acts can be affected by a host of variables, such as the degree of danger, the importance of the outcome, the need for confidentiality and secrecy, the call for intentional ambiguity, political discourse contexts, locations, time, being an agent for a special "cause," and intercultural contexts.

Danger

In order to cope with a situation involving great danger, communicators might approach truth-telling in a way not employed in a less dangerous context. Responding to hijackers, kidnappers, or other dangerous individuals, people might understandably be less than candid, truthful, and open to save their own lives or those of others. The desire to live understandably takes precedence over truth-telling at that moment. Government officials or military commanders in charge of national defense might mislead audiences with their statements or withhold information to make life more secure for those very people, to unify the country, to give impetus to a military action, and to negotiate with a foreign adversary. As Winston Churchill put it, "In wartime truth is so precious that it must be shielded by a bodyguard of lies." During the Persian Gulf War in 1991, the Allies listed specific topics on which the press was not to report. When the Cambodian Communists were massacring large numbers of people, many professionals had to lie about their educated backgrounds lest they be piled up with the massacred. Prisoners of war have to cope with the dilemma of talking to save their lives, yet not revealing information that endangers the lives of their comrades. There are examples, of course, of prisoners of war refusing to answer their interrogators even when it meant a martyr's death, but that is hardly the norm. Gandhi once spoke to a person who said to him, to justify a questionable action the person had taken, "I had to save my own life, didn' t I?" Gandhi responded, "Did you?" ,to indicate that individual integrity and other values may be more important. Few of us are Gandhis or are in his unique position to wield extraordinary moral and political power. We break civil, religious, and cultural laws and mores when the situation seems to demand it; for example, we exceed the speed limit when rushing a loved one to the hospital, one may feel compelled to heal someone on the sabbath, or if cultural mores forbid men from touching women, a man would nevertheless rescue a drowning woman. The 1995 Beijing United Nations Conference on Women highlighted the tension between the concepts of universal human rights and regional cultural and religious values. Which takes precedence, under what circumstances? Parents might tell their children to lie to a stranger who telphones and tell him or her that there is an adult in the house. Police might think it necessary to withhold information or give disinformation to apprehend drug dealers or other wrongdoers. A law enforcement officer in a small town intentionally deceived reporters by saying that there were no known suspects in a murder case, when indeed there was a suspect. The officer wanted the reporters to leave town because their presence intimidated the local people, and stopped them from coming to the police with information to aid the investigation. The ends of calming community fears, apprehending the murderer, and serving justice might indeed elevate the ethical quality of the officer's communicative decision, but not necessarily to the top of the EQ Scale.

Professional guidelines are occasionally bent when a higher ethical concern is operating. Doctors might decide to lie to a patient about his or her condition. Editors of two U.S. newspapers, the *New York Times* and the *Washington Post*, agreed to print a lengthy manifesto by a terrorist who said he would cease his violent acts if they published his writings. To acquiesce meant putting public safety over the profession's axiom of never letting outside sources dictate the newspapers' content. Such an exception does not of course negate the principle, but might in the long run strengthen it. (As this passage is being written, the suspected Unabomber has just been apprehended.)

High Stakes

Many communicative contexts do not involve life or death dangers but nevertheless have extremely high stakes that create ethical concerns. Business leaders can be faced with impending financial crises, and public officials or professional people might have to cope with impending disasters in their realms of operation. The desire to continue to live as an institution as well as an individual understandably evokes sympathy for their plight but also shows others the mettle of their character. When a person continues to seek employment after many disappointments, honesty can be severely tested during the interview. The high stakes of courtship, the significant enterprise of choosing a mate for life (at least in most cases), challenges the participants to be honest with each other. Concern for others should guide people's statements and actions in their desire to win the prize. Many would not give a low ethical quality rating to a married woman who took off her wedding ring when applying for a desperately needed job at a company that discriminated against married women.

Confidentiality

The honoring or breaching of confidentiality is often a difficult balancing act. Executive sessions in business, government, and education, sometimes exclude the public to protect freedom of expression, to ensure a full airing of the issues, to protect innocent people in or out of the group. In university departments, full professors meet to discuss the strengths and weaknesses of assistant and associate professors to determine tenure, promotions, and merit salary increases. If such discussions of weaknesses were made public, the candidates might be deeply hurt, and the fabric of the group would be weakened. In the election of a new pope, the College of Cardinals of the Roman Catholic Church meets in secret to make its choice. The deliberations in choosing winners of Nobel prizes are supposed to remain secret for 50 years, and British Cabinet sessions are supposed to be kept secret for 25 years. Some members of the British Cabinet of the U. S. Congress have published diaries that many feel jeopardize the obligation of confidentiality, and injustice to named individuals and to the system of governance itself by making current or future lawmakers hesitate to speak their minds, to the detriment of democracy. Doctors have to keep confidential their patients' medical information. People with AIDS or with partners who have AIDS agonize over to whom they can reveal this information and with whom they can comfortably discuss it. They or people with other medical disorders might keep that information from their employers or fellow employees in order not to be shunned or even lose their job.

Secrecy

Withholding information—secrecy—is sometimes rated lower on the EQ Scale than at other times. Governments might keep secret serious health problems of presidents or other high officials, in order not to unnerve the populace. Intimate friends might keep their shared secrets to themselves, and even invent codes when being overheard by third parties. But the burden of justifiying secrecy rests on the communicators, and although a situation might require modifying communicative acts, it does not relieve people of the agony of the decision making and of living with the consequences.

Secrecy is often positive. Surprise events, marking and celebrating birthdays, housewarmings, job changes, retirements, farewells, or special accomplishments, are pleasant experiences in human interaction. To keep such parties secret from the honored guest heightens the drama, deepens the pleasure, and brings a focus and a crescendo to the occasion. With such a noble purpose a high ethical quality rating would be appropriate. Inventors, authors, and other creative people keep secret their creations until they wish them to be publicly known. Storytellers do not prematurely reveal a narrative's ending. Secrecy and deceptive twists of plot are the very stuff of fiction, but these devices are not equally appropriate for nonfiction narratives of life. Nevertheless, there are indeed occasions in which "fun" depends on keeping things secret from others.

Intentional Ambiguity

A number of contexts cry out for justification of intentional ambiguity. Diplomats engage in it to keep potentially dangerous foes and strong competitors from fully understanding the true position of the diplomat's own nation. Politicians might be intentionally vague on a controversial subject so that voters do not turn against them because of that single issue and jeopardize other equally important issues. Negotiators in behalf of labor, management, home sellers, and other groups, justify ambiguity to serve their clients' interests. Lawyers employ purposively vague terminology, and advertisers make tantalizing but fuzzy claims for their products. Teachers might make lectures and comments purposely unclear so that students must work diligently to provide their own clarity and understanding. Kierkegaard, the late 19th century Danish philosopher and theologian, purposefully presented confusing material so that his students would have to think through their positions for themselves. This, he thought, was the best way to awaken people from their cozy status quo religious and philosophical views (Anderson, 1963). Parents at times warn their misbehaving children "You' ll be sorry", and leave the penalty unclear. These communicators all claim to have good reasons for their messages, and are convinced that their motives are for the best. The burden of proof rests on them.

Political Discourse

Some contexts related to political discourse may permit communicative acts considered of low ethical quality in other situations. The electorate implicitly understands that campaigners' oratory is exaggerated and emotional; hence the ethical quality is not so low as it would be for an officeholder whom the public expects to communicate carefully, thoughtfully, and rationally. In political caucus sessions where all participants share a common view, their strong and frank language is appropriate among friendly peers and hence would not be rated so low in ethical quality as it might be if openly expressed in public. Social protest oratory, often laced with emotion, slogans, and intemperateness and usually claimed to be motivated by righteous indignation, might rate higher in ethical quality than would other public discourse that has those same characteristics.

Location

Communication in certain places might rate lower on the EQ Scale than when occurring in other locations. Whether a shopping center is a public area in which speech can be freely expressed is under debate. So far the Supreme Court and most state courts have held that shopping centers are not public forums for free speech. California is one state that considers shopping centers to be public forums, and owners or renters of shops in shopping areas claim that their property rights are being violated. Since ancient times, the marketplace, or the public square, which modern shopping malls recall, were common locations for religious and political discourse, but critics assert that this analogy does not hold true. Open areas on college and university campuses are often used for public discourse, usually with no major problem except when loudspeakers disturb nearby classrooms (and hence the freedom of speech therein). Political speaking in places of worship in most Christian churches in the United States is held to be an inappropriate mixture of church and state, whereas in Muslim mosques the political and religious are fundamentally intertwined so such discourse would be expected. Picketing, shouting, and similar behavior near homes of political officials and other public figures has to conform to local regulations.

Time

Ethical quandaries in communication are often caused by the time factor. Deadlines facing newspaper reporters and editors can push them to write and select for publication unverified material. Lingering on ethical concerns would be considered a luxury impeding the dash toward publication. Students trying to complete a term paper on time might be tempted to falsify documentation or plagiarize material. They "don' t want to," but the time pressure is so great that their ethical standards are weakened. Time should not be an excuse for shoddiness or for low ethical quality discourse. Quoting someone out of historical context can be an act of low ethical quality; for good reasons people may hold views today that are different from their earlier, possibly less mature, views. Also, what is considered inappropriate at one time is accepted at another. Baseball fans might remember that years ago a pitcher's curve ball was deemed unfair and deceptive, but today is a highly honored pitch. In

international diplomacy, today's friends can become tomorrow's enemies, and vice versa; to cite a public official's comments about a nation
out of temporal context can be unfair to that person and misleading to
the public.

Agent of a "Cause"

Situations in which communicators feel they are the agents of a cause
sometimes stimulate discourse of low ethical quality. In some religions
and cults members are permitted to lie to protect and further the faith.
Some political orientations encourage adherents to lie to entrench and
advance the party. Here again the issue of the interrelationship between
ends and means prompts me to assert that any cause that needs or
welcomes such low ethical quality discourse to preserve itself probably
rests on questionable foundations.

Intercultural Communication

As noted in Chapters 2 and 6, intercultural communication contexts
challenge us to be sensitive to important variations. Openness, frankness, and truth-telling are more honored in some cultures than they are
in others where a concern for harmony and a reticence to hurt other's
feelings or cause them to lose face are more highly valued. Expressing
disagreement in U.S. politics and classrooms is encouraged; in many
countries it is considered highly inappropriate. We need to respect
different cultures' varying attitudes toward time (Jaffe, 1995). Many
cultures accept and respect class differences, age differentials, and ances-
tral linkages, whereas in the United States and elsewhere these distinc-
tions are blurred to achieve a more egalitarian society. In many Western
nations courtship and the freedom to choose a mate in marriage are
encouraged, whereas many Asian cultures favor arranged marriages.
Western "decadence" in sexual, religious, political, and other areas is
sharply criticized by countries who contend that the supremacy of mass
media in the industrialized world produces a cultural imperialism that
spreads alien values and floods the world with slanted information about
national and world affairs. Theses countries charge that there is no free
flow of information when a few countries have all the facilities for mass
communication and others have very little; the flow is unidirectional.
Such contoversies can affect the fabric of a society and bring further
charges of unfair and unethical communication interchange. As a
counter-assertion, however, some societal fabrics perhaps need to be

torn, to be modified, to be improved in the process. For example, when apartheid was in force in South Africa international media messages challenging the political framework helped to bring about a shredding of that fabric. Although local advocates of apartheid criticized outside cultural interference, others within and outside the country saw it as a way to enforce new attitudes that respected all races and all people.

Some cultures do not have a tradition of press impartiality (Halvorsen, 1992), so it is not considered to be of low ethical quality to demonstrate strong partisan views. In the United States and other nations, nepotism is a serious negative, but in some cultures nepotism is a positive and appropriate way to help family and extended family when a person is in a position to do so. In U.S. culture, giving bribes is frowned on, but in countries where government salaries are low, extra money is accepted and expected to be given to someone who renders a service, much as we consider tipping a person for a service as appropriate. In some cultures it is disrespectful not to show emotion by, for example, wailing and crying at a funeral, whereas in other cultures keeping a dignified silence is respectful. All societies think that their mores and morals are correct and superior to others; changes, when they occur, are gradual and usually reluctant. Only when sufficient trust is built up, can people hope to alter the ways of others.

SITUATION ETHICS

The specific concerns and demands of a communicative situation are sometimes so compelling that the ethical quality of the discourse should be judged by that situation. In the last three decades situation ethics has come to be viewed as an appropriate source of ethical standards. I think it more appropriate, however, to view situation ethics not as a source but as a modifier of communicative behavior; still deeper levels of oughtness are operating but are being adjusted to cope with the particular context. In 1966 Joseph Fletcher's book *Situation Ethics: The New Morality* appeared, followed by Harvey Cox's collection of essays, *The Situation Ethics Debate* (1968) both published by Westminster Press. These books crystallized the idea and publicized the label *situation ethics*. Fletcher (1966) clarified his approach in this manner:

> The situationist enters into every decision-making situation fully armed with the ethical maxims of his community and its heritage, and he treats them with respect as illuminators of his problems. Just the same he is

prepared in any situation to compromise them or set them aside in the situation if love seems better served by doing so. . . . The situationist follows a moral law or violates it according to love's need . . . Only the commandment to love is categorically good. (p. 26)

Fletcher held that "for the situationist what makes the lie right is its loving purpose" (p. 65). Drawing heavily on the New Testament emphasis on love, Fletcher claimed that the object is to do the "loving" thing, not necessarily the "right" thing (although, the former can become the latter). People are more important than principles, he would maintain. The variables of a situation include the purpose, motivation, and function of the communicator, the degree of urgency and danger involved, the high stakes in the transaction, the expectations, goals, characteristics, sophistication, and values of the audience, the means of communication employed, the worthiness of the ends, and the likely immediate and long range consequences.

Nilsen (1974) wrote: "The adaptation of principle to circumstances is not the abrogation of principle, but its application so that the greater good is served in the long run" (p. 35). When we find ourselves bending our commitment to a cherished principle, we ought to do so with thoughtfulness and soul-searching, not with flippancy or crass opportunism. Not obeying a particular principle can mean obeying a higher guide; cult members might reveal a group's secrets for the welfare of the larger society and the furtherance of reason. A Hebrew proverb (Harris, 1901) emphasizes such a situation: "Hold no man responsible for his utterances in times of grief" (p. 336).

Fletcher's (1966) exposition on situation ethics, specifically his use of metaphors, created the idea that principles other than love are excluded from operating. He wrote of the necessity "to cut loose from" rules and laws, of "moving over from" law to love, "to set aside", "to throw aside" rules and prescriptions. These phrases suggest that only one value operates. I prefer to emphasize that in any given situation multiple principles continue to operate but in shifting degrees of priority in relation to each other. For example, suppose a father and his young child are suddenly confronted on the sidewalk by a snarling dog. The father is strongly committed to the values of protecting his child's well-being, being kind to animals, and miscellaneous other potentially relevant beliefs. If the father perceives that his child's welfare is in danger, he, with the "loving purpose" of a situationist, might threaten, kick, injure, or even kill the dog. At that moment, in that situation, one value (the child's welfare) takes precedence. But the degree of the father's commitment to the other values plays a part in defining the situation (is the dog a serious threat?) and in deciding the nature, severity, and duration of the action taken (e.g., yell at the dog, hit him gently with a stick, hit him forcefully, once or many times). The blending, the consubstantial operating of many values, determines whether the father repeats the act in a future similar situation or urges others to duplicate his actions.

In replying to his critics, Fletcher (1968) insisted that "situationism" was in between "legalism" and "extemporism" and thus put it in the rhetorically secure middle-ground position, doing battle with the two extremes of blind obedience to rules and irresponsible opportunism. Situationalism attempts to mediate "between unprincipled behavior on the one hand and overprincipled conscience on the other" (p. 264).

Ramsey (1978) provided a guide for grappling with the ethical demands of particular situations: "In ethics, an exception ought not to be assumed to weaken a rule of practice, nor should exceptions add up to the revision of the rule" (p. 165).

EXERCISES

1. Write an essay in which you discuss in general terms the rightsabilities and opportunities of receivers of communicative messages. Give examples from your own experiences. Apply specific ethical guidelines in your analysis.

2. From your own experiences and from your reading, discuss ethical concerns about communicating with those who are in intense emotional conditions, both sad and joyous. Include people with terminal illnesses.

3. If you had the power and opportunity to create television programs for children, what would you do to produce a highly ethical fare? How would your ideas contrast with existing programming?

4. Write a paper in which you discuss the ethical aspects of communicative contexts in which power differential between sender and receiver plays a considerable role. How would you suggest that such situations be made more ethical?

5. Write an essay on the importance of trust in various communicative contexts, and weave in some personal examples from your experience.

6. Read about how during the Persian Gulf War or Vietnam conflicts the news the populace received was restricted, even deceptive, in the interest of national security during a time of great danger. Evaluate the ethics of those wartime communications.

7. During the heightened atmosphere of political campaigns, we often expect, and excuse, strong language and emotionalism that we would not condone in calmer situations. As long as audiences expect such rhetoric, how serious is the ethical lapse in such contexts? Include some specific examples.

8. Is it ethical for political extremists to demonstrate near the homes of adversaries and for pro-life advocates to demonstrate near the homes of doctors? In other words, are there private locations that should be protected from such intimidating discourse?

9. Write a paper in which you discuss the ethics of communication in an intercultural situation. Give examples from your reading or your own experiences.

10. Write an essay in which you attack or defend *situation ethics*.

8

Conclusion

As we approach the 21st century, numerous ethical issues are bubbling to the surface in all areas of society—politics, medicine, law, religion, science and technology, academia, business, sports, entertainment, and the mass media. Newspaper and magazine articles, popular and scholarly books, and professional treatises are addressing these ethical concerns. Scores of conferences and seminars enable interested people to interact face to face. Ethics centers have come into being and are increasingly active. Educational institutions, , from elementary level through graduate and professional schools, are including ethics and values in their offerings and activities. In colleges and universities, new courses in applied ethics are being introduced in various departments.

Speech communication and mass communication departments are among those seeking to sharpen the ethical maturity of their students. In addition to the creation of new courses in ethics, established courses are making room for a section on ethics. Scholarly conferences on the international, national, regional, and state levels are including a growing number of papers and panels on ethics, and scholarly journals are analyzing the ethical dimensions of human communication. But this healthy growth is far from even, and I hope that this book provides impetus to hasten toward a mature treatment of ethics.

I have defined ethics as the "moral responsibility to choose intentionally and voluntarily oughtness in values like rightness, goodness, truthfulness, justice, and virtue, which may, in a communicative transaction, significantly affect ourselves and others." The key terms embedded in that definition have been kept in mind throughout the book and should be assimilated by the readers.

Throughout the book I have emphasized the *degree* of ethical quality rather than a two-valued polarized mind-set. Making ethical judgments on a 7-point Likert-type scale enables us to be more precise and flexible, sensitively attuned to the variables of each situation. It enables us to think more explicitly of positive, laudable instances of ethically commendable communication as well as those communicative acts that are

178

low on the Ethical Quality Scale. Using the EQ Scale stimulates us to look for opportunities to bring greater richness to the communicative landscape.

Throughout I have emphasized the intimate interrelationship of rights and responsibilities, a connection so intricate that I have suggested a new single term, *rightsabilities*. Even if the term is awkward, I hope that the mind-set will be firmly established and that we will act accordingly.

A number of major objectives have undergirded this book: to deepen and broaden our command of many relevant sources for ethical standards that enlarge our reservoir from which to draw far into the future; to sharpen ethical sensitivity and to enable ourselves to be aware of ethical issues previously not perceived; to develop a set of readily available ethical guidelines to apply when facing ethical dilemmas; to strengthen the linkage between ethics and reasoning, so that moral reasoning is more firmly implanted. Further objectives include gaining insight into the presence and power of metaphorical terminology employed in the ethical domain; gaining an improved insight into ourselves, our values and habits of mind, our need for improvement, and our need to experience the healthy pleasure of building an inner integrity capable of standing up to external scrutiny; understanding, and appreciating those who differ from us; preventing low ethical quality communication from occurring; seeing not only negative episodes but also the positive examples of high ethical quality communication all around us.

Drawbacks in the teaching of ethics at colleges and universities seem outweighed by the potential advantages. The cost of not attending to ethics is simply too high.

The sources for standards of ethics are indeed numerous, and we ought to widen our horizons as to the possible guides available. Millions of people on this planet are guided by religious admonitions with ancient roots; Jews, Christians, and Muslims have a common monotheistic heritage. They trace their origins to Abraham and Jehovah, God, and Allah, and claim that the Bible and the Koran are uniquely inspired scriptures. Hinduism, Buddhism, Taoism, and Confucianism have given ethical guidance for many centuries. Despite the need to sift the abundant chaff from the wheat, ancient writings have much to tell us about communication ethics: warnings against untruthfulness, slander, blasphemy, insincere flattery, vain speech, and gossiping; emphasis on the importance of trustworthiness and on the need to use the gift of communication to edify those around us.

Personal role models, contemporary and historical, help us grapple with ethical dilemmas. The groups to which we belong—family, place of employment, social clubs, academic units, civic affiliations—also exert a strong influence on ethical decision making. Formal codes often grow out of professional networks, which carry potential sanctions against low ethical behavior.

The political, social and cultural values of our society serve as a moral compass. In our democratic context we honor the dignity and intrinsic worth of the individual, and value egalitarianism and freedom of expression and tolerance for all. Societies eventually find it necessary to construct and enforce laws in order to function successfully, and these become an elementary guideline for ethical behavior.

On a more philosophical level, consequentialism serves as a crucial ethical guideline. Here our concern is focused on the effects of communicative acts on immediate and long-range audiences and also on ourselves and by extension on those with whom we associate regularly. Consequentialism stresses the utilitarian goal of the greatest good for the greatest number with the least possible harm to those not benefiting, and is thus result oriented. Its philsophical cousin, nonconsequentialism, is rule oriented and stresses the obligation to live up to an ideal, or principle, regardless of the consequences. In this philosophy rules are followed because they are right and should not be modified by circumstances.

Another ethical guideline focuses on the enhancement of human nature, and emphasizes nurturing the unique qualities of human nature, such as rationality, and communicative ability, and the enrichment of values such as freedom. To dehumanize another person or group is an act low on the EQ Scale. Closely related is the dialogical ethical guideline. Drawing on some of the previous guidelines, the dialogical spirit emphasizes that all communicatees should be respected as humans, not treated as things to be manipulated. It stresses openness, spontaneity, honesty, mutual equality, empathy, and supportiveness and encourages dialogic interchange rather than a monologue.

A final ethical guideline is the Golden Rule. Rooted in ancient Western and Easten religious beliefs, its simplicity has made it a helpful guide, emphasizing that humans need to reverse roles with others, to place themselves imaginatively and empathically into the place of others, considering how a similar reciprocal act would be appreciated.

A number of ethical issues revolving around the communicator have been discussed in this book. Freedom of expression in democratic societies is considered necessary for personal self-fulfillment and for a safer, richer society. To arrive at the closest possible approximation of truth and to develop the best possible mechanisms for societal living, democracies need and cherish freedom of speech for all. That free speech must be used responsibly is a corollary not so often subscribed to, and here is a main battlefield for those of us who are committed to the highest possible ethical communication. We need to realize that multiple purposes and motives often are operating in most of our communicative acts, and we have an obligation to see theses motives clearly and to prioritize them. Conflicts of interests should haunt sensitive communicators, especially professionals like news reporters, and need to be dealt with openly and responsibly.

When playing the role of a gatetender in a communication context, we need to be sensitive to the ethical considerations involved. The manipulation of the ethos factor in such a way as to deceive the audience, that is, to lead them to confer a higher credibility than is deserved, is something a highly ethical communicator would shun. The higher a person's ethos stands with a particular audience, the greater the responsibility not to misuse it. We assume in a democracy that the larger the number of voices heard, the more likely a healthy society will result; thus many observers are deeply troubled when in the mass communication arena mergers place ownership and power in the hands of a very few. We ought not overlook the instances in which low ethical communication results from not communicating, from sins of omission. Through such means we might do a significant injustice to the neglected communicatee, especially those who are lonely, ill, or otherwise vulnerable. We also may be harming ourselves and society.

Ethical issues in contexts centering on the gathering and processing of material were discussed at some length. Plagiarism is universally condemned; to pass off in an oral or written message another's material as if it were one's own damages the integrity of academic institutions and the stability and health of society.

The job description of journalists calls for vigorous and effective pursuit of information. A host of ethical issues become intertwined with their efforts and should be handled conscientiously. Journalists seek to give confidentiality to many sources and sometimes obtain data under false pretenses or other secret means. They are tempted by perks from people or groups in society about whom they will be writing and are enticed by public relations handouts to have their work done for them. When they interview people, respect for the interviewee should be a major concern. Accuracy, fairness, objectivity, and reasonable completeness need to be constant guides in securing as well as in reporting data.

Legislative bodies at all levels of government need to be guided by high ethical standards in their pursuit of relevant information needed to enact laws, if society is to be wisely and fairly governed. Academic researchers likewise need to be firmly committed to ethical guidelines as they carry out their mission of discovering and publicizing information about people, society, and the natural world. Whether securing data in controlled experiments or in natural settings, scholars must employ high ethical standards. Selecting and handling subjects in an experimental enterprise demands ethical commitment, and in cross-cultural projects the researcher needs special empathy as well as skill. Being fair with colleagues and research assistants goes without saying.

Various government agencies including law enforcement agencies engage in securing data about people, and in so doing carry a heavy ethical obligation not to violate their trust. Corporations need to honor high ethical standards as they engage in product research and monitor their employees and their competitors. Professionals need to protect the confidentiality of the information they secure from their clients. Even family members, especially parents, need to secure information about each other in a loving and fair manner. It should be clear, then, that data gathering and processing, initial steps for communicators in all walks of life, must be on a high ethical plane.

I have discussed three major categories of communicators that inherently possess strong ethical concerns—ghostwriters, hemispheric communicators, and whistle-blowers. people have long been intrigued with the ethicality of ghostwriting. Defenders of ghostwriting state that the need for extremely busy people in high positions in government, business, and other walks of life to have help in constructing their speeches is a given, and as the presenter takes responsibility for what is said, there is little to be concerned about. But many have strongly condemned ghostwriting; the audience might not gain entry into the true mind, character, and capability of the communicator; and public speaking, in which the presenter and the message are supposed to be intimately intertwined, can be demeaned. In classroom contexts in which speakers are being trained and graded, it is mandatory that the students indeed present a product created by them. The contemporary rhetorical critic has a difficult task to find the real rhetor in public addresses, to separate the multiple rhetors in those situations where many ghosts were present at the creation. The critic who seeks to analyze those speeches delivered in the dim past of history has always had the difficult task of trying to determine whether the extant versions of a speech were actually spoken or were somehow altered after the fact. Finally, we need to realize that *ghostwriter* is a perjorative label, and should be replaced by a more neutral term such as *speech assistant*.

I defined hemispheric communicators as those who by nature of their defined roles, like lawyers, advertisers, lobbyists, and public relations practitioners, present messages that speak only to half the landscape, to only the bright side of the moon. In presenting one-sided, incomplete, skewed, and simplistic messages, these communicators have many ethical dimensions with which to grapple, including potentially misleading and deceiving the audience. But hemispheric communicators perform a real service to society, by supplying helpful information and advice, which contribute to the people making their own eventual decisions. The audience might well be on their guard against exaggerations and embellishments, but they have the right to expect truthfulness and fairness from rhetors. Brainwashing and its counteragent, deprogramming, should be used with sensitivity to ethical dimensions. The use of surrogate communicators should bear close scrutiny, as should those rhetors who pride themselves on speaking for those who are voiceless.

The familiar phenomenon of the whistle-blower in society generates a host of ethical concerns. Whistle-blowing is a communicative act characterized as intentional, responsive, accusatory, public, and refutational. Any whistleblowing episode usually continues for a long time, seeks to enlist support from the public, and can appear in varied media. Whistle-blowing strains contractual agreements. A whistle-blower usually is one person and is subordinate to those against whom charges are made. He or she is a well-informed member of the group who is morally agitated and claims to be guided by laudatory ideals. Whisle-blowers come to be viewed as heroes or villains, and the ensuing rhetoric is cast in this two-valued framework.

A number of procedural ethical tension points present themselves to the conscientious person who would be a whistle-blower. How serious is the problem? Has the information been handled carefully, and have a person's motives been adequately explored? Has there been a sufficiently serious attempt to have the problem corrected within the organization? Should whistle-blowing occur when a person is still a member of the organization or afterward? Should whistle-blowing be done openly or anonymously? With what intensity and how often should it occur? Who is the proper audience? How proper is it for a person to shift roles from being a participant to being a judge? How ethical is it to undertake an effort that is likely to be expensive for many people in terms of time, money, and emotional involvement?

Substantive ethical tension points are also numerous and agonizing. People must live up to their obligations to the organization, give conscientious service and loyalty, but not succumb to the notion that the organization can do no wrong. Whistle-blowers usually think that their revelations will in the long run benefit the organization. Obligation to co-workers in the organization is also central, for their financial and emotional security can be adversely affected. Whistle-blowers might have moral obligations to their profession, and the need to balance loyalty to its ethical standards and the well being of the corporation can create a dilemma. A whistle-blower's family might be subjected to psychological agony and financial worry. "To thine ownself be true" haunts most whistle-blowers, as they try to cope with their need for a sense of inner integrity and self-worth and with what they feel is their obligation to the public. The effect of a whistle-blowing act can be a strengthening or a lessening of basic societal values such as freedom of speech, courage, fairness, human dignity, safety, efficiency, and loyalty. Whistleblowing usually depends on prioritizing "good" values, an agonizing exercise indeed.

A host of ethical concerns swirl around the message in a communicative transaction. The truth of a message is a central issue. Two components, accuracy and completeness, need to be recognized; when one is served, the other might not be. The harm that lying can cause the deceived, the deceiver, and the larger society is significant and includes weakening of trust, which in turn leads to many other negative results. Truth carries precedence over falsehood, and when falsehood is justified in special contexts, the one who lies carries the burden of proof and must offer sound explanations. Lies are usually in response to a query or situation, told to superiors, and offered to escape pain or acquire personal gain. The detection of lies is often extremely difficult, and problematic at best; reading nonverbal cues or using polygraphs leave much to be desired. In the final analysis, truth is a pearl of great value and must be demonstrated in those messages that would be highly ethical.

A promise has been defined here as a first-person intentional assertion, usually voluntary, tying the present to the future, committing a person to believe something or to act in a specified way. In various contexts, synonyms are employed, such as oath, pledge, vow, agreement, covenant, contract, commitment, or assurance. The ethical dimension is inherent; promises not kept can bring disastrous consequences to many people. Not only should concern be focused on promise-keeping but on promise-making, on the ethical obligation to make well grounded, wise promises in the first place.

The intertwining of reason and emotion in messages calls for careful ethical scrutiny. Those utterances that further an audience's reasoning and symbol-using capabilities, and thus avoid dehumanizing, are considered high in ethical quality. Propaganda, large-scale persuasion, relying heavily on emotional appeals, deemphasizing rationality and careful use of evidence, and presenting a message in a sharply two-valued framework is usually ranked low on the EQ Scale.

Our discussion of the ethics of exit communication in interpersonal, organizational, public speaking, and mass communication contexts was guided by the premise that the well-being, satisfaction, and humanity of all participants (especially the leaver) should be maximized. In interpersonal communication transactions, verbal and nonverbal acts need to be thoughtfully and compassionately used, and we should watch for sins of omission. Deceiving or misleading others at exit moments is ethically suspect. We need to be sensitive to cross-cultural considerations in our leave takings. Pre-exit messages can be helpful in reducing sadness and heightening well-being when exit moments subsequently occur.

Too many organizations give crude and cruel exit messages to their employees in termination cases, whereas conscientious organizations try to smooth the transition period by various means serving to tell departing and remaining employees that they are highly valued. Throughout society there are many verbal, nonverbal and written exit messages that need to be handled with care and compassion.

In public speaking, farewell speeches must be uttered not only effectively but also ethically. Presidential farewell addresses in the United States act as a rite of passage to the next administration, and hence need to be constructed with great sensitivity, and to avoid undue exaggeration and faulty guidance. Other farewell speeches in many other contexts throughout society also need to be highly ethical as well as technically effective in order to enhance the lives of those involved.

Withholding messages , which involves such areas as secrecy, confidentiality and censorship, can have a strong ethical impact. The positive and negative aspects of secrecy need to be carefully and conscientiously assessed. Lawyers, doctors, counselors, clergy, and others are bound by their professional obligations to maintain confidentiality in client relationships. Confidentiality encourages clients to seek professional help without fear that the information will become public knowledge and allows caregivers to render appropriate help. Mass media personnel protect the confidentiality of sources of information. In domestic or international negotiations, confidentiality is often needed at sensitive stages. But there may well be times in these contexts when the value of confidentiality is overridden by the public welfare. Censorship can result from our own desire not to utter certain messages, or it can come from a government or religious agency that seeks to stop certain messages from being expressed. The power wielded in these contexts needs to be employed conscientiously, and should be balanced with a deep concern for the well-being of the specific audience and the general society. The disadvantages of withholding might seriously outweigh any anticipated benefits.

On the other hand, releasing messages also carries potential ethical concerns. The leaking of information can cause serious harm and weaken bonds of trust. Government committees, award-granting committees, and other such bodies need to protect their deliberations to achieve their appointed tasks. A person might leak information from high or low ethical motives; if the claim is made that such an act works to the benefit of the larger community, then a heavy burden of proof is demanded. Gossip is usually unconfirmed, injurious and demeaning messages about an individual, and as such carries a low ethical quality. Spreading rumors about a group or impending event is usually ethically suspect, but there are situations, such as in tightly controlled totalitarian states, where rumors play a positive role in communicating the true state of affairs. I use the metaphor of *flooding* to express the overwhelming feeling of being drowned in the sea of electronic messages, breathtaking in speed and endless in quantity. How we and future generations cope with these often untrustworthy, demeaning, and unwanted messages is a serious and difficult task.

I have discussed ethical issues revolving around the many mediums used in communicative transactions. The concerns about language use are based on the premise that the human capability of language ought not to injure others. Defamation, whether orally (slander) or in writing (libel), remains, as it has for centuries, a central villain. Blatant or subtle forms of racist language is to be strongly deprecated. Stereotyping of racial groups in all communicative contexts including the mass media is to be avoided. The use of sexist language, demeaning to women, likewise must be eliminated. Name-calling, flattery, and ad hominem arguments all carry their own negative effects. Two-valued God and Devil terminol-

ogy exaggerates polarities and generates emotion that impedes thoughtful discussion. In language use we need to choose qualifiers, quantifiers,
and reservations with care. Figurative language, with its powerful im-
agery, can be a positive medium, but can also raise ethical concerns.
Infiltrating our minds with the ease of subliminal advertising, it can
subtly and firmly mold thought processes, and obscure rather than
clarify. Slogans, anecdotes, and stories, with considerable appeal and
power, can be used inappropriately and in ethically questionable ways.
Statistics, supposedly precise, can distort and conceal the truth if used
inappropriately and irresponsibly. Obscenity and profanity, despite the
difficulty in defining them to everyone's satisfaction, fall low on the
ethical scale in their dehumanizing effect on individuals and in their
polluting of the social atmosphere. Humor, for all its pleasant appeal,
carries with it a potential for hurting people and groups and should be
used carefully and responsibly.

Many nonverbal cues used in communicating carry with them considerable potential for mischief. Vocal cues can intimidate an audience,
and reduce a demand for sound reasoning and solid evidence. Body cues,
such as obscene gestures, misleading facial expressions, or inappropriate
hugging might be unappreciated at the very least. Clothing or objects
worn on the body also speak, and should be considered in ethical terms.
Body rhetoric, using the body usually in concert with others in marches,
or gatherings, can have significant ethical concerns. Personal encountering acts, gifts, flags, postage stamps, mechanical devices, and an endless
number of artifacts surrounding us all communicate nonverbal messages
with ethical dimensions.

Technological advances have enabled us to extend the voice's range, and
have brought great advantages to communicating possibilities. But with
each new opportunity comes potential misuse, and ethical sensitivity is
needed. Microphones and public address systems need to be used effectively to make the transaction with the audience enriching. The telephone
permits hucksters, crank callers, and other unwanted messengers to intrude
into our homes. In capturing and preserving messages, tape recordings can
be positive or harmful. Radios have enriched our lives for many decades,
and bring us information, entertainment , and guidance in personal and
societal decision making. But bullying talk shows, excessive commercials,
unbalanced political material, obnoxious profanity, and low-level intellectual substance all make us wish for higher ethical quality.

Technological advances in the visual dimension have greatly enriched
our lives; they allow us to see things close at hand, on the other side of

the globe, or in outer space. But again, this opportunity brings with it serious ethical concerns. Still photography might show an unflattering camera angle or an unfair moment of tension, and its published frame may leave out significant elements. The motion picture camera has created the movie and television industries, with all of their possibilities but also with their troublesome aspects. Worshipping the gods of motion, violence, singularity, magnitude, brevity, recency, sensationalism, simplification, problem-orientation, and the bizarre, these media generate a host of ethical questions. The cartoon is a powerful, usually humorous, visual creation but can be unfair, even ruthless, in newspapers or magazines. Cartoons in motion pictures multiply the fun but also the ethical concerns , especially with heavy use of violence. Visual aids in public speaking presentations demand effective use as well as the communicator's concern not to substitute form for substance.

Printed mass media are significant in our lives, and the ethical quality of their messages is of prime importance. Newspapers rushing to meet daily deadlines run the risk of presenting inaccurate and incomplete material, and in their desire to catch attention and sell their product they sensationalize and pander to mass audience tastes. Magazines likewise in their fierce competitive world can produce ethically suspect material.

Electronic advances in mass communication allow millions of people to communicate by sending messages via E-mail, fax, and the Internet, and the misuse of these astounding facilities increases apace, with hackers being a serious threat. Many developing nations accuse the highly industrialized nations of cultural imperialism and of exporting low moral values via these electronic facilities.

Additional mediums of communication mingle their many positive features with ethical concerns. Music, such as marches, hymns, jazz, jingles, national anthems, protest songs, makes a positive contribution, but listeners can be stimulated to violent or thoughtless behavior or can be lulled into nonrational passivity. Silence is a medium of communication used by people with positive results, but also with serious ethical concerns, when we contemplate the devasting effects of the silent treatment, of hiding information, or of letting ignorance and bullying go unanswered.

A number of ethical issues revolve around the audience. In communicative transactions, receivers have rights, responsibilities, and opportunities, just as senders do. We have the right not be forced into a communicative response, and the Fifth Amendment protects us in a court of law; observers should not read guilt or other negative implications into the choice not to respond. We have the right to protect our privacy, within reasonable limits. As members of an audience in a public speaking situation we have the right to receive sufficient information on which to make a significant choice. But we also have responsibilities to give respectful attention to the communicator and to judge carefully the message aimed at us. Beyond rightsabilities is the domain of opportunities; a highly ethical receiver of communication can in turn communicate sympathy, praise, or other feedback to enrich the life of the initial communicator.

Highly ethical listeners refrain from making distractions, from not paying attention, from heckling, or from inappropriate interruptions. When participating in group discussions or other forum events where listeners are expected to become speakers, we need to contribute appropriately. Audience members have an ethical obligation and an opportunity to give accurate and supportive feedback

The audience's emotional condition, state of health, age, and disability should serve as special considerations when evaluating the ethical quality of communicative acts. For instance, when a receiver is intensely sorrowful, fearful, or seriously ill, the communicator should be especially sensitive. Very young and older people are potentially vulnerable and hence deserve special empathy, as do those who are disabled.

Relationships between receivers and senders are central to the ethical quality of communicative transactions. When a sender holds considerably more power than the receiver, the highly ethical communicator uses that advantage sensitively. The greater the power, the greater the responsibility and the opportunity to enrich lives of others. The degree of trust between receivers and senders is one of the most important dimensions in human communication, and thus important in considering ethical quality. Delicate yet strong, trust holds together individuals, groups, and societies. Slow to grow, trust needs nurturing, and can quickly collapse. Blind, unthinking trust can dehumanize participants and endanger society. When receivers are too friendly with or too prejudiced against the communicator, objectivity and fairness can be seriously compromised.

The emphasis in effective communication to adapt appropriately to an audience might submerge the ethical dimension, and justify questionable methods and content in the name of the need to adapt. Having multiple audiences for the same message can tempt a communicator to be simplistic, ambiguous and unclear to reach them all.

Ethical sensitivity in communicative acts can be affected by many situational variables. In trying to cope with a situation involving great danger, communicators might modify their commitment to truth-telling. They might break civil, religious, and cultural laws and mores when the situation demands it. Police might think it necessary to withhold information or to give misleading disinformation to apprehend dangerous criminals. High stakes in such situations as crucial business dealings, impending disasters, unemployment straits, or courtship contexts test ethical commitments. The honoring or breaching of confidentiality depending on circumstances troubles many conscientious professionals and public officials. Secrecy can likewise challenge ethical commitment. Intentional ambiguity is justified by some diplomats, politicians, labor-management negotiators, teachers, lawyers, and parents. Place, time, and cultural factors can create situations in which ethical decisions differ from those made in other places, times, and cultures. Situations in which communicators think they are speaking for a cause can stimulate discourse that is low on the EQ Scale.

The specific demands of a given situation are sometimes felt to be so compelling that we measure the degree of a discourse's ethical quality according to that situation, hence the term *situation ethics*. Various situation ethics have emerged, but one approach stresses that existing mores and principles are honored but are assigned a lower priority when love serves better the needs of the individuals and the society. Multiple strands of ethical guidance continue to operate, but the demands of the situation shift the priorities of those strands according to the prompting of compassion. Situation ethics of this type would claim to be a middle ground between blind obedience to rules and irresponsible opportunism.

The subjects I have discussed in this book are intended to provoke readers to think for themselves about the ethical issues in all areas of the communication process. By offering ways of analyzing communicative acts in ethical terms, I hope to make the landscape of human communication more humane as well as more effective. By broadening and sharpening ethical insights and suggesting helpful applications in ethical decision making, this book seeks to provide an undergirding to communicative transactions that will enrich the lives of the individuals involved and strengthen the fabric of the larger society. As students become more skillful communicators, I hope that exposure to this volume will deepen their commitment to high ethical quality, not only in their professions, but in every part of life.

Appendix A:
Some Ethics Centers
Across the Nation

Association for Practical and Professional Ethics
Indiana University
410 North Park Ave.
Bloomington, IN 47405
phone: (812) 855-6450
fax: (812) 855-3315

Cal Turner Program in Moral Leadership
Vanderbilt University
110 Divinity School
Nashville, TN 37240
phone: (615) 343-3960

Carnegie Council on Ethics and International Affairs
Merrill House
170 East 64th Street
New York, NY 10021-7478
(212) 838-4120

Cary M. Maguire Center for Ethics and Public Responsibility
Southern Methodist University
Dallas, TX 75275
phone: (214) 768-3467

Center for Academic Ethics
Wayne State University
311 Education Building
Detroit, MI 48202
phone: (313) 577-8290

Center for Applied Ethics
Dyson College of Arts & Sciences
Pace University
41 Park Row
Pace Plaza
New York, NY 10038

Center for Applied and Professional Ethics
Department of Philosophy
California State University—Chico
Chico, CA 95929
phone: (916) 898-6183

Center for Applied and Professional Ethics
University of Tennessee
Department of Philosophy
801 McClung Tower
Knoxville, TN 37996
phone: (615) 974-3255

Center for Biomedical Ethics
Case Western Reserve University
10900 Euclid Avenue
Cleveland, OH 44106
phone: (216) 368-4196

Center for Biomedical Ethics
2221 University Ave. SE, Suite 110
University of Minnesota
Minneapolis, MN 55414
phone: (612) 626-9756
fax: (612) 626-9786

The Center for Business, Society & Ethics
Carlow College
3333 Fifth Ave.
Pittsburgh, PA 15213

Center for Ethics Across the University
Loyola University of Chicago
6525 No. Sheridan Road

Chicago, IL 60626
phone: (312) 508-8349

Center for Ethics and Human Rights
American Nurses Association
600 Maryland Avenue, SW
Suite 100 West
Washington, DC 20024-2571
phone: (202) 554-4444, ext. 294

Center for Ethics, Medicine and Public Issues
Baylor College of Medicine
One Baylor Plaza
Houston, TX 77030

Center for Ethics in Public Policy and the Professions
Emory University
428A Candler Library
Atlanta, GA 30322
phone: (404) 727-4954

Center for Ethics Studies
Marquette University
Academic Support Faculty 336
Milwaukee, WI 53233
phone: (414) 288-5824

Center for Health Care Ethics
Duquesne University
Graduate School of Liberal Arts and Sciences
Pittsburgh, PA 15282
phone: (412) 396-6530

Center for Moral Development and Education
Larsen Hall
Harvard University
Cambridge, MA 02138

Center for Professional and Applied Ethics
The University of North Carolina at Charlotte
9201 University City Boulevard

Charlotte, NC 28223
phone: (704) 547-3542

Center for Professional Ethics
Case Western Reserve University
129 Yost Hall
Cleveland, OH 44106
phone: (216) 368-5349

Center for Religion, Ethics and Social Policy (CRESP)
Cornell University
123 Anabel Taylor Hall
Ithaca, NY 14853

Center for Study of Applied Ethics (CSAE)
University of Virginia
Darden Graduate School of Business Administration
P.O. Box 6550
Charlottesville, VA 22906

Center for the Study of Ethical Development
141 Burton Hall
University of Minnesota
Minneapolis, MN 55455
(612) 624-0876

Center for the Study of Ethics in the Professions
Illinois Institute of Technology
3101 So. Dearborn St., Room 166
Life Sciences Bldg.
Chicago, IL 60616-3793
phone: (312) 567-3017
fax: (312) 567-3016

Center for the Study of Ethics in Society
Western Michigan University
320 Moore Hall
Kalamazoo, MI 49008
phone: (616) 387-3142 or 4380
fax: (616) 387-3990 or 3999

Center for the Study of Values
University of Delaware
Newark, DE 19716

Center for the Study of Values and Social Policy
University of Colorado
Campus Box 232
Boulder, CO 80309

Center for Technology, Policy and Industrial Development
Massachusetts Institute of Technology
Cambridge, MA 02139

Center for Values of Business
Loyola University
10 East Pearson Ave.
Chicago, IL 60611

Centre for Practical Ethics
York University
Room 102, McLaughlin College
4700 Keele Street
North York, Ontario
M3J 1P3 Canada
phone: (416) 736-5128, ext. 30446

Donald McGannon Communication Research Center for the Study of
Issues in Policy & Ethics
Fordham University
Department of Communications
Rose Hill Campus
Bronx, NY 10458
(212) 579-2693

Ethics in Public Affairs Program
The Maureen and Mike Mansfield Center
University of Montana
Missoula, MT 59812
phone: (406) 243-2181
fax: (406) 243-2988

Gannett Center For Media Studies
Columbia University
2950 Broadway
New York, NY 10027

The Hastings Center (Institute of Society, Ethics and the Life Sciences,
Inc.)
255 Elm Road
Briarcliff Manor, NY 10510
phone: (914) 762-8500

Institute for Applied and Professional Ethics
Ohio University
301 Gordy Hall
Athens, OH 45701
phone: (614) 593-4596

Institute for Business and Professional Ethics
DePaul University
One East Jackson Boulevard
Chicago, IL 60604
phone: (312) 362-6569

Institute of Communication Research
College of Communication
222 B Armory Building
University of Illinois
505 East Armory Ave.
Champaign, IL 61820

Institute for Communication Research
Emerson College
100 Beacon St.
Boston, MA 02116

Institute for Ethics and Policy Studies
University of Nevada–Las Vegas
45055 S. Maryland Parkway
Box 455049
Las Vegas, NV 89154
phone: (702) 597-4029

Institute for Global Ethics
P.O. Box 563
21 Elm Road
Camden, ME 04843
phone: (207) 236-6658

Institute for Philosophy and Public Policy
University of Maryland at College Park
3111 Van Munching Hall
College Park, MD 20742
phone: (301) 405-4753

Institute for Social Responsibility
San Jose State University
FO 201, One Washington Square
San Jose, CA 95192
phone: (408) 924-4523

Institute for the Study of Applied and Professional Ethics
Dartmouth University
6031 Parker House
Hanover, NH 03755
(603) 646-1263

John Hazen White, Sr., Center for Ethics and Public Service
University of Rhode Island
206 Washburn Hall
Kingston, RI 02881
phone: (401) 792-2183

The Josephson Institute for the Advancement of Ethics
4640 Admiralty Way, Suite 1001
Marina del Rey, CA 90292
phone: (310) 306-1868

The Kennedy Institute of Ethics
Poulton Hall
37th & P Streets, N.W.
Georgetown University
Washington, DC 20007

Lincoln Center for Applied Ethics
Arizona State University
College of Business
Tempe, AZ 85287
phone: (602) 965-2710

The Park Ridge Center for the Study of Health, Faith, and Ethics
211 East Ontario, Suite 800
Chicago, IL 60611
phone: (312) 266-2222
fax: (312) 266-6086

Philosophy and Technology Studies Center
Polytechnic Institute of New York
333 Jay Street
Brooklyn, NY 11201
(718) 260-3442

The Poynter Center for the Study of Ethics and American Institutions
Indiana University
1410 North Park Avenue
Bloomington, IN 47405
phone: (815) 855-0261

The Poynter Institute for Media Studies
801 Third Street South
St. Petersburg, FL 33701

Program in Applied Ethics
Fairfield University
Fairfield, CT 06430-7524

Program in Applied Ethics
John Carroll University
University Heights
Cleveland, OH 44118
phone: (216) 397-4466

Program in Business Ethics
School of Religion, University of Southern California
Los Angeles, CA 90089

The Program in Ethics and the Professions
Harvard University
79 John F. Kennedy Street
Cambridge, MA 02138
phone: (617) 495-1336
fax: (617) 496-9053

Program for Science, Society and Human Values
Duke University
206 E. Duke Bldg.
Durham, NC 27708

Program in Values, Technology and Society
Bldg. 370, Room 372
Stanford University
Stanford, CA 94305

Project in Professional Ethics
University of Houston—Clear Lake
2700 Bay Area Boulevard
Houston, TX 77058
phone: (713) 283-3571

Science, Technology & Society
128 Willard Building
The Pennsylvania State University
University Park, PA 16802

Silha Center for the Study of Media Ethics & Law
University of Minnesota, School of Journalism & Mass Communication
111 Murphy Hall
Minneapolis, MN 55455
phone: (612) 625-3421

Society & The Professions: Studies in Applied Ethics
Washington & Lee University
Lexington, VA 24450

Society for Values in Higher Education
409 Prospect Street
New Haven, CT 06510

The Starkoff Institute of Ethics and Contemporary Moral Problems
Hebrew Union College—Jewish Institute of Religion
3101 Clifton Ave.
Cincinnati, OH 45220
phone: (513) 221-1875

Stein Center for Ethics and Public Interest Law
Fordham University School of Law
140 West 62nd Street
New York, NY 10023
phone: (212) 636-6851

University Center for Human Values
Princeton University
Louis Marx Hall
Princeton, NJ 08544
phone: (609) 258-4798

Warren W. Hobbie Center for Values and Ethics
Catawba College
2300 W. Innes Street
Salisbury, NC 28144
phone: (704) 637-4429

Westminster Institute for Ethics and Human Values
361 Windermere Road
London, Ontario N6G 2K3
Canada
phone: (519) 673-0046

Youngstown State University Ethics Center
Youngstown State University
410 Wick Avenue
Youngstown, OH 44555
phone: (216) 742-1465

Appendix B

**Eulogy for the Late President John F. Kennedy.
Delivered on Sunday, November 24, 1963, in the
Capitol Rotunda by Senator Mike Mansfield,
Senate Majority Leader (D, Montana)**

There was a sound of laughter;
In a moment it was no more.
And so, she took a ring from her finger and placed it in his hands.

There was a wit in a man neither young nor old;
But a wit full of an old man's wisdom, and of a child's wisdom,
And then, in a moment it was no more.
And so, she took a ring from her finger and placed it in his hands.

There was a man marked with the scars of his love of country,
A body active with the surge of a life far, far from spent,
And, in a moment, it was no more.
And so, she took a ring from her finger and placed it in his hands.

There was a father with a little boy and a little girl
And a joy of each in the other.
In a moment it was no more,
And so, she took a ring from her finger and placed it in his hands.

There was a husband who asked much and gave much,
And, out of the giving and the asking,
Wove with a woman what could not be broken in life,
And, in a moment, it was no more.
And so, she took a ring from her finger and placed it in his hands,
And kissed him and closed the lid of a coffin.

A piece of each of us died at that moment.
Yet, in death he gave of himself to us.
He gave us of a good heart from which the laughter came.
He gave us of a profound wit, from which a great leadership emerged.
He gave us of a kindness and a strength fused into a human courage to
    seek peace without fear.

He gave us of his love that we, too, in turn, might give.
He gave that we might give of ourselves,
That we might give to one another until there would be no room,
No room at all,
For the bigotry, the hatred, the prejudice and the arrogance
Which converged in that moment of horror to strike him down.

In leaving us—
These gifts, John Fitzgerald Kennedy, president of the United States,
    leaves with us.
Will we take them, Mr. President?
Will we have, now, the sense and the responsibility and the courage to
    take them?
I pray to God that we shall
And under God we will.

Note: I shared this poetic arrangement with Senator Mansfield and asked
him if he had had this poetic structure in mind when he composed the
speech. He responded (letter to author, October 31, 1977) that he had
not. Thus, it apparently was a spontaneous boiling up from within,
stimulated by the meaning and depth of sadness of the occasion, generated by private and public sorrow and apprehension.

References

Alexander, N. (1995). Academic boycotts: Some reflections on the South African case. *Perspectives on the Professions, 15* (1), 6–7.

American Association of Museums. (1978). *Museum ethics* [Brochure]. Washington, DC: Author.

American Revision Committee. (1901). *The Holy Bible.* New York: Thomas Nelson & Sons.

Ames, R. (1984). Religiousness in classical Confucianism: A comparative analysis. *Asian Culture Quarterly, 12* (2), 7–23.

Anderson, R. E. (1963). Kierkegaard's theory of communication. *Speech Monographs, 30,* 1–14.

Arnett, R. C. (1992). *Dialogic education: Conversation about ideas and between persons.* Carbondale, IL: Southern Illinois University Press.

Augustine, Saint of (Hippo). (1949). *The confessions of Saint Augustine.* (E.B. Pusey, Trans.) New York: Modern Library.

Baelz, T. (Ed.). (1932). *Awakening Japan: The diary of a German doctor* (E. & C. Paul, Trans.) New York: Viking Press. (Original work published 1930)

Bakhurst, D. (1992). On lying and deceiving. *Journal of Medical Ethics, 18,* 63–66.

Baldwin, D. (1985, January / February). The loneliness of the government whistleblower. *Common Cause Magazine,* 32–34.

Barton, H. A. (Ed.). (1975). *Letters from the promised land: Swedes in America, 1840–1914.* Minneapolis: University of Minnesota Press.

Beatty, M. J. & Kruger, M. W. (1978). The effects of heckling on speaker credibility and attitude change. *Communication Quarterly, 26* (2), 46–50.

Bebeau, M. J. (1994). Influencing the moral dimensions of dental practice. In J.R. Rest & D. Narvaez (Eds.), *Moral development in the professions* (pp. 121–146). Hillsdale, NJ: Lawrence Erlbaum Associates.

Bennett, M.J. (1979). Overcoming the Golden Rule: Sympathy and empathy. In D. Nimmo (Ed.), *Communication Yearbook, 3* (pp. 407–422). New Brunswick, NJ: Transaction Books.

Benson, T. W. (1974). Conversation with a ghost: A postscript. *Today's Speech, 22* (3), 13–15.

The Bhagavad Gita. (Y. Ramacharka, Trans.) (1935). Chicago: Yogi Publication Society.

Black, J. (1994). *Areopagetica* in the information age. *Journal of Mass Media Ethics, 9,* 131–134.

Black, J. (1995). Novel insights into journalism ethics. *Media Ethics, 7,* (1), 1, 9–13.

Bok, D. (1988). Moral and ethical education in colleges: Theoretical and practical considerations. *Ethics: Easier Said Than Done, 1,* 9–15.

Bok, S. (1979). *Lying: Moral choice in public and private life.* New York: Vintage Books.

Bok, S. (1982). *Secrets: On the ethics of concealment and revelation.* New York: Pantheon Books.

Bollinger, L. C. (1991). *Images of a free press.* Chicago: University of Chicago Press.

Bonhoeffer, D. (1972). *Letters and papers from prison* (E. Bethge, Trans. and Ed.). New York: Macmillan. (Original work published 1951).

Borden, S. L. (1993). Empathic listening: The interviewer's betrayal. *Journal of Mass Media Ethics, 8,* 219–226.

Borden, S. L. (1996). Gotcha! Deciding when sources are fair game. *Journal of Mass Media Ethics, 10,* 223–235.

Bormann, E. G. (1961). Ethics of ghost–written speeches. *Quarterly Journal of Speech, 47,* 262–267.

Bormann, E. G. (1975). *Discussion and group methods: Theory and practice* (2nd ed.). New York: Harper & Row.

Bormann, E. G. (1985). Ethics and small group communication. *The Speech Association of Minnesota Journal, 12,* 20–25.

Bosmajian, H. A. (1983). *The language of oppression.* Lanham, MD: University Press of America.

Brembeck, W. L. & Howell, W. S. (1976). *Persuasion: A means of social influence* (2nd ed.). Englewood Cliffs, NJ: Prentice–Hall.

British orations. (1960). London: J. M. Dent & Sons.

Bryant, S. (1995). Electronic surveillance in the workplace. *Canadian Journal of Communication, 20,* 505–521.

Cahn, S. M. (Ed.). (1990). *Morality, responsibility, and the university: Studies in academic ethics.* Philadelphia: Temple University Press.

Callahan, J. C. (Ed.). (1988). *Ethical issues in professional life.* New York: Oxford University Press.

Cameron, M. E. (1993). *Living with AIDS: Experiencing ethical problems.* Newbury Park, CA: Sage.

Campbell, K. K. & Jamieson, K. H. (1990). *Deeds done in words: Presidential rhetoric and the genres of governance.* Chicago: University of Chicago Press.

Carmichael, C. W. (1985). Cultural patterns of the elderly. In L.A. Samovar & R. E. Porter (Eds.), *Intercultural communication: A reader* (4th ed.) (pp. 136–141).Belmont, CA: Wadsworth.

Carpenter, R. H. (1990). American tragic metaphor: Our twentieth-century combatants as frontiersmen. *Quarterly Journal of Speech, 76,* 1–72.

Chin, R. (1993, August 3). Changes in age, race are plotted through 2020 (pp. 1A, 6A). St. Paul, MN: *Pioneer Press.*

Chen, Q. (1993, March 29–April 4). Lei Feng: For three decades the face of altruism. *Beijing Review,* 16–18.

Christensen, R. with Thornley, S. (1993). *Golden memories.* Minneapolis: Nodin Press.

Christians, C. G. (1986). Reporting and the oppressed. In D. Elliott (Ed.), *Responsible journalism* (pp. 109–130). Beverly Hills: Sage.

Christians, C. G. (1995). Connie Chung and Kathleen Gingrich: The republic likely will survive them both. *Journal of Mass Media Ethics, 10* (2), 125–127.

Christians, C. G., Rotzoll, K. B., & Fackler, M. (1995). *Media ethics: Cases and moral reasoning* (4th ed.). New York: Longman.

Church, G. (1993, April 19). Goody to the Godzilla myth. *Time, 141,* 44.

Confucius. (1938). *The analects of Confucius* (A. Waley, Trans.) New York:Vintage Books.

Conze, E. (Trans.). (1984). *Buddhist scriptures.* Harmondsworth, England: Penguin Books.

Cooke, A. (1979). *The Americans: Fifty talks on our life and times.* New York: Alfred A. Knopf.

Cooper, T. W., assisted by Carey, C. (1996). Racism, hoaxes, epistemology, and news as a form of knowledge: The Stuart case as fraud or norm? *Howard Journal of Communication, 7,* 75–95.

Corgan, V. C. (1995). *Controversy, courts, and community: The rhetoric of Judge Miles Welton Lord.* Westport, CT: Greenwood Press.

Cox, H. (Ed.). (1968). *The situation ethics debate.* Philadelphia: Westminster Press.

Crossen, C. (1994). *Tainted truth: The manipulation of facts in America.* New York: Simon & Schuster.

Cunningham, S. B. (1992). Sorting out the ethics of propaganda. *Communication Studies, 43,* 233–245.

Daniloff, N. (1988). *Two lives, one Russia.* Boston: Houghton Mifflin.

DeGeorge, R. T. (1985). Ethical responsibilities of engineers in large organizations: The Pinto case. *Business & Professional Ethics Journal, 1,* 1–17.

DeGeorge, R. T. (1986). *Business ethics* (2nd ed.). New York: Macmillan.

Dei, S. (1989). *The international speech–making of Yasuhiro Nakasone: A case study in intercultural rhetoric.* Unpublished doctoral dissertation, University of Minnesota, Minneapolis.

Devlin, L. P. (1974). The influences of ghostwriting on rhetorical criticism. *Today's Speech, 22* (3), 7–12.

Dijk, T.A. van. (1987). *Communicating racism: Ethnic prejudice in thought and talk.* Newbury Park, CA: Sage.

Donne, J. (Wiley, B., Ed.) (1959). In G.B. Harrison (Gen. Ed.), Major British writers (Vol 2, pp. 357–399). New York: Harcourt, Brace.

Dorff, E. N. & Newman, L. E. (1995). Jewish morality. In E.N. Dorff & L.E. Newman (Eds.), *Contemporary Jewish ethics and morality: A reader* (pp. 247–250). New York: Oxford University Press.

Douglas, W. O. (1974). *Go east, young man: The autobiography of William O. Douglas, the early years.* New York: Dell Publishing.

Ekman, P. (1986). *Telling lies: Clues to deceit in the marketplace, politics, and marriage.* New York: Berkley Books.

Elliott, D. (Ed.). (1995a). *The ethics of asking: Dilemmas in higher education fund raising.* Baltimore: Johns Hopkins University Press.

Elliott, D. (1995b). Connie Chung and Kathleen Gingrich: A lesson on the seduction of sources. *Journal of Mass Media Ethics, 10,* 127–128.

Elmer–Dewitt, P. (1994, July 25). Battle for the soul of the Internet. *Time, 145,* 50–56.

Eveland, W. C. (1980). *Ropes of sand: Americas failure in the Middle East.* London: W. W. Norton.

Falk, E. (1995, November). *Jewish laws of speech: Towards intercultural rhetoric.* Paper presented at the 81st annual meeting of the Speech Communication Association, San Antonio, TX.

Fallows, J. (1996). *Breaking the news.* New York: Pantheon.

Fields, W. (1996). *Union of words: A history of presidential eloquence.* New York: The Free Press.

Fletcher, J. (1966). *Situation ethics: The new morality.* Philadelphia: Westminster Press.

Fletcher, J. (1968). Reflection and reply. In H. Cox (Ed.), *The situation ethics debate* (pp. 249–264). Philadelphia: Westminster Press.

Freidan, B. (1993, September). My quest for the fountain of age. *Time, 142,* 61–64.

Gaylin, W. (1990). Fooling with Mother Nature. *Hastings Center Report, 20* (1), 17–21.

Glazer, M. Ten whistleblowers and how they fared. *Hastings Center Report, 13* (6), 33–41.

Gleick, E. (1996a, February 12). Where there's smoke.... *Time, 147,* p. 54.

Gleick, E. (1996b, March 11). Tobacco blues. *Time, 147,* pp. 54–55, 57–58, 60.

Glendon, M. A. (1991). *Rights talk: The impoverishment of political discourse.* New York: The Free Press.

Glosserman, B. (1996, June 17–23). Seeking needles in the haystack. *The Japan Times Weekly International Edition,* p. 15.

Golden, J. L. & Corbett, E. P. J. (Eds.). (1968). *The rhetoric of Blair, Campbell, and Whately.* New York: Holt, Rinehart and Winston.

Gonzales, A. & Bradley, C. (1990). Breaking into silence: Technology transfer and mythical knowledge among the Acomas of *Nuevo Mexico.* In M. J. Medhurst, A. Gonzales, & T. R. Peterson (Eds.), *Communication and the culture of technology* (pp. 63–76). Pullman, WA: Washington State University Press.

Goodman, E. (1995, June 25). High–tech pushes up high anxiety. *Manchester Guardian Weekly* (U.K.), p. 18.

Gore, A. (1992). *Earth in the balance: Ecology and the human spirit.* Boston: Houghton Mifflin.

Gorlin, R. A. (Ed.). (1994). *Codes of professional responsibility* (3rd ed.). Washington, DC: The Bureau of National Affairs.

Greenwald, J. (1993, June 21). A matter of honor. *Time, 141,* 33–34.

Greenwald, J. (1995, August 28). The spy who cried help. *Time, 146,* 53.

Griffin, C. J. G. (1992). New light on Eisenhower's farewell address. *Presidential Studies Quarterly, 22,* 469–480.

Grow, D. (1992, June 23). Minister didn't finish speaking, but invocation got people talking. *Star Tribune* (Minneapolis), p. 3B.

Halderness, M. (1996, April 14). Sense and censorship's moving battlefront. *Manchester Guardian Weekly (U.K.),* p. 22.

Halvorsen, D. E. (1992, June). *Confucianism defies the computer: The conflict within the Korean press.* Honolulu: The East–West Center.

Hammarskjold, D. (1964). *Markings* (L. Sjoberg & W. H. Auden, Trans.). New York: Alfred A. Knopf. (Original work published 1963).

Hample, D. (1980). Purpose and effects of lying. *Southern Speech Communication Journal, 46* (3), 33–47.

Harris, M. H. (Trans.). (1901). *Hebraic literature: Translations from the Talmud, Midrashim and Kabbala.* New York: M. Walter Dunne.

Hausman, C. (1995, December/1996, January). Business–ethics education: Shining light into the "gray areas". *Insights on Global Ethics, 5,* (10), 1,4–5.

Havel, V. (1992). *Open letters: Selected writings, 1965-1990* (P. Wilson, Ed.). New York: Vintage Books.

Henkin, L. (1990). *The age of rights.* New York: Columbia University Press.

Henkoff, R. (1995, September 4). So who is this Mark Whitacre, and why is he saying these things about ADM? *Fortune, 132,* pp. 64–66, 68.

Herodotus. (1942). *The Persian Wars* (G. Rawlinson, Trans.). New York: Modern Library.

Hilts, P. J. (1995, August 3). Study finds tobacco ads nearer schools. *New York Times*, p. A11.

Himmelfarb, G. (1995). *The de–moralization of society: From Victorian virtues to modern values.* New York: Alfred A. Knopf.

Hodges, L. W. (1988). When is lying and deception justified?: Undercover, masquerading, surreptitious taping in investigative journalism *Ethics: Easier Said Than Done, 2* (2), 45–49.

Hodges, L. W. (1994). The journalist and privacy. *Journal of Mass Media Ethics, 9,* 197–212.

Hoffer, E. (1951). *The true believer.* New York: Mentor Books.

Holmberg, C. B. (1985). Toward the rhetoric of music: Dixie. *Southern Speech Communication Journal, 51* (3), 71–82.

Huff, D. (1993). *How to lie with statistics.* New York: W. W. Norton. (Originally published 1954)

Humphrey, H. H. (1976). *The education of a public man: My life and politics* (N. Sherman, Ed.). Garden City, NY: Doubleday.

Hunsaker, D. M. (1979). Freedom and responsibility in First Amendment theory: Defamation law and media credibility. *Quarterly Journal of Speech, 65,* 25–35.

Information Office of the State Council. (1991, November 4–11). Human rights in China. *Beijing Review, 34,* 8–45.

Jaffe, C. I. (1995). Chronemics: Communicating temporal cycles to Russian Old Believer students. *World Communication, 24* (1), 1–12.

Jaksa, J. A. (1993, November). *Organizational communication ethics: A case study approach.* Paper presented at the 79th annual meeting of the Speech Communication Association, Miami Beach, FL.

Jaksa, J. A. & Pritchard, M. S. (1994). *Communication ethics: Methods of analysis* (2nd ed.). Belmont, CA: Wadsworth.

Jensen, J. V. (1967). London's outdoor oratory. *Today's Speech, 15* (1), 3–6.

Jensen, J. V. (1973). Communicative functions of silence. *ETC.: A Review of General Semantics, 30,* 249–257.

Jensen, J. V. (1977). British voices on the eve of the American Revolution: Trapped by the family metaphor. *Quarterly Journal of Speech, 63,* 43–50.

Johannesen, R. L. (1990a). Virtue ethics, character, and political communication. In J. A. Jaksa (Ed.), *Proceedings of the First National Communication Ethics Conference* (pp. 219–256). Kalamazoo: Western Michigan University.

Johannesen, R. L. (1996). *Ethics in human communication* (4th ed.). Prospect Heights, IL: Waveland Press.

Johnson, E. (with Novak, W.). (1992). *My life.* New York: Random House.

Jordan, B. (1993, August). General letter urging support of Teaching Tolerance Project. Austin, TX: Author.

Joseph, J. A. (1995). On moral imperatives. *Foundation News & Commentary, 36* (6), 10–13.

King, C. S. (1969). *My life with Martin Luther King, Jr.* New York: Holt, Rinehart & Winston.

Kirkwood, W. (1989). Truthfulness as a standard for speech in ancient India. *Southern Communication Journal, 54,* 213–234.

Krauss, B. (1977). *The island way.* Norfolk Island, Australia: Island Heritage, Ltd.

Küng, H. & Kuschel, K. (Eds.). (1993). *A global ethic: The declaration of the parliament of the world's religions.* New York: Continuum Publishing Co.

Labitzky, A. M. (1995, November). *'Do as I say and not as I do?': A challenge for change to our future scholars.* Paper presented at the 81st annual meeting of the Speech Communication Association, San Antonio, TX.

Lin, Y. (Ed.). (1942). *The wisdom of China and India.* New York: The Modern Library.

Lind, R. A. & Rarick, D. L. (1994). The concept of ethical sensitivity in the study of communication ethics: Issues in definition, measurement, and application. In J. A. Jaksa (Ed.), *Proceedings of the Third National Communication Ethics Conference* (pp. 370–381). Annandale, VA: Speech Communication Association.

Lind, R. A. & Rarick, D. L. (1995). Assessing ethical sensitivity in television news viewers: A preliminary investigation. *Journal of Mass Media Ethics, 10,* 69–82.

Litfin, A. D. (1974). Eisenhower on the military–industrial complex: Critique of the rhetorical strategy. *Central States Speech Journal, 25,* 198–209.

Loveridge–Sanbonmatsu, J. (1993). Benazir Bhutto: Feminist voice for democracy in Pakistan. *Howard Journal of Communication, 4,* 295–316.

Lu, X. (1994). The theory of persuasion in Han Fei Tzu and its impact on Chinese communication behaviors. *Howard Journal of Communications, 5,* 108–122.

Mann, P. (1995, December 10). Too good to be famous (Review of the book *Rabindranath Tagore: The myriad–minded man) New York Times Book Review,* p. 28.

Martin, H. H. (1976). A generic explanation: Staged withdrawal, the rhetoric of resignation. *Central States Speech Journal, 27,* 247–257.

McDowell, B. (1991). *Ethical conduct and the professional's dilemma: Choosing between service and success.* New York: Quorum Books.

McGee, J. (1996, July 14). Federal wiretaps increase. *Manchester Guardian Weekly* (U.K.), p. 16.

McIntyre, B. T. (1995). VCR Use in Hong Kong. *Communication Research Reports, 12,* 61–70.

McMasters, P. (1996). Ethics and free expression. *Media Ethics, 7*(2), 1, 17, 18, 23.

McNamara, R. with VanDeMark, B. (1995). *In retrospect: The tragedy and lessons of Vietnam.* New York: Times Books.

McNeel, S. P. (1994). College teaching and student moral development. In J.R. Rest & D. Narvaez (Eds.), *Moral development in the professions* (pp. 27–49). Hillsdale, NJ: Lawrence Erlbaum Associates.

McPhail, M. L. (1994a). *The rhetoric of racism.* Lanham, MD: Rowman & Littlefield.

McPhail, M. L. (1994b). The politics of complicity: Second thoughts about the social construction of racial equality. *Quarterly Journal of Speech, 80,* 343–357.

McPhail, M.L. (1996). Race and sex in black and white: Essence and ideology in the Spike Lee discourse. *Howard Journal of Communications, 7,* 127–138.

Medhurst, M. J. (1994). Reconceptualizing rhetorical history: Eisenhower's farewell address. *Quarterly Journal of Speech, 80,* 195–218.

Medhurst, M. J. (1995). Robert L. Scott plays Dwight D. Eisenhower. *Quarterly Journal of Speech, 81,* 502–506.

Mencius (Meng–tzu). (1960). *The sayings of Mencius* (J.R. Ware, Trans.). New York: Mentor Books.

Mendelson, E. (1996, June 2). The word and the Web. *The New York Times Book Review,* p. 35.

Merton, T. (1959). *The silent life.* New York: Farrar, Straus & Cudahy.

Messenger, P. M. (Ed.). (1989). *The ethics of collecting: Whose culture? Cultural Property: Whose property?* Albuquerque: University of New Mexico Press.

Miceli, M.P., & Near, J.P. (1992). *Blowing the Whistle: The organizational and legal implications for companies and employees.* New York: Lexington Books.

Miller, G. R. (1983). Telling it like it isn't and not telling it like it is: Some thoughts on deceptive communication. In J. I. Sisco (Ed.), *Jensen lectures: Contemporary communication studies* (pp. 91–116). Tampa, FL: University of South Florida.

Minneapolis Tribune. (1982, February 5). 115, p. 11A.

Morreim, E. H. (1993). Am I my brother's warden? Responding to the unethical or incompetent colleague. *Hastings Center Report, 23* (3), 19–27.

Nakayama, T. K. & Krizek, R. L. (1995). Whiteness: A strategic rhetoric. *Quarterly Journal of Speech, 81,* 291–309.

Nazario, S. L. (1990, April 6). Schoolteachers say it's wrongheaded to try to teach students what's right. *The Wall Street Journal,* pp. B1, B8.

Nehru, J. (1942). *Toward freedom.* New York: John Day Co.

Nilsen, T. R. (1974) *Ethics of speech communication* (2nd ed.). Indianapolis: Bobbs–Merrill.

Noonan, P. (1990). *What I saw at the revolution: A political life in the Reagan era.* New York: Random House.

Oliver, R. T. (1962). Syngman Rhee: A case study in transnational oratory. *Quarterly Journal of Speech, 48,* 116–127.

Oliver, R. T. (1971). *Communication and culture in ancient India and China.* Syracuse, NY: Syracuse University Press.

Oliver, R. T. (1993, Winter). My life as a Korean ghost. *Korea Journal,* 68–80.

Overmyer, D. L. (Ed.). (1995). Chinese religions: The state of the field. *The Journal of Asian Studies, 54,* 314–395.

Palmer, E. H. (Trans.). (1947). *The Koran*. London: Oxford University Press. (original work published 1900).

Paraschos, M. (1996). News media and "conflict": 1896 and 1996. *Media Ethics, 7*(2), 3, 18, 19.

Parker, J. & Johnson, C. (Eds.). (1995). *Sir Walter Raleigh's speech from the scaffold: A translation of the 1619 Dutch edition, and comparison with English texts*. Minneapolis: James Ford Bell Library.

Parry–Giles, S. J. (1994). Rhetorical experimentation and the Cold War, 1947–1953: The development of an internationalist approach to propaganda. *Quarterly Journal of Speech, 80,* 448–467.

Patterson, B. R. (1995). Communication network activity: Network attributes of the young and elderly. *Communication Quarterly, 43,* 155–166.

Pearce, J. (1993, February 8–14). *The Japan Times International Edition*, p. 7.

Pellegrino, E. D. (1991). Trust and distrust in professional ethics. In Pellegrino, E. D., Veatch, R. M., & Langan, J. P. (Eds.), *Ethics, trust, and the professions: Philosophical and cultural aspects* (pp. 69–89). Washington, DC: Georgetown University Press.

Peters, C. & Branch, T. (1972). *Blowing the whistle: Dissent in the public interest*. New York: Praeger.

Peterson, S. E. (1993, April 4). U. S. Supreme Court offers peace of mind to Minnesotans. *Star Tribune* (Minneapolis), p. D1.

Pickthall, M. M. (Trans.). (1953). *The meaning of the glorious Koran*. New York: Mentor Books.

Pike, J. A. (1966). *Doing the truth* (2nd ed.). London: Victor Gallancz.

Pippert, W. G. (1989). *An ethics of news: A reporter's search for truth*. Washington, DC: Georgetown University Press.

Pooley, E. (1996, March 4). Nuclear warriors. *Time, 147,* pp. 46–54.

Powell, C. L. with Persico, J. E. (1995). *My American journey*. New York: Random House.

Quittner, J. (1996, June 24). Free speech for the Net. *Time, 147,* 56–57.

Ramsey, P. (1978). *Ethics at the edges of life: Medical and legal intersections*. New Haven: Yale University Press.

Redding, C. (1990). Ethics and the study of organizational communication: A case of culpable neglect. In J. A. Jaksa (Ed.), *Proceedings of the First National Communication Ethics Conference* (pp. 120–147). Annandale, VA: Speech Communication Association.

Reece, D. (1996). Covering and communication: The symbolism of dress among Muslim women. *Howard Journal of Communications, 7,* 35–52.

Rest, J. R. (1988). Can ethics be taught in professional schools? The psychological research. *Ethics: Easier Said Than Done, 1* (1), 22–26.

Rest, J. R. & Narvaez, D. F. (Eds.). (1994). *Moral development in the professions: Psychology and applied ethics*. Hillsdale, NJ: Lawrence Erlbaum Associates.

Safire, W. (Ed.). (1992). *Lend me your ears: Great speeches in history*. New York: W. W. Norton.

Sarasohn, J. (1993). *Science on trial: The whistle–blower, the accused, and the Nobel Laureate*. New York: St. Martin's Press.

Schnell, J. (1995). The lack of political cartoons in The People's Republic of China. *Communication and Theater Association of Minnesota Journal, 22,* 91–96.

Scott, R. L. (1990). Eisenhower's farewell: The epistemic function of argument. In R. Trapp & J. Schuetz (Eds.), *Perspectives on argumentation: Essays in honor of Wayne Brockriede* (pp. 151–161). Prospect Heights, IL: Waveland Press.

Scott, R. L. (1995). Eisenhower's farewell address: Response to Medhurst. *Quarterly Journal of Speech, 81,* 496–501.

Self, D. J. & Baldwin, D. C., Jr. (1994). Moral reasoning in medicine. In J. R. Rest & D. Narvaez (Eds.), *Moral development in the professions* (pp. 147–162). Hillsdale, NJ: Lawrence Erlbaum Associates.

Sharkey, W. F. (1992). Use and responses to intentional embarrassment. *Communication Studies, 43,* 257–275.

Simon, T. W. (1994). Fighting racism: Hate speech detours. In M.N.S. Sellers (Ed.), *An ethical education* (pp. 171–186). Providence, RI: Berg Publishers.

Smilgis, M. (1989, November 27). The celebs' golden mouthpiece. *Time, 134,* p. 82.

Smith, D. K. (1979). Rhetoric of and in the learning society. *Communication Education, 28,* 97–103.

Smolowe, J. (1996, January 22). My boss, big brother. *Time, 147,* p. 56.

Star Tribune (Minneapolis, MN). (1992, January 18). p. 13A.

Steglitz, I. E. (1993). *Intercultural perspective-taking: The impact of study abroad.* Unpublished doctoral dissertation, University of Minnesota, Minneapolis.

Sunstein, C. R. (1993). *Democracy and the problem of free speech.* New York: The Free Press.

Taylor, R. L. & Arbuckle, G. (1995). Confucianism. *The Journal of Asian Studies, 54,* 347–354.

Thoma, S. (1994). Moral judgments and moral action. In J. R. Rest & D. Narvaez (Eds.), *Moral development in the professions* (pp. 199–211). Hillsdale, NJ: Lawrence Erlbaum Associates.

Thonssen, L. & Baird, A. C. *Speech criticism: The development of standards for rhetorical appraisal.* New York: Ronald Press.

Tracey, M. & Redal, W. W. (1995). The new parochialism: The triumph of the populist in the flow of international television. *Canadian Journal of Communication, 20,* 343–365.

Trueblood, D. E. (1944). *The predicament of modern man.* New York: Harper & Brothers.

Tuan, Y. (1977). *Space and place: The perspective of experience.* Minneapolis: University of Minnesota Press.

Veatch, R. M. (1989). *Death, dying, and the biological revolution: Our last quest for responsibility.* New Haven: Yale University Press.

Wentworth, E. B. (1995). Introduction: The ethical landscape. In D. Elliott (Ed.), *The ethics of asking: Dilemmas in higher education fund raising* (pp. 1–15). Baltimore: The Johns Hopkins University Press.

Werhane, P. (1983). Individual rights in business. In T. Regan (Ed.), *Just business: New introductory essays in business ethics* (pp. 114–119). Philadelphia: Temple University Press.

Westbrook, T. (1994). Tracking the moral development of journalists: A look at them and their work. In J. R. Rest & D. Narvaez (Eds.), *Moral development in the professions* (pp. 189–197). Hillsdale, NJ: Lawrence Erlbaum Associates.

Westin, A. F. (Ed.). (1981). *Whistle blowing: Loyalty and dissent in the corporation.* New York: McGraw–Hill.

Whereatt, R. (1992, June 21). Minister's mention of abortion rights in prayer draws boos at IR convention. *Star Tribune* (Minneapolis, MN), pp. 1A, 7A.

Whitacre, M. (1995, September 4). My life as a corporate mole for the FBI. *Fortune, 132,* pp. 52–56, 60, 62.

Wiesel, E. (1990). *From the kingdom of memory: Reminiscences.* New York: Summit Books.

Winegar, K. (1994, July 24). Study: TV coverage of female athletes is better but not equal. *Star Tribune* (Minneapolis), pp. 1A, 15A.

Wintour, P. (1995, August 13). Doctors to become whistleblowers. *Manchester Guardian Weekly* (U.K.), p. 9.

Wright, P. (1987). *Spycatcher.* New York: Viking Penguin.

Yu, T.H. & Kessel, R.G. (1995, November). *A survey of Confucius' views on the ethics of spoken language.* Paper presented at the 81st annual meeting of the Speech Communication Association, San Antonio, TX.

Zoglin, R. (1996, October 21). The news wars. *Time, 148,* 58–64.

Suggested Additional Readings

Adam, G. S. (1992). Truth, the state, and democracy: The scope of the legal right of free expression. *Canadian Journal of Communication, 17,* 343–360.

Aguilar, F. J. (1994). *Managing corporate ethics: Learning from America's ethical companies how to supercharge business performance.* New York: Oxford University Press.

Allen, D. S. (1996). Separating the press and the public. *Journal of Mass Media Ethics, 10,* 197-209.

Allen, D. S. & Jensen, R. (Eds.). (1995). *Freeing the First Amendment: Critical perspectives on freedom of expression.* New York: New York University Press.

Altman, A. (1993). Liberalism and campus hate speech: A philosophical examination. *Ethics, 103,* 302–317.

Andersen, K. E. (1984). Communication ethics: The non–participant's role. *Southern Speech Communication Journal, 49,* 219–228.

Andersen, K. E. (1993). The role of ethical-value issues in campaigns: A longer–term view of family values. *American Behavioral Scientist, 37,* 292–302.

Andre, J. (1992). Learning to see: Moral growth during medical training. *Journal of Medical Ethics, 18,* 148–152.

Antczak, F. J. (1989). Teaching rhetoric and teaching morality: Some problems and possibilities of ethical criticism. *Rhetoric Society Quarterly, 19,* 15–22.

Arnett, R. C. (1986). *Communication and community: Implications of Martin Buber's dialogue.* Carbondale, IL: Southern Illinois University Press.

Arnett, R. C. (1987). The status of communication ethics scholarship in speech communication journals from 1915 to 1985. *Central States Speech Journal, 38,* 44–61.

Arnett, R. C. (1988). Communication ethics and the basic texts: An uncommon theoretical relationship. *Speech Association of Minnesota Journal, 15,* 23–48.

Arnett, R. C. (1990). The practical philosophy of communication ethics and free speech as the foundation for speech communication. *Communication Quarterly, 38,* 208–217.

Ashe, A., & Rampersad, A. (1993). *Days of grace: A memoir.* New York: Knopf.

Asuncion-Lande, N. C. (1980). *Ethical perspectives and critical issues in intercultural communication.* Annandale, VA: Speech Communication Association.

Atkin, D. (1993–1994). The role of race and gender as determinants of local TV news coverage. *Howard Journal of Communications, 5* (1 & 2), 123–137.

Bales, F. (1992). Televising executions: An obscenity? *Media Ethics Update, 4*(2), 15–16.

Barney, R. D. (1986). The journalist and a pluralistic society: An ethical approach. In D. Elliott (Ed.), *Responsibile journalism* (pp. 60–80). Beverly Hills, CA: Sage.

Bates, S. (1995). Who is the journalist's client? *Media Ethics, 7* (1), 3, 14–16.

Beall, M. L. (1987). Censorship and self–censorship: A problem in the schools. *Communication Education, 36,* 313–316.

Bebeau, M. J. with Pimple, K. D., Muskavitch, K. M. T., Borden, S. L., & Smith, D. H. (1995). *Moral reasoning in scientific research: Cases for teaching and assessment.* Bloomington, IN: Indiana University Press.

Bellingham, R., & Cohen, B. (1990). *Ethical leadership: A competitive edge.* Amherst, MA: Human Resource Development Press.

Bezanson, M. E. (1987). The right to receive through the school library. *Communication Education, 36,* 339–346.

Bick, P. A. (1988). *Business ethics and responsibility: An information sourcebook.* Phoeniz: Oryx Press.

Bivins, T. H. (1989). Are public relations texts covering ethics adequately? *Journal of Mass Media Ethics, 4* (1), 39–52.

Black, E. (1988). Secrecy and disclosure as rhetorical forms. *Quarterly Journal of Speech, 74,* 133–150.

211

Black, J. & Barney, R. (Eds.) (1994). *Exploring questions of media morality: Special issue: Privacy I and II. Journal of Mass Media Ethics, Vol. 9, Numbers 3 & 4.* Mahwah, NJ: Lawrence Erlbaum Associates.

Black, J. & Steele, R. (1991). Professional decision making and personal ethics. *Journalism Educator, 46* (3), 3–17.

Bloom, M. M. (1990). Sex differences in ethical systems: A useful framework for interpreting communication research. *Communication Quarterly, 38,* 244–254.

Boileau, D. M. (1985). Ethics and speech: An inherent or irrelevant relationship? *Communication Education, 34,* 258–264.

Bormann, E. G. (1981). Ethical standards for interpersonal/small group communication. *Communication, 6,* 267–285.

Bosmajian, H. A. (1972). Freedom of speech and the heckler. *Western Speech, 36,* 218–232.

Bosmajian, H. A. (1991). Celebrating the bicentennial of the Bill of Rights. *Western Journal of Speech Communication, 55,* 305–318.

Bosmajian, H. A. (1994). The freedom not to speak. *Legal Studies Forum: An Interdisciplinary Journal, 18,* 425–448.

Bovee, W. G. (1991). The end can justify the means—but rarely. *Journal of Mass Media Ethics, 6,* 135–145.

Bowie, N. E. (1994). *University–business partnerships: An assessment.* Lanham, MD: Rowman & Littlefield.

Braun, P. (1988). Deception in journalism. *Journal of Mass Media Ethics, 3* , 77–83.

Braxton, J. M. (Ed.) (1994). Special issue: Perspectives on research misconduct. *Journal of Higher Education,* 65.

Bredemeier, B. J. L., & Shields, D. L. L. (1994). Applied ethics and moral reasoning in sport. In J.R.Rest & D. Narvaez (Eds.), *Moral development in the professions* (pp. 173–187). Hillsdale, NJ: Lawrence Erlbaum Associates.

Brislin, T. (1992). "Just Journalism": A moral debate framework. *Journal of Mass Media Ethics, 7,* 209–219.

Brislin, T. (1996). Value hierarchies: U.S. and Chinese journalists. *Media Ethics, 7*(2), 6, 23, 24.

Brislin, T. & Williams, N. (1996). Beyond diversity: Expanding the canon in journalism ethics. *Journal of Mass Media Ethics, 11,* 16-27.

Brody, C. M. & Wallace, J. (Eds.). (1994). *Ethical and social issues in professional education.* Albany, NY: State University of New York Press.

Brown, M. T. (1990). *Working ethics: Strategies for decision–making and organizational responsibility.* San Francisco: Jossey–Bass.

Brown, W. J. & Singhal, A. (1990). Ethical dilemmas of prosocial television. *Communication Quarterly, 38,* 268–280.

Bryant, D. C., Arnold, C. C., Haberman, F. W., Murphy, R., & Wallace, K. R. (Eds.). (1967). *An historical anthology of select British speeches.* New York: Ronald Press.

Bugeja, M.J. (1996). *Living ethics: Developing values in mass communication.* Boston: Allyn & Bacon.

Burrowes, C. P. (1989). Measuring freedom of expression cross–culturally: Some methodological and conceptual problems. *Mass Communication Review, 16* (1 & 2), 38–51.

Cahn, D. D. (1985). Telling it exactly like it is: An experimental study of oral truth cues. *Communication Research Reports, 2,* 86–89.

Cahn, S. M. (1986). *Saints and scamps: Ethics in academia.* Totowa, NJ: Rowman & Littlefield.

Callahan, D., (1992). Ethics committees and social issues: Potentials and pitfalls. *Cambridge Quarterly of Health Care Ethics, 1* (1), 5–10.

Callahan, D. & Bok, S. (Eds.). (1980). *Ethics teaching in higher education.* New York: Plenum Press.

Campbell, C. S. (1992). Religious ethics and active euthanasia in a pluralistic society. *Kennedy Institute of Ethics Journal, 2,* 253–277.

Canary, D. J., & Cody, M. J. (1994). *Interpersonal communication: A goals–based approach.* New York: St. Martin' s Press.

Cannon, A. (1995, September 2). Language of racial hatred re–emerging in public. *St. Paul (MN) Pioneer Press,* pp. 1A, 6A.

Capo, J. A. (1994). Ethical issues in the information infrastructure. *Media Ethics, 6* (2), 4, 17, 21.

Carman, J., & Jürgensmeyer, M. (Eds.). (1991). *A bibliographic guide to the comparative study of ethics.* Cambridge, U.K.: Cambridge University Press.

Carrns, A. (1993). Nurses bring holistic view to ethical decision making. *Medical Ethics Advisor, 9* (5), 49–51, 54–55.

Chang, F.Y. (1994). School teachers' moral reasoning. In J. R. Rest & D. Narvaez (Eds.), *Moral development in the professions* (pp. 71–83). Hillsdale, NJ: Lawrence Erlbaum Associates.

Charron, L. N. (1995). *Qualitative thematic critical analysis of communication ethics in interpersonal communication textbooks.* Unpublished doctoral dissertation, University of Minnesota, Minneapolis.

Chesebro, J. W. (1969). A construct for assessing ethics in communication. *Central States Speech Journal, 20,* 104–114.

Ching, J. (1977). The problem of God in Confucianism. *International Philosophical Quarterly, 17* (1), 3–32.

Christians, C. G. (1977). Fifty years of scholarship in media ethics. *Journal of Communication, 27* (3), 19–29.

Christians, C. G. (1988). Can the public be held accountable? *Journal of Mass Media Ethics, 3* (1), 50–58.

Christians, C. G. (Ed.). (1991). Communication ethics and contemporary theory [Special issue]. *Communication, 12.*

Christians, C. G. (1991). Books in media ethics. In *Two bibliographies on ethics* (3rd ed.), pp. 3-13 Minneapolis, MN: Silha Center for the Study of Media Ethics and Law.

Christians, C. G. & Covert, C. L. (1980). *Teaching ethics in journalism education.* Hastings-on-Hudson, NY: Hastings Center Institute of Society, Ethics and the Life Sciences.

Christians, C. G. & Fackler, M. (1980). Liberty within the bounds of virtue, with special reference to John Milton' s political prose. In A. van der Meiden (Ed.), *Ethics and mass communication* (pp. 16–41). Utrecht, Netherlands: State University of Utrecht Press.

Christians, C. G., Ferré, J. P., & Fackler, P. M. (1993). *Good news; Social ethics and the press.* New York: Oxford University Press.

Churchill, R. P. (Ed.). (1994). *The ethics of liberal democracy: Morality and democracy in theory and practice.* Providence, RI: Berg.

Cloud, S. & Olson, L. (1996). *The Murrow boys: Pioneers on the front lines of broadcast journalism.* Boston: Houghton Mifflin.

Cohen, A. A., & Itzhak, R. (1990). A five–version tale of one jeep, one Palestinian and two Israelis: Some secrets of tv news editing that only comparative viewing reveals. *Feedback, 31* (3), 6–12.

Colby, D. C., & Cook, T. E. (1991). Epidemics and agendas: The politics of nightly news coverage of AIDS. *Journal of Health Politics, Policy and Law, 16,* 215–249.

Collier, L. M. (1995). College campus hate speech codes: A personal view from an absolute perspective. *Howard Journal of Communications, 5,* 263–278.

Committee on Science, Engineering, and Public Policy. (1995). *On being a scientist: Responsible conduct in research.* Washington, DC: National Academy Press.

Condit, C. M. (1987). Crafting virtue: The rhetorical construction of public morality. *Quarterly Journal of Speech, 73,* 79–87.

Condon, J. (1981). Values and ethics in communication across cultures: Some notes on the North American case. *Communication, 6,* 255–265.

Conway, D. W. (1991). Nietzsche and autonomy in communication ethics. *Communication, 12,* 217–230.

Cook, P. G. & Ruggles, M. A. (1992). Balance and freedom of speech: Challenge for Canadian broadcasting. *Canadian Journal of Communication, 17,* 37–59.

Cooper, T. W. (1990). Comparative international media ethics. *Journal of Mass Media Ethics, 5* (1), 3–14.

Cooper, T. W. (1994). Double invasion: The ethics of communication about communicable diseases. *Media Ethics, 6* (2), 6, 19–20.

Cooper, T. W. (Ed.). (1988). *Television and ethics: An annotated bibliography.* Boston: G. K. Hall.

Cooper, T. W. (Ed.) with Christians, C. G., Plude, F. F., & White, R. A. (1989). *Communication ethics and global change.* White Plains, NY: Longman.

Coye, R. & Belohlov, J. (1989). Disciplining: A question of ethics? *Employee Responsibilities and Rights Journal, 2,* 155–162.

Cramer, C. E. Ethical problems of mass murder coverage in the mass media. *Journal of Mass Media Ethics, 9,* 26–42.

Crowley, J. H. (1993). The advertising industry' s defense of its First Amendment rights. *Journal of Mass Media Ethics, 8,* 5–16.

Cunningham, S. B. (1990). Between moral theory and utterance: The need for heuristic principles in communication ethics. In J.A. Jaksa (Ed.), *Proceedings of the First National Communication Ethics Conference* (pp. 51–74). Kalamazoo, MI: Western Michigan University.

Cunningham, S. B. (1993). A place in the sun: Making room for media ethics. *Journal of Mass Media Ethics, 8,* 147–155.

Cushman, D., & King, S. S. (1989). Communication, knowledge, and ethics: A twentieth century perspective. In S. S. King (Ed.), *Human communication as a field of study* (pp. 233–240). Albany, NY: State University of New York Press.

Dandekar, N. (1991). Can whistleblowing be *fully* legitimated? A theoretical discussion. *Business and Professional Ethics Journal, 10* (1), 89–108.

Davis, J. F. (1992). The power of images: Creating the myths of our time. *Media & Values,* No. 57, 4–6.

Davis, M. (1995). Academic boycotts. *Perspectives on the Professions, 15* (1), 1–2.

Day, L. A. (1991). *Ethics in media communication: Cases and controversies.* Belmont, CA: Wadsworth.

Deakins, A. H. (1991). Eavesdropping for data: Gender and topic. *World Communication, 20* (2), 67–77.

Dee, J. (1993). "Disgorging Benefits" and plugging dikes: An analysis of the legal arguments advanced by the United States and the United Kingdom to stop former intelligence agents from publishing what they know. *Communication, 13,* 303–326.

Dee, J. (1995). Twins separated at birth: The strange cases of Michael Levin and Leonard Jeffries. *Howard Journal of Communications, 5,* 279–294.

Deetz, S. (1990). Reclaiming the subject matter as a guide to mutual understanding: Effectiveness and ethics in interpersonal interaction. *Communication Quarterly, 38,* 226–243.

Demers, F. (1989). Journalistic ethics: The rise of the "good employee' s model": A threat for professionalism? *Canadian Journal of Communication, 14* (2), 15–27.

Dennis, E.E. (1986). Social responsibility, representation, and reality. In D. Elliott (Ed.), *Responsible journalism* (pp. 99–108). Beverly Hills, CA: Sage.

Dennis, E. E., & Merrill, J. C. (1991). *Media debates: Issues in mass communication.* New York: Longman.

Denton, R. E., Jr. (Ed.). (1991). *Ethical dimensions of political communication.* Westport, CT: Praeger.

DePaulo, B. M., & Rosenthal, R. (1979). Telling lies. *Journal of Personality and Social Psychology, 37,* 1713–1722.

Devroy, A. (1990, February 25). A distaste for rhetoric. *Manchester Guardian Weekly* (U. K.), pp. 17–18.

Dicken-Garcia, H. (1989). *Journalistic standards in nineteenth century America.* Madison, WI: University of Wisconsin Press.

Donaldson, J. (1992). *Business ethics: A European casebook.* London: Academic Press.

Donaldson, T. J., & Freeman, R. E. (Eds.). (1994). *Business as a humanity.* New York: Oxford University Press.

Donaldson, T. J., & Werhane, P. (Eds.). (1988). *Ethical issues in business* (3rd ed.). Englewood Cliffs, NJ: Prentice-Hall.

Douglas, W. O. (1953). *Beyond the high Himalayas.* Garden City, NY: Doubleday.

Dresser, R., & Whitehouse, P. J. (1994). The incompetent patient on the slippery slope. *Hastings Center Report, 24,* 6–12.

Dryzek, J. S. (1990). Green reason: Communicative ethics for the biosphere. *Environmental Ethics, 12,* 195–210.

Duckett, L. J., & Ryden, M. B. (1994). Education for ethical nursing practice. In J. R. Rest & D. Narvaez (Eds.), *Moral development in the professions* (pp. 51–69). Hillsdale, NJ: Lawrence Erlbaum Associates.

Dyk, T. B., & Wilkins, W. J. (1989). Regulation and ownership: Washington' s influence on who owns the media. *Gannett Center Journal, 3,* 74–91.

Ehrlich, M. C. (1995). The ethical dilemma of television news sweeps. *Journal of Mass Media Ethics, 10,* 37–47.

Ekman, P., with Ekman, M. A. M., & Ekman, T. (1989). *Why kids lie: How parents can encourage truthfulness.* New York: Scribners.

Ellin, J. S. (1988). Special professional morality and the duty of veracity. In J. C. Callahan (Ed.), *Ethical issues in professional life* (pp. 130–139). New York: Oxford University Press.

Elliott, C. (1992). Where ethics comes from and what to do about it. *Hastings Center Report, 22* (4), 28–35.

Elliott, D. (1986a). Foundations for news media responsibility. In D. Elliott (Ed.), *Responsible journalism* (pp. 32–44). Beverly Hills, CA: Sage.

Elliott, D. (1988). All is not relative: Essential shared values and the press. *Journal of Mass Media Ethics, 3* (1), 28–32.

Elliott, D. (1991) Moral development theories and the teaching of ethics. *Journalism Educator, 46* (3), 18–24.

Elliott, D. (Ed.). (1986b). *Responsible journalism.* Beverly Hills, CA: Sage.

Elliott, D. & Culver, C. (1992). Defining and analyzing journalistic deception. *Journal of Mass Media Ethics, 7,* 69–84.

Ellis, A. L. (Ed.). (1996). *First we must listen: Living in a multicultural society.* New York: Friendship Press.

Elliston, F. A. (1986). Anonymous whistleblowing: An ethical analysis. *Business & Professional Ethics Journal, 5,* 5–22.

Ellul, J. (1981). The ethics of propaganda: Propaganda, innocence, and amorality. *Communication, 6,* 159–175.

Emanuel, L. L., & Emanuel, E. J. (1993). Decisions at the end of life: Guided by communities of patients. *Hastings Center Report, 23* (5), 6–14.

Emord, J. W. (1991). *Freedom, technology, and the First Amendment.* San Francisco: Pacific Research Institute.

Englehardt, H. T., Jr. (1989). Can ethics take pluralism seriously? *Hastings Center Report, 19* (5), 33–34.

Everett, S. C. (1996). Mirage multiculturalism: Unmasking the Mighty Morphin Power Ranger. *Journal of Mass Media Ethics, 11,* 28-39.

Ferré, J. P. (1985). Religious perspectives on commercial television in the United States. *Critical Studies in Mass Communication, 2,* 290–295.

Ferré, J. P. (1988a). The dubious heritage of media ethics: Cause–and–effect criticism in the 1890s. *American Journalism, 5,* 191–203.

Ferré, J. P. (1988b). Grounding an ethics of journalism. *Journal of Mass Media Ethics, 3* (1), 18–27.

Ferré, J. P. (1990). Communication ethics and the political realism of Reinhold Niebuhr. *Communication Quarterly, 38,* 218–225.

Ferré, J. P., & Willihnganz, S. C. (1991). *Public relations and ethics: A bibliography.* Boston: G. K. Hall.

Fish, S. (1993). *There' s no such thing as free speech: And it' s a good thing, too.* New York: Oxford University Press.

Fitzpatrick, B. (1992, June). Communicating poverty. *One World* (176), 13–15.

Fitzsimon, M. & McGill, L. T. (1995). The citizen as media critic. *Media Studies Journal, 9* (2), 91-101.

Fletcher, J. (1988). The moral limits of knowledge. *Virginia Quarterly Review, 64,* 565–584.

Forester, T., & Morrison, P. (1993). *Computer ethics: Cautionary tales and ethical dilemmas in computing* (2nd ed.). Cambridge, MA: MIT Press.

Fortado, B. (1990). The responsibilities of a semistructured interviewer. *Employee Responsibilities and Rights Journal, 3,* 31–46.

Fortenbaugh, W. W. (1992). Aristotle on persuasion through character. *Rhetorica, 10,* 207–244.

Fraleigh, D. (1995). University limitation on intentional infliction of emotional distress: Constitutional remedy for hate speech. *Howard Journal of Communications, 5,* 295–306.

Francois, W. E. (1994). *Mass media law and regulation* (6th ed.). Prospect Heights, IL: Waveland Press.

Frey, L. R., Botan, C. H., Friedman, P. G. & Kreps, G. L. (1991). *Investigating communication: An introduction to research methods*. Englewood Cliffs, NJ: Prentice Hall.

Fritschler, A. L. (1995). Colleges and the numbers game. *Insights on Global Ethics, 5* (6), 1, 4–5.

Fry, D. (1989). What do our interns know about journalism ethics? *Journal of Mass Media Ethics, 4,* 186–192.

Fuller, J. (1996). *News values: Ideas for an information age*. Chicago: University of Chicago Press.

Gamble, T., & Gamble, M. (1994). Speaking of ethics. *Public speaking in an age of diversity* (pp. 14–16, 80–81, 112–113, 195–196, 322–325, 446). Boston: Allyn & Bacon.

Gandhi, S. (Ed.). (1993). *Two alone, two together: Letters between Indira Gandhi and Jawaharlal Nehru, 1940–1964* (pp. 179–184), letter of Nehru, April 16, 1943. London: Hodder & Stoughton.

Garramone, G. M., & Kennomer, J. D. (1989). Ethical considerations in mass communication research. *Journal of Mass Media Ethics, 4,* 174–185.

Garrison, B., & Splichal, S. (1994). Reporting on private affairs of candidates: A study of newspaper practices. *Journal of Mass Media Ethics, 9,* 169–183.

George, R. J. (1987). Teaching business ethics: Is there a gap between rhetoric and reality? *Journal of Business Ethics, 6,* 513–518.

Gerald, J. E. (1963). *The social responsibility of the press*. Minneapolis, MN: University of Minnesota Press.

Gibson, D. C. (1987). The communication dilemma of the CIA. *Public Relations Review, 13,* (2), 27–38.

Gillmor, D. M. (1990). Libel as sedition: Public officials should have *no* libel law remedy. *Media Ethics Update, 3* (1), 12–13.

Gillmor, D. M. (1992). Principle before policy. *Media Ethics Update, 5* (2), 13, 15.

Gillmor, D. M. (1993). A look at media ethics. *Media Ethics, 6* (1), 21–22.

Gladney, G. A. (1991). Technologizing of the word: Toward a theoretical and ethical understanding. *Journal of Mass Media Ethics, 6,* 93–105.

Gladney, G. A. (1993). *USA Today,* its imitators, and its critics: Do newsroom staffs face an ethical dilemma? *Journal of Mass Media Ethics, 8,* 17–36.

Glasser, I. (1991). *Visions of liberty: The bill of rights for all Americans*. New York: Arcade.

Glasser, T. L. (1986). Press responsibility and First Amendment values. In D. Elliott (Ed.), *Responsible journalism* (pp. 81–98). Beverly Hills, CA: Sage.

Glasser, T. L. (1988). Protecting the reporter at the editor's expense. *Media Ethics Update, 1* (3), 4, 10.

Glasser, T. L. (1991). Communication and the cultivation of citizenship. *Communication, 12,* 235–248.

Glasser, T. L., & Ettema, J. S. (1989). Investigative journalism and the moral order. *Critical Studies in Mass Communication, 6* (1), 1–20.

Glenn, J. (1986). *Ethics in decision making*. New York: Wiley.

Godfrey, D. G. (1993). Ethics in practice: Analysis of Edward R. Murrow's WWII radio reporting. *Journal of Mass Media Ethics, 8,* 103–118.

Golden, J. (1966). John F. Kennedy and the ghosts. *Quarterly Journal of Speech, 52,* 348–357.

Goldzwig, S. R. (1989). A social movement perspective on demagoguery: Achieving symbolic realignment. *Communication Studies, 40,* 202–228.

Goodpaster, K. (1991). Can ethics be taught? A conversation with M. Kelly. *Business Ethics, 5* (2), 26–28.

Goodwin, H. E., & Smith, R. F. (1994). *Groping for ethics in journalism* (3rd ed.). Ames, IA: Iowa State University Press.

Gordon, D., & Merrill, J. C. (1988). Power — the key to press freedom: A four–tiered social model. *Journal of Mass Media Ethics, 3,* 38–49.

Gordon, R. D. (1988). Social responsibility and communication research. *Speech Communication Annual, 2,* 93–102.

Gordon, W. I. (1988). Range of employee voice. *Employee Responsibilities and Rights Journal, 1,* 283–299.

Gori, M. S. (1984, October). Ben Elliott. *Bucknell World*, Lewisburg, PA: Bucknell Uniersity.

Grant, M. R. (1992). Gibralter killings: British media ethics. *Journal of Mass Media Ethics*, 7, 31–40.

Grant, V. J. (1991). Teaching medical ethics: Consent in paediatrics, a complex teaching assignment. *Journal of Medical Ethics, 17*, 199–204.

Gray, P. (1992, October 5). Lies, lies, lies. *Time*, 140, 32–38.

Gray, P. (1994, July 25). Nice guys finish first? *Time*, 144. 48–49.

Greenberg, K. J. (Ed.). (1991). *Conversations on communication ethics*. Norwood, NJ: Ablex.

Greenwald, J. (1995a, July 24). Harvest of subpoenas. *Time*, 146, 53.

Greipp, M. E. (1992). Greipp's model of ethical decision making. *Journal of Advanced Nursing, 17*, 734–738.

Grierson, D. (1991). Herbert Matthews and Castro's revolution: A lapse in discretion at *The New York Times. World Communication, 20*, 3–10.

Griffith, T. (1989). Press lords and media barons. *Gannett Center Journal, 3*, 1–10.

Gronbeck, B. (1968). From "is" to "ought": Alternative strategies. *Central States Speech Journal, 19*, 31–39.

Gross, L., Katz, J. S., & Ruby, J. (Eds.). (1988). *Image ethics: The moral rights of subjects in photography, film and television.* New York: Oxford University Press.

Gustainis, J. J. (1990). Demagoguery and political rhetoric: A review of the literature. *Rhetoric Society Quarterly, 20*, 155–161.

Haarsager, S. (1991). Choosing silence: A case of reverse agenda setting in depression era news coverage. *Journal of Mass Media Ethics, 6*, 35–46.

Haefner, M. J. (1991). Ethical problems of advertising to children. *Journal of Mass Media Ethics, 6*, 83–92.

Haiman, F.S. (1952). A re-examination of the ethics of persuasion. *Central States Speech Journal, 3* (2), 4-9.

Haiman, F. S. (1958). Democratic ethics and the hidden persuaders. *Quarterly Journal of Speech, 44*, 385–392.

Haiman, F. S. (1967). The rhetoric of the streets: Some legal and ethical considerations. *Quarterly Journal of Speech, 53*, 99–114.

Haiman, F. S. (1972). Speech v. privacy: Is there a right not to be spoken to? *Northwestern University Law Review, 67*, 153–199.

Haiman, F. S. (1978). The rhetoric of 1968: A farewell to rational discourse. In W. A. Linkugel, R. R. Allen, and R. L. Johannesen, (Eds.), *Contemporary American speeches* (pp. 156–169). Dubuque, IA: Kendall–Hunt.

Haiman, F. S. (1981). *Speech and law in a free society.* Chicago: University of Chicago Press.

Haiman, F. S. (1982). Nonverbal communication and the First Amendment: The rhetoric of the streets revisited. *Quarterly Journal of Speech, 68*, 371–383.

Haiman, F. S. (1984a). Ghostwriting and the cult of leadership. *Communication Education, 33*, 301–307.

Haiman, F. S. (1984b). Justice Brennan and the First Amendment, 1956–1984. *Free Speech Yearbook: 1983*, (pp. 33–42). Annandale, VA: Speech Communication Association.

Haiman, F. S. (1987). School censors and the law. *Communication Education, 36*, 327–338.

Haiman, F. S. (1993). *"Speech acts" and the First Amendment.* Carbondale, IL: Southern Illinois University Press.

Hale, J. L. (1987). Plagiarism in classroom settings. *Communication Research Reports, 4* (4), 66–70.

Hall, R. N. (1965). Lyndon Johnson's speech preparation. *Quarterly Journal of Speech, 51*, 168–176.

Hall, R. N. (1973). Professional accountability. *Association for Communication Administration Bulletin, 2*, 18–20.

Hamilton, K. R., & Krueger, D. A. (1990). The state-of-the-art in corporate ethics shows big changes taking place. *Ethics: Easier Said Than Done, 9*, 38–44.

Hamilton, M. A. (1989). Reactions to obscene language. *Communication Research Reports, 6* (2), 67–69.

Handy, B. (1996, January 15). Out with the sleaze. *Time*, 147, 64–66.

Hanson, W. (1992). Ethical issues in the philanthropic and nonprofit community. *Ethics: Easier Said Than Done, 18*, 31–43.

Hardy–Short, D. C. (1988). "Send me your huddled masses": Ethical considerations, communication, and the English First movement. *World Communication, 17,* 169–191.

Harless, J. D. (1990). Media ethics, ideology, and personal constructs: Mapping professional enigmas. *Journal of Mass Media Ethics, 5,* 217–232.

Harmon, M. D. (1991). Hate groups and cable public access. *Journal of Mass Media Ethics, 6,* 146–155.

Harris, C. E., Jr., Pritchard, M. S., & Robins, M. J. (1995). *Engineering ethics: Concepts and cases.* Belmont, CA: Wadsworth.

Harris, C. R. (1991). Digitization and manipulation of news photographs. *Journal of Mass Media Ethics, 6,* 164–174.

Harrison, R. P. (1981). *The cartoon: Communication to the quick.* Beverly Hills: Sage.

Harrison, S. L. (1990a). Ethics and moral issues in public relations curricula. *Journalism Educator, 45* (3), 32–38.

Harrison, S. L. (1990b). Pedagogical ethics for public relations and advertising. *Journal of Mass Media Ethics, 5,* 256–262.

Haskins, W. A. (1989, November). Teaching ethics in the basic survey speech communication course. *Basic Course Communication Annual, 1,* 95–105.

Hausman, C. (1992a). *Crises of conscience: Perspectives on journalism ethics.* New York: HarperCollins.

Hausman, C. (1992b). Private lives, public figures: Examining the ethics of privacy. *Insights on Global Ethics, 2*(10), 5–7.

Hausman, C. (1994). Information age ethics: Privacy ground rules for navigating in cyberspace. *Journal of Mass Media Ethics, 9,* 135–144.

Hausman, C., & Palombo, P. J. (1994). Information age and privacy issues: Hot new ethical dilemmas. *Insights on Global Ethics, 4* (6), 1, 4–5.

Haynes, P. (1991). Dangerous omissions and the importance of context. *Media Ethics, 6* (2), 11–13.

Heath, R. L. (1988). The rhetoric of issue advertising: A rationale, a case study, a critical perspective–and more. *Central States Speech Journal, 39,* 99–109.

Heath, R. L. ,& Ryan, M. (1989). Public relations' role in defining corporate social responsibility. *Journal of Mass Media Ethics, 4,* 21–38.

Hebert, P. C., Meslin, E. M. & Dunn, E. V. (1992). Teaching medical ethics: Measuring the ethical sensitivity of medical students: A study at the University of Toronto. *Journal of Medical Ethics, 18,* 142–147.

Heider, D. (1996). Completeness and exclusion in journalism ethics: An ethnographic case study. *Journal of Mass Media Ethics, 11,* 4-15.

Hemmer, J. J., Jr. (1995). Hate speech: The egalitarian/libertarian dilemma. *Howard Journal of Communications, 5,* 307–330.

Henry, G. (1989, March 12). BBC code sets curbs on violence. *Manchester Guardian Weekly* (U. K.), p. 5.

Hentoff, N. (1992). *Free speech for me–but not for thee: How the American left and right relentlessly censor each other.* New York: HarperCollins.

Herring, M. Y. (1988). *Ethics and the professor: An annotated bibliography, 1970–1985.* New York: Garland.

Herzog, W. (1991). Issues for development communication ethics. *Journal of Mass Media Ethics, 6,* 210–221.

Hess, J. A. (1993). Teaching ethics in introductory public speaking: Review and proposal. In L. W. Hugenberg (Ed.), *Basic communication course annual, 5,* (pp. 101–126). Boston: American Press.

Hill, M., & Thrasher, B. (1994). A model of respect: Beyond political correctness in the campus newsroom. *Journal of Mass Media Ethics, 9,* 43–55.

Hills, J., & Papathanassopoulos, S. (1991). *The democracy gap: The politics of information and communication technologies in the U.S. and Europe.* New York: Praeger.

Hitt, W. D. (1990). *Ethics and leadership: Putting theory into practice.* Columbus, OH: Battelle Press.

Hocking, J. E., & Leathers, D. G. (1980). Nonverbal indicators of deception: A new theoretical perspective. *Communication Monographs, 47,* 119–131.

Hodges, L. W. (1986). Defining press responsibility: A functional approach. In D. Elliott (Ed.), *Responsible journalism* (pp. 13–31). Beverly Hills, CA: Sage.

Hodges, L. W., Corey, A. E., Jr., Meyer, T. P., & Rotzoll, K. (1992) Cases and commentaries: Old Joe Camel. *Journal of Mass Media Ethics, 7,* 121–128.

Hodley, R. (1989). Television news ethics: A survey of television news directors. *Journal of Mass Media Ethics, 4,* 249–264.

Hoffman, W. M., & Moore, J. M. (Eds.). (1984). *Business ethics: Readings and cases in corporate morality.* New York: McGraw–Hill.

Holden, C. (1988). Whistle–blowers air cases at House hearings. *Science, 240,* 386–387.

Hopper, R., & Ball, R. A. (1984). Broadening the deception construct. *Quarterly Journal of Speech, 70,* 288–302.

Howell, W. S. (1982). *The empathic communicator.* Belmont, CA: Wadsworth.

Hulteng, J. L. (1985). *The messengers' motives: Ethical problems of the news media* (2nd ed.). Englewood Cliffs, NJ: Prentice–Hall.

Husselbee, L. P. (1994). Respecting privacy in an information society: A journalist' s dilemma. *Journal of Mass Media Ethics, 9,* 145–156.

Hyde, M. J. (1993). Medicine, rhetoric and euthanasia: A case study in the workings of a postmodern discourse. *Quarterly Journal of Speech, 79,* 201–224.

Ikenaga, C. S. (1985). Electronic eavesdropping: Which conversations are protected from interception? *University of Hawaii Law Review, 7,* 227–237.

Ingelfinger, F. J. (1972). Informed (but uneducated) consent. *New England Journal of Medicine, 287,* 465–466.

Iyengar, S. (1991). *Is anyone responsible? How television frames political issues.* Chicago: University of Chicago Press.

Jackson, J. (1991). Telling the truth. *Journal of Medical Ethics, 17,* 5–9.

James, E. L., Pratt, C. B., & Smith, T. V. (1994). Advertising ethics: Practitioner and student perspectives. *Journal of Mass Media Ethics, 9,* 69–83.

James, G. G. (1988). In defense of whistle blowing. In J. C. Callahan (Ed.), *Ethical issues in professional life* (pp. 315–322). New York: Oxford University Press.

Jamieson, K. (1992). The paradox of political ads: Reform depends on voter savvy. *Media & Values, 58,* 13–14.

Jenkinson, C. (1992). From Milton to media: Information flow in a free society. *Media & Values, 58,* 3–6.

Jennings, B., Nelson, J. L., & Parens, E. (1994). *Values on campus: Ethics and values programs in the undergraduate curriculum.* Special Report from the Hastings Center. Briarcliff Manor, NY: The Hastings Center.

Jensen, J. V. (1959). An analysis of recent literature on teaching ethics in public address. *Speech Teacher, 8,* 219–228.

Jensen, J. V. (1981). *Argumentation: Reasoning in communication.* Belmont, CA: Wadsworth.

Jensen, J. V. (1985a). Ethics in speech communication: Focus on Minnesota. *The Speech Association of Minnesota Journal, 12,* 1–10.

Jensen, J. V. (1985b). Teaching ethics in speech communication. *Communication Education, 34,* 324–331.

Jensen, J. V. (1987). Ethical tension points in whistleblowing. *Journal of Business Ethics, 6,* 321-328.

Jensen, J. V. (1989). The communicative act of whistleblowing. In C.A.B. Osigweh, Yg. (Ed.). *Managing employee rights and responsibilities* (pp. 187-198). New York: Quorum Books.

Jensen, J. V. (1990). Directions to consider in communication ethics. In J. A. Jaksa (Ed.), *Proceedings of the First National Communication Ethics Conference* (pp. 1–13). Kalamazoo, MI: Western Michigan University.

Jensen, J. V. (1991). Ethics in speech communication. In *Two bibliographies on ethics* (3rd ed.), pp. 1-62 Minneapolis, MN: Silha Center for the Study of Media Ethics and Law.

Jensen, J. V. (1992). Ancient Eastern and Western religions as guides for contemporary communication ethics. In J. A. Jaksa (Ed.), *Conference Proceedings of the Second National Communication Ethics Conference* (pp. 58–67). Annandale, VA: Speech Communication Association.

Jensen, R. (1994). Banning "Redskins" from the sports page: The ethics and politics of Native American nicknames. *Journal of Mass Media Ethics, 9,* 16–25.

Jensen, R. (1996). The politics and ethics of lesbian and gay "wedding" announcements in newspapers. *Howard Journal of Communications, 7,* 13-28.

Johannesen, R. L. (1971a). The crisis of public confidence in public communication. *Free Speech Yearbook: 1971,* 43–49.

Johannesen, R. L. (1971b). The emerging concept of communication as dialogue. *Quarterly Journal of Speech, 57,* 373–383.

Johannesen, R. L. (1971c). On teaching and social responsibilities of a speaker. In J. J. Auer & E. Henkinson (Eds.), *Essays on teaching speech in the high schools* (pp. 219–243). Bloomington: Indiana University Press.

Johannesen, R. L. (1974). Attitude of speaker toward audience: A significant concept for contemporary rhetorical theory and criticism. *Central States Speech Journal, 25,* 95–104.

Johannesen, R. L. (1978). Richard M. Weaver on standards for ethical rhetoric. *Central States Speech Journal, 29,* 127–137.

Johannesen, R. L. (1980). Teaching ethical standards for discourse. *Journal of Education, 162,* 5–20.

Johannesen, R. L. (1981). Issue editor' s introduction: Some ethical questions in human communication. *Communication, 6,* 145–158.

Johannesen, R. L. (1985). An ethical assessment of the Reagan rhetoric: 1981–1982. In K. R. Sanders, L. L. Kaid, & D. Nimmo (Eds.), *Political Communication Yearbook, 1984,* (pp. 226–241). Carbondale, IL: Southern Illinois University Press.

Johannesen, R. L. (1988). What should we teach about formal codes of communication ethics? *Journal of Mass Media Ethics, 3* (1), 59–64.

Johnson, B. M. (1990). The ripple effect of blowing the whistle. *Ethics: Easier Said Than Done, 9,* 26–32.

Johnstone, C. L. (1980). An Aristotelian trilogy: Ethics, rhetoric, politics, and the search for moral truth. *Philosophy and Rhetoric, 13,* 1–24.

Johnstone, C. L. (1981). Ethics, wisdom, and the mission of contemporary rhetoric: The realization of human being. *Central States Speech Journal, 32,* 177–188.

Johnstone, C. L. (1983). Dewey, ethics, and rhetoric: Toward a contemporary conception of practical wisdom. *Philosophy and Rhetoric, 16,* 185–207.

Johnstone, H. W., Jr. (1981). Toward an ethics of rhetoric. *Communication, 6,* 305–314.

Johnstone, H. W., Jr. (1982). Communication: Technology and ethics. In M. J. Hyde (Ed.), *Communication philosophy and the technological age* (pp. 38–53). University, AL: University of Alabama Press.

Jones, J. C. (1980). *Mass media codes of ethics and councils: A comparative international study on professional standards.* Paris: UNESCO.

Josephson, M. (1988). Teaching ethical decision making and principled reasoning. *Ethics: Easier Said Than Done, 1,* 27–33.

Josephson, M. (1991). The best of times, the worst of times. *Ethics: Easier Said Than Done, 13-14,* 39–51.

Josephson, M. (1992). The hole in the moral ozone: Ethical values, attitudes, and behaviors in American schools. *Ethics: Easier Said Than Done, 19-20,* 35–45.

Judd, L. R. (1989). Credibility, public relations and social responsibility. *Public Relations Review, 15* (2), 34–40.

Kalbfleisch, P. J. (1992). Deceit, distrust and the social milieu: Application of deception research in a troubled world. *Journal of Applied Communication Research, 20,* 308-334.

Kamisar, Y. (1993). Are laws against assisted suicide unconstitutional? *Hastings Center Report, 23* (3), 32–41.

Kane, P. (1991). *Errors, lies, and libel.* Carbondale, IL: Southern Illinois University Press.

Kantar, M. J. (1990). *Children' s responses to televised adaptations of literature.* Unpublished doctoral dissertation, University of Minnesota, Minneapolis.

Kaplan, H. (1990, Fall). "I didn' t think of it that way": On teaching ethics in broadcasting curricula. *Feedback, 31,* 14–18.

Kaplar, R. T. & Maines, P. D. (1996). The role of government in undermining journalistic ethics. *Journal of Mass Media Ethics, 10,* 236-247.

Kass, L. R. (1990). Practicing ethics: Where' s the action? *Hastings Center Report, 20* (1), 5–12.

Keller, P. W. (1981). Interpersonal dissent and the ethics of dialogue. *Communication, 6,* 287–303.

Kelsey, D. (1991). Computer ethics: An overview of the issues. *Ethics: Easier Said Than Done, 15,* 30–33.

Kennedy, C., & Alderman, E. (1995). *The right to privacy.* New York: Knopf.

Kennerly, E. (1986–1987). Mass media and mass murder: American coverage of the Holocaust. *Journal of Mass Media Ethics, 2* (1), 61–70.

Kern–Foxworth, M. (1990). Ethnic inclusiveness in public relations textbooks and reference books. *Howard Journal of Communications, 2* (2), 226–237.

Kidder, R. M. (1994). *Shared values for a troubled world: Conversations with men and women of conscience.* San Francisco: Jossey–Bass.

Kidder, R. M. (1995). *How good people make tough choices.* New York: William Morrow.

Killenberg, G. M. (1993). What is a quote? Practical, rhetorical, and ethical concerns for journalists. *Journal of Mass Media Ethics, 8,* 37–54.

Klaidman, S., & Beauchamp, T. L. (1988). *The virtuous journalist.* New York: Oxford University Press.

Knowlton, S. R. & Parsons, P. R. (Eds). (1995). *The journalist's moral compass: Basic principles.* Westport, CT: Praeger.

Koen, C. M., Jr. (1989). Sexual harassment: Criteria for defining hostile environment. *Employee Responsibilities and Rights Journal, 2,* 289–301.

Koppel, T. & Gibson, K. (1996). *Nightline: History in the making and the making of television.* New York: Random House.

Koshland, D. E., Jr. (1988, April 29). Science, journalism, and whistle–blowing. *Science, 240,* 585.

Kostyn P. E. (1990). Doing what is right: Teaching ethics in journalism programs. *Journal of Mass Media Ethics, 5,* 45–48.

Kowal, J. P. Responsible science reporting in a technological age. *Journal of Technical Writing and Communication, 4,* 307–314.

Kreiner, A. (1995). Whistle-blowing: A challenge of workplace ethics. *Insights on Global Ethics, 5* (8), 1, 4–5.

Krippendorff, K. (1991). The power of communication and the communication of power: Toward an emancipatory theory of communication. *Communication, 12,* 175–196.

Kruckeberg, D. (1989). The need for an international code of ethics. *Public Relations Review, 15* (2), 6–18.

Kultgen, J. (1988). *Ethics and professionalism.* Philadelphia: University of Pennsylvania Press.

Küng, H. (1991) *Global responsibility: In search of a new world ethic.* New York: Crosswood.

Küng, H. (1993). The history, significance and method of the Declaration Toward a Global Ethic. In H. Küng & K. Kuschel (Eds.), *A global ethic: The declaration of the parliament of the world's religions* (pp. 43-76). New York: Continuum.

Labunski, R. (1989). *Libel and the First Amendment.* New Brunswick, NJ: Transaction Books.

Ladenson, R. F. (1988). Free expression in the workplace: Does the public–private distinction matter? *Employee Responsibilities and Rights Journal, 1,* 91–99.

LaFollette, M. C. (1988). *Ethical misconduct in research publication: An annotated bibliography.* Boston: MIT Press.

Lake, J. B. (1991). Of crime and consequence: Should newpapers report rape complainants' names? *Journal of Mass Media Ethics, 6 ,* 106–118.

Lambeth, E. B. (1988). Marsh, mesa, and mountain: Evolution of the contemporary study of ethics of journalism and mass communication in North America. *Journal of Mass Media Ethics, 3* (2), 20–25.

Lambeth, E. G. (1990a). *Committed journalism: An ethic for the profession* (2nd ed.). Bloomington, IN: Indiana University Press.

Lambeth, E. G. (1990b). Communication ethics and the quest for ecumenic wisdom: A North American perspective. *Media Ethics Update, 5* (2), 6, 22–23.

Lancaster, F. W., & Haricombe, L. (1995). The academic boycott of South Africa: Symbolic gesture or effective agent of change? *Perspectives on the Professions, 15* (1), 3–5.

Lauritzen, P. (1992). Reflections on the nether world: Some problems for a feminist ethic of care and compassion. *Soundings, 75* (2 & 3), 383–402.

Lawson, M. (1988, October 8). It's just not me, dear. *The Independent Magazine (London),* 38–40.

Leander, T. (1988). "Intellectual property" raises ethical questions in the computer industry. *ethikos, 1* (6), 1–3, 15–16.

Leslie, L. Z. (1988). Ethics as communication theory: Ed Murrow' s legacy. *Journal of Mass Media Ethics, 3* (2), 7–19.

Leslie, L. Z. (1992). Lying in prime time: Ethical egoism in situation comedies. *Journal of Mass Media Ethics, 7,* 5–18.

Lester, P. M. (1991). *Photojournalism: An ethical approach.* Hillsdale, NJ: Lawrence Erlbaum Associates.

Lester, P. M. (1995). *Visual communication: Images with messages.* Belmont, CA: Wadsworth.

Levine, G. F. (1990). Television journalism on trial: Westmoreland v. CBS. *Journal of Mass Media Ethics, 5,* 102–116.

Levine, T. R., & McCornack, S. A. (1991). The dark side of trust: Conceptualizing and measuring types of communicative suspicion. *Communication Quarterly, 39,* 325–340.

Levy, L. W. (1995). *Blasphemy: Verbal offense against the sacred, from Moses to Salman Rushdie.* Chapel Hill, NC: University of North Carolina Press.

Lind, R. A., (1995). Can you walk (man) and talk at the same time? The effect of personal stereo use on college students' interpersonal communication. *Communication and Theater Association of Minnesota Journal, 22,* 19–31.

Lind, R. A. (1996a). Diverse interpretations: The "relevance" of race in the construction of meaning in, and the evaluation of, a television news story. *Howard Journal of Communications, 7,* 53-74.

Lind, R. A. (1996b). Race and viewer evaluations of ethically controversial TV news stories. *Journal of Mass Media Ethics, 11,* 40-52.

Lind, R. A. (1996c). Women in British broadcasting: An examination of perceived opportunities and constraints. *Communication and Theater Association of Minnesota Journal, 23,* 3-14.

Lind, R. A. & Rarick, D. L. (1992). Public attitudes toward ethical issues in TV programming: Multiple viewer orientations. *Journal of Mass Media Ethics, 7,* 133–150.

Linsky, M. (1986). Practicing responsible journalism: Press impact. In D. Elliott (Ed.), *Responsible journalism* (pp. 133–150). Beverly Hills, CA: Sage.

Lippke, R. L. (1995). *Radical business ethics.* Lanham, MD: Rowman & Littlefield.

Lipson, M. (1993). What do you say to a child with AIDS? *Hastings Center Report, 23* (2), 6–12.

Logan, R. A. (1989). The unworkable compromise: The knowledge tablet, ethics and public policy for the future. *Mass Comm Review, 16* (1 & 2), 14–25.

Lowenstein, R. L. & Merrill, J. C. (1990). *Macromedia: Mission, message and morality.* New York: Longman.

Lu, X. (1995, November). *A metaphorical approach to persuasion in Zhan–Guo Ce: A reflection of Chinese culture and communication.* Paper presented at the 81st annual meeting of the Speech Communication Association, San Antonio, TX.

Lucas, S. E. (1995). Ethics and public speaking. In *The art of public speaking* (5th ed., pp. 28–47). New York: McGraw–Hill.

Lundstedt, S. B. (Ed.). (1991). *Telecommunications, values and the public interest.* Norwood, NJ: Ablex.

Lyon, D. (1994). *The electronic eye: The rise of surveillance society.* Minneapolis: University of Minnesota Press.

MacKinnon, C. A. (1993). *Only words.* Cambridge, MA: Harvard University Press.

Mahoney, J. & Vallance, E. (Eds.). (1992). *Business ethics in a new Europe.* Dordrecht, Netherlands: Kluwer.

Makau, J. M. (1984). Judicial invention in First Amendment governmental regulation cases. *Free Speech Yearbook, 1983,* 1–19.

Makau, J. M. (1990). Communication ethics and argumentation instruction. In J. A. Jaksa (Ed.), *Proceedings of the First National Communication Ethics Conference* (pp. 92–110). Kalamazoo, MI: Western Michigan University.

Mangum, G. C., & Mangum, A. B. A. (1983). Forensic rhetoric and invention: Composition students as attorneys. *College Composition and Communication, 34,* 43-56.

Marion, G., & Szard, R. (1986). The journalist in life–saving situations: Detached observer or Good Samaritan? *Journal of Mass Media Ethics, 1* (2), 61–67.

Markie, P. J. (1994). *A professor's duties: Ethical issues in college teaching.* Lanham, MD: Rowman & Littlefield.

Martin, E. (1991). On photographic manipulation. *Journal of Mass Media Ethics, 6,* 156–163.

Martinson, D. L. (1994). Enlightened self–interest fails as an ethical baseline in public relations. *Journal of Mass Media Ethics, 9,* 100–108.

Martinson, D. L. (1996). Ethical public relations practitioners must not ignore "public interest". *Journal of Mass Media Ethics, 10,* 210–222.

Matelski, M. J. (1991). *TV news ethics.* Boston: Focal Press.

McCaleb, J., & Dean, K. (1987). Ethics and communication education: empowering teachers. *Communication Education, 36,* 414–416.

McCoy, R. E. (1993). *Freedom of the press: An annotated bibliography: Second supplement, 1978–1992.* Carbondale, IL: Southern Illinois University Press.

McEuen, V. S., Gordon, R. D., & Todd–Mancillas, W. R. (1990). A survey of doctoral education in communication research ethics. *Communication Quarterly, 38,* 281–290.

McGuire, J., Stauble, C., Abbott, D., & Fisher, R. (1995). Ethical issues in the treatment of communication apprehension: A survey of communication professionals. *Communication Education, 44,* 98–109.

McKenzie, R. (1993). Comparing breaking TV newscasts of the 1989 San Francisco earthquake: How socially responsible was the coverage? *World Communication, 22* (1), 13–20.

McKerrow, R. E. (1987). The ethical implication of a Whatelian rhetoric. *Rhetoric Society Quarterly, 17,* 321–327.

McManus, J. (1992). Serving the public and serving the market: A conflict of interest? *Journal of Mass Media Ethics, 7,* 196–208.

McQuarrie, F. A. E. (1992). The cracked mirror: An imperfect case of press self–examination. *Journal of Mass Media Ethics, 7,* 19–30.

Medhurst, M. J. (1987). Ghostwritten speeches: Ethics isn't the only lesson. *Communication Education, 36,* 241–249.

Media and violence: Part two: Searching for solutions. (1993). *Media & Values (63).*

Merrill, J. C. (1986). Three theories of press responsibility and the advantages of pluralistic individualism. In D. Elliott (Ed.), *Responsible journalism* (pp. 47–59). Beverly Hills, CA: Sage.

Merrill, J. C. (1989). *The dialectic in journalism: Toward a responsible use of press freedom.* Baton Rouge, LA: Louisiana State University Press.

Merrill, J. C. (1990). *The imperative of freedom: A philosophy of journalistic autonomy.* New York: Freedom House.

Merrill, J. C. (1992). Machiavellian journalism: With a brief interview on ethics with Old Nick. *Journal of Mass Media Ethics, 7,* 85–96.

Merrill, J. C. (1994). *Legacy of wisdom: Great thinkers and journalism.* Ames, IA: Iowa State University Press.

Merritt, D. (1995). *Public journalism and public life: Why telling the news is not enough.* Hillsdale, NJ: Lawrence Erlbaum Associates.

Meyer, P. (1987). *Ethical journalism: A guide for students, practitioners, and consumers.* New York: Longman.

Meyers, C. (1990). Blueprint of skills, concepts for media ethics course. *Journalism Educator, 45* (3), 25–31.

Meyers, C. (1993). Justifying journalistic harms: Right to know vs. interest in knowing. *Journal of Mass Media Ethics, 8,* 133–146.

Miceli, M. P., & Near, J. P. (1992). *Blowing the whistle: The organizational and legal implications for companies and employees.* New York: Lexington Books.

Middleton, K. R., & Chamberlin, B. F. (1994). *The law of public communication* (3rd ed.). White Plains, NY: Longman.

Minow, N. N., & Lamay, C. L. (1995). *Abandoned in the wasteland: Children's television and the First Amendment.* New York: Hill & Wang.

Moore, R. L. (1995). *Mass communication law and ethics.* Hillsdale, NJ: Lawrence Erlbaum Associates.

Moreno, J. D. (1993). Who's to choose? Surrogate decision making in New York state. *Hastings Center Report, 23* (1), 5–11.

Moskowitz, R. (1989). Hospital ethics committees: The healing function. *Hospital Ethics Committee Forum, 1*, 309–315.

Mowery, D., & Duffy, E. (1990). The power of language to efface and desensitize. *Rhetoric Society Quarterly, 20*, 163–171.

Mowlana, H. (1989). Communication, ethics, and the Islamic tradition. In T. W. Cooper, C. G. Christians, F. F. Plude, & R. A. White (Eds.). *Communication ethics and global change* (pp. 137–146). White Plains, NY: Longman.

Nelson, J. L. (1992). Taking families seriously. *Hastings Center Report, 22* (4), 6–12.

Niemira, D. (1993). Life on the slippery slope: A bedside view of treating incompetent elderly patients. *Hastings Center Report, 23*, (3), 14–17.

Northington, K. B. (1992). Split allegiance: Small–town newspaper community involvement. *Journal of Mass Media Ethics, 7*, 220–232.

Nyberg, D. (1993). *The varnished truth: Truth telling and deceiving in ordinary life.* Chicago: University of Chicago Press.

Obermayer, H. J. (1994). Eastern European publishers face ethical dilemmas. *Journal of Mass Media Ethics, 9*, 94–99.

O' Brien, S. (1993). Eye on Soweto: A study of factors in news photo use. *Journal of Mass Media Ethics, 8*, 69–87.

Ognianova, E. V. (1993). On forgiving Bulgarian journalists / spies. *Journal of Mass Media Ethics, 8*, 156–167.

Olen, J. (1988). *Ethics in journalism.* Old Tappan, NJ: Prentice Hall.

O' Neil, R. M. (1972). *Free speech: Responsible communication under law* (2nd ed.). Indianapolis, IN: Bobbs-Merrill.

O' Neil, R. M. (1993). *The rights of public employees: The basic ACLU guide to the rights of public employees* (2nd ed.). Carbondale, IL: Southern Illinois University Press.

Panitz, B. (1995, October). Ethics instruction: An undergraduate essential. *ASEE [American Society for Engineering Education] Prism*, 20–25.

Park, M. S. & Klopf, D. W. (1994). Comparing human values in Korea and the United States. *Journal of the Communication Association of Korea, 2*, 70–83.

Parry–Giles, S. J. (1993). The rhetorical tension between propaganda and democracy: Blending competing conceptions of ideology and theory. *Communication Studies, 44*, 117–131.

Patterson, P., & Wilkins, L. (1994). *Media ethics: Issues and cases* (2nd ed.). Madison, WI & Dubuque, IA: W.C. Brown & Benchmark.

Pease, E. C. (1994). The ethics of image and intervention: Diplomacy and media in the post–Cold War world. *Insights on Global Ethics, 4* (7), 1, 4–5.

Perez, G. (1992). Communication ethics in today' s Latin America. *Media Ethics Update, 5* (2), 7, 24.

Perry, D. K. (1992). Assessing the import of media–related effects: Some contextualist considerations. *World Communication, 21* (2), 69–82.

Peters, J. D., & Cmiel, K. (1991). Media ethics and the public sphere. *Communication, 12*, 197–215.

Peters, T. J., & Austin, N. (1985). *A passion for excellence: The leadership difference.* New York: Random House.

Peters, T. J., & Waterman, R. H., Jr. (1982). *In search of excellence: Lessons from America' s best–run companies.* New York: Warner Books.

Pfau, M., & Burgoon, M. The efficacy of issue and character attack message strategies in political campaign communication. *Communication Reports, 2*, 53–61.

Pinker, S. (1994). *The language instinct.* London: Penguin.

Plumley, J., & Ferragina, Y. (1990). Do advertising texts cover ethics adequately? *Journal of Mass Media Ethics, 5*, 247–255.

Ponemon, L. A., & Gabhart, D. R. L. (1994). Ethical reasoning research in the accounting and auditing professions. In J. R. Rest & D. Narvaez (Eds.), *Moral development in the professions* (pp. 101–119). Hillsdale, NJ: Lawrence Erlbaum Associates.

Pool, I. S. (1983). *Technologies of freedom.* Cambridge, MA: Harvard University Press.

Pratt, C. A., & Renter, T. L. (1989). What' s really being taught about ethical behavior? *Public Relations Review, 15* (1), 53–66.

Pribble, P. T. (1990). Making an ethical commitment: A rhetorical case study of organizational socialization. *Communication Quarterly, 38,* 255–267.

Primoratz, I. (1995). Boycott of Serbian academics. *Perspectives on the Professions, 15* (1), 8–9.

Pritchard, M. S. (1990). Virtues in political life. In J. A. Jaksa (Ed.), *Proceedings of the First National Communication Ethics Conference* (pp. 257–263).

Purdy, M. (1993). Ethics and communication consulting. In R. L. Ray (Ed.), *Bridging both worlds: The communication consultant in corporate America.* Lanham, MD: Rowman & Littlefield.

Pym, A. (1995). A response to Johannesen. *Southern Communication Journal, 61,* 178–182.

Rada, J. A. (1996). Color blind-sided: Racial bias in network television' s coverage of professional football games. *Howard Journal of Communications, 7,* 231–239.

Rasmussen, K. (1973). Nixon and the strategy of avoidance. *Central States Speech Journal, 24,* 193–202.

Ratzan, S. C. (1994). Ethical health communication. *Media Ethics, 6* (2), 7, 21.

Rawitch, C. Z. (1989). Teaching ethics in J-School. *Ethics: Easier Said Than Done, 2,* 55–57.

Reaves, S. (1991). Digital alteration of photographs in consumer magazines. *Journal of Mass Media Ethics, 6,* 175–181.

Rest, J. R. (1979). *Development in judging moral issues.* Minneapolis, MN: University of Minnesota Press.

Rest, J. R. (1982). A psychologist looks at the teaching of ethics. *Hastings Center Report, 12*(2), 29–36.

Rest, J. R., Barnett, R., Bebeau, M., Deemer, D., Getz, I., Moon, Y. L., Spicklemeir, J., Thomas, S., & Volker, J. (1986). *Moral development: Advances in research and theory.* New York: Praeger.

Reynolds, P. D. (1982). *Ethics and social science research.* Englewood Cliffs, NJ: Prentice-Hall.

Rice, D. B. (1985). Criminal law: Informant bugging–When is a private conversation really private? *Washburn Law Journal, 24,* 376–385.

Richards, J. I. (1990). *Deceptive advertising: Behavioral study of a legal concept.* Hillsdale, NJ: Lawrence Erlbaum Associates.

Richardson, B. (1994). Four standards for teaching ethics in journalism. *Journal of Mass Media Ethics, 9,* 109–117.

Rivers, W. L., & Mathews, C. (1988). *Ethics for the media.* Old Tappan, NJ: Prentice-Hall.

Rodey, C. (1990). Telling stories: Creative literature and ethics. *Hastings Center Report, 20* (6), 25.

Rosen, J. (1991). Making journalism more public. *Communication, 12,* 267–284.

Salwen, M. B. (1992). The influence of source intent: Credibility of a news media health story. *World Communication, 21* (2), 63–68.

Samarajiva, R. (1994). Privacy in electronic public space: Emerging issues. *Canadian Journal of Communication, 19* (1), 87–99.

Schwartz, D. (1992). To tell the truth: Codes of objectivity in photojournalism. *Communication, 13,* 95–109.

Seib, P. (1994). *Campaigns and conscience: The ethics of political journalism.* Westport, CT: Praeger.

Seib, P., & Fitzpatrick, K. (1995). *Public relations ethics.* Orlando: Harcourt Brace Jovanovich.

Self, D. J., Olivarez, M., & Baldwin, D. C., Jr. (1994). Moral reasoning in veterinary medicine. In J. R. Rest & D. Narvaez (Eds.), *Moral development in the professions* (pp. 163–171). Hillsdale, NJ: Lawrence Erlbaum Associates.

Sellers, M. (Ed.). (1994). *An ethical education: Community and morality in the multicultural university.* Providence, RI: Berg.

Shapiro, W. (1989, July 10). Is it right to publish rumors? *Time, 134,* 53.

Shayon, R. L. (1995). Dialogue of a troubled minority. *Media Ethics, 7,* (1), 5, 17.

Shibles, W. H. (1985). *Lying: A critical analysis.* Whitewater, WI: Language Press.

Shipman, M. (1995). Ethical guidelines for televising or photographing executions. *Journal of Mass Media Ethics, 10,* 95–108.

Singer, A. W. (1989, March–April). Whistleblowers: Spearheading a new ethical movement. *ethikos, 2,* 9–11, 17, 24.

Slattery, K. L. (1994). Sensationalism versus news of the moral life: Making the distinction. *Journal of Mass Media Ethics, 9,* 5–15.

Smeltzer, M. A. (1994). *Lying as a standard of ethical communication: A critical case study of the arguments on the veracity of Anita Hill and Clarence Thomas.* Unpublished doctoral dissertation, University of Minnesota, Minneapolis.

Smeltzer, M. A. (1996). Lying and intersubjective truth: A communication based approach to understanding lying. *Argumentation, 10,* 361-373.

Smith, C. R. (1989). *Freedom of expression and partisan politics.* Columbia, SC: University of South Carolina Press.

Smolla, R. A. (1992). *Free speech in an open society.* New York: Knopf.

Sneed, C. (1993). Campus editors confront the Holocaust controversy. *Journal of Mass Media Ethics, 8,* 168-181.

Snoeyenbos, M., Almeder, R., & Humber, J. (Eds.). (1983). *Business ethics: Corporate values and society.* New York: Prometheus Books.

Solomon, R. C. (1994). *The new world of business: Ethics and free enterprise in the global 1990s.* Lanham, MD: Rowman & Littlefield.

Soloski, J., & Bezanson, R. P. (Eds.). (1992). *Reforming libel law.* New York: Guilford.

Sommers, C. H. (1984). Ethics without virtue: Moral education in America. *The American Scholar, 53,* 381-389.

Spielman, B. (1992). Expanding the boundaries of informed consent: Disclosing alcoholism and HIV status to patients. *The American Journal of Medicine, 93,* 216-218.

Sprinthall, N. A. (1994). Counseling and social role taking: Promoting moral and ego development. In J. R. Rest & D. Narvaez (Eds.), *Moral development in the professions* (pp. 85-99). Hillsdale, NJ: Lawrence Erlbaum Associates.

Sproule, J. M. (1987). Whose ethics in the classroom? An historical survey. *Communication Education, 36,* 317-326.

Steele, R. M. (1992). To comfort and afflict: Truth telling, independence, courage and openness. *Media Ethics Update, 4* (2), 1, 16-19.

Starr, D. (1996). Reporters' rights, credibility, and objectivity. *Media Ethics, 7* (2), 15, 26.

Steere, J., & Dowdall, T. (1990). On being ethical in unethical places: The dilemmas of South African clinical psychologists. *Hastings Center Report, 20* (2), 11-15.

Steiner, L. (1991). Feminist theorizing and communication ethics. *Communication, 12,* 157-173.

Stevens, J. D. (1983). *Shaping the First Amendment: The development of free expression.* Beverly Hills, CA: Sage.

Stewart, L. P. (1992). Ethical issues in postexperimental and postexperiential debriefing. *Simulation and Gaming, 23,* 196-211.

Stewart, L. P. (Ed.). (1990). Communication ethics [Special issue]. *Communication Quarterly, 38* (3).

Stoker, K. (1995). Existential objectivity: Freeing journalists to be ethical. *Journal of Mass Media Ethics, 10,* 5-22.

Stovall, J. G., & Cotter, P. R. (1992). The public plays reporter: Attitudes toward reporting on public officials. *Journal of Mass Media Ethics, 7,* 97-106.

Stryk, L. (Ed.). (1969). *World of the Buddha: A reader.* Garden City, NY: Doubleday.

Sundar, Shyam. (1991). Techno-ethics: As a matter of fax. *Journal of Mass Media Ethics, 6,* 24-34.

Swain, B. M. (1978). *Reporters' ethics.* Ames, IA: Iowa State University Press.

Taylor, R. L. (1990). *The religious dimensions of Confucianism.* Albany, NY: State University of New York Press.

Tedford, T. L. (1985). *Freedom of speech in the United States.* New York: Random House.

Tedford, T. L., Makay, J. J., & Jamison, D. (Eds.). (1987). *Perspectives on freedom of speech: Selected essays from the journals of the Speech Communication Association.* Carbondale, IL: Southern Illinois University Press.

Thayer, L. (Ed.). (1980). *Ethics, morality and the media: Reflections on American culture.* New York: Hastings House.

Thomassen, N. (1992). *Communicative ethics in theory and practice.* New York: St. Martin's Press.

Thompson, D. F. (1992). The nature of practical ethics. *Ethically Speaking, 1*(2), 1-3.

Tomlinson, D. E. (1991). Where morality and law diverge: Ethical alternatives in the soldier of fortune cases. *Journal of Mass Media Ethics, 6,* 69-82.

Trianosky, G. What is virtue ethics all about? *American Philosophical Quarterly, 27,* 335-344.

Tucker, D. F. B. (1985). *Law, liberalism and free speech.* Towata, NJ: Rowman & Allanheld.

Tyner, C. L. (1991a). Building fences for the electronic village. *Ethics: Easier Said Than Done* 15, 34–39.

Tyner, C. L. (1991b). Political ethics: Yesterday, today, and tomorrow. *Ethics: Easier Said Than Done* 13-14, 58–67.

Tyner, C. L., (1991). Teaching ethics in our schools. *Ethics: Easier Said Than Done* 11, 36–56.

Veatch, R. M. (1977). *Case studies in medical ethics.* Cambridge, MA: Harvard University Press.

Veatch, R. M. (1981). *A theory of medical ethics.* New York: Basic Books.

Vergabbi, D. J. (1992). Journalist as source: The moral dilemma of news rescue. *Journal of Mass Media Ethics, 7,* 233–245.

Verwoerdt, A. (1966). *Communication with the fatally ill.* Springfield, IL: Charles C. Thomas.

Viall, E. K. (1992). Measuring journalistic values: A cosmopolitan/community continuum. *Journal of Mass Media Ethics, 7,* 41–53.

Vibbert, C. B. (1990). Freedom of speech and corporations: Supreme Court strategies for the extension of the First Amendment. *Communication, 12,* 19–34.

Vickers, B. (1995). [Review of the book *The pianist as orator: Beethoven and the transformation of keyboard style].* *Rhetorica, 13,* 98–101.

Waithe, M. E., & Ozar, D. T. (1990). The ethics of teaching ethics. *Hastings Center Report, 20* (4), 17–21.

Walker, M. U. (1993). Keeping moral space open: New images of ethics consulting. *Hastings Center Report, 23,* (2), 33–40.

Walton, C. C. (Ed.). (1990). *Enriching business ethics.* New York: Plenum Press.

Ward, J., & Hansen, K. A. (1996). *Search strategies in mass communication,* (3rd ed.). White Plains, NY: Longman.

Weaver, P. H. (1994). *News and the culture of lying.* New York: Free Press.

Weber, C. E. (1995). *Stories of virtue in business.* Lanham, MD: Rowman & Littlefield.

Weber, W. S. (1991). Leaving their free speech rights at the door: The anti–speech movement in California higher education. *Jesse Marvin Unruh Assembly Fellowship Journal, 2,* 21–42.

Weil, V. (Ed.). (1983). *Beyond whistleblowing: Defining engineers' responsibilities.* Chicago: Center for the Study of Ethics in the Professions, Illinois Institute of Technology.

White, M.D. (1989). Plagiarism and the news media. *Journal of Mass Media Ethics, 4,* 265–280.

White-Newman, Julie Belle. (1990). Position paper on teaching communication ethics in the 1990's: Avoiding those pitfalls which promote naivete/cynicism. In J.A. Jaksa (Ed.) *Proceedings of the First National Communication Ethics Conference* (pp. 264–278). Kalamazoo, MI: Western Michigan University.

Wilkins, L. (1994). Journalists and the character of public officials / figures. *Journal of Mass Media Ethics, 9,* 157–168.

Wilkins, L. (1995). Covering *Antigone:* Reporting on conflict of interest. *Journal of Mass Media Ethics, 10,* 23–36.

Williams, F., & Pavlik, J. V. (Eds.). (1993). *The people's right to know: Media, democracy, and the information highway.* Hillsdale, NJ: Lawrence Erlbaum Associates.

Williams, J. W. (1990). Teaching broadcast ethics: An alternative course plan. *Feedback, 31* (4), 14–15, 24–26.

Williams, O. V., & Hauch, J. W. (Eds.). (1992). *A virtuous life in business: Stories of courage and integrity in the corporate world.* Lanham, MD: Rowman & Littlefield.

Williams, R. B. (1995). Ethical reasoning in television news: Privacy and AIDS testing. *Journal of Mass Media Ethics, 10,* 109–120.

Winder, D. (1995). Rising fundamentalism, retreating secularism: A new dimension in world politics. *Insights on Global Ethics, 5* (9), 1, 4–6.

Winegarden, A. D., Fuss–Reineck, M., & Charron, L. J. (1993). Using *Star Trek: The Next Generation* to teach concepts in persuasion, family communication, and communication ethics. *Communication Education, 42,* 179–188.

Wolf, S. M. (1994). Health care reform and the future of physician ethics. *Hastings Center Report, 24* (2), 28–41.

Woodward, B. (1987). *Veil: The secret wars of the CIA, 1981-1987.* New York: Simon & Schuster.

Wright, D. K. (1989). Examining ethical and moral values of public relations people. In D. K. Wright (Ed.), Public relations ethics [Special issue], *Public Relations Review, 15* (2), 19–33.

Wueste, D. E. (Ed.). (1994). *Professional ethics and social responsibility.* Lanham: MD.: Rowman & Littlefield.

Wulfemeyer, K. T. (1985–1986). Ethics in sport journalism: Tightening up the code. *Journal of Mass Media Ethics, 1* (1), 57–67.

Wulfemeyer, K. T., (1989). Freebies and moonlighting in local TV news: Perceptions of news directors. *Journal of Mass Media Ethics, 4,* 232–248.

Wulfemeyer, K. T. & Frazier, L. (1992). The ethics of video news releases: A qualitative analysis. *Journal of Mass Media Ethics, 7,* 151–168.

Wylie, F. W. (1989). Ethics in college and university public relations. *Public Relations Review, 15,* (2), 63–67.

Young, L. W. L. (1994). *Crosstalk and cullture in Sino-American communication.* Cambridge (UK): Cambridge University Press.

Ziesenis, E. B. (1991). Suicide coverage in newspapers: An ethical consideration. *Journal of Mass Media Ethics, 6,* 234–244.

Ziff, H. M. (1986). Practicing responsible journalism: Cosmopolitan versus provincial models. In D. Elliott (Ed.), *Responsible journalism* (pp. 151–166). Beverly Hills, CA: Sage.

Zolten, J. J. (1996). The media-driven evolution of the African American hard gospel style as a rhetorical response to hard times. *Howard Journal of Communications, 7,* 185-203.

Zuckerman, L. (1989, February 27). Knocking on death' s door. *Time, 133,* 49.

Jensen (1991) lists additional older sources.

Author Index

Subject Index